THERAPY
TECHNIQUES

FAMILY THERAPY TECHNIQUES

INTEGRATING AND TAILORING TREATMENT

JON CARLSON, LEN SPERRY, JUDITH A. LEWIS

Routledge
Taylor & Francis Group

NEW YORK AND HOVE

Published in 2005 by
Routledge
270 Madison Avenue
New York, New York 10016
www.routledge-ny.com

Published in Great Britain by
Routledge
2 Park Square
Milton Park, Abingdon
Oxon OX14 4RN U.K.
www.routledge.co.uk

10 9 8 7 6 5 4 3 2 1

Library of Congress Cataloging-in-Publication Data

Carlson, Jon.
  Family therapy techniques: integration and tailoring / Jon Carlson, Len
Sperry, Judith A. Lewis.
     p. cm.
  Includes index.
  ISBN 1-58391-360-2 (pbk.)
  1. Family psychotherapy. I. Sperry, Len. II. Lewis, Judith A., 1939- III. Title.

  RC488.5.C3633 2005
  616.89'156--dc22

                                    2004019945

This book is dedicated to our friend and colleague
Don C. Dinkmeyer

TABLE OF CONTENTS

Foreword   xi

Preface   xvii

One   Family Therapy in the 21st Century   1

     New Strategies for a Changing Environment   1
     The New Realities of Family Life   2
     Responses to Change   5
     The False Hope of Divorce   6
     The New Realities of Professional Practice   7
     The New Practice of Family Therapy   11
     Summary   13

Two   Theories of Family Therapy   17

     Goals, Treatment Process, and Techniques   17
     Adler   19
     Bowen/Intergenerational   22
     Satir/Communication   25
     Experiential   29
     Milan   31
     Constructivist/Narrative   34
     Solution-Focused   36
     Strategic   39
     Structural   42
     Behavioral and Cognitive–Behavioral   46
     Object Relations   48
     Summary   50

Three	Integrative Treatment with Couples and Families	53
	The Basis for Treatment Efficacy	53
	Integration	54
	Transtheoretical Therapy	58
	Integrative Problem-Centered Approach	61
	Integrative Behavioral Couples Therapy (IBCT)	64
	Emotionally Focused Couple Therapy (EFCT)	66
	Olsen's Integrative Family Therapy	68
	Integrative Treatment	70
	Snyder's Pluralistic Approach to Couples Therapy	72
	Additional Models	75
	Concluding Notes	75
Four	Tailoring Treatment for Couples and Families	79
	Models and Protocols for Tailoring and Matching	79
	Tailoring Terminology and Resistance	80
	Perspectives of Tailoring	81
	A Clinical Protocol for Matching and Tailoring Treatment	87
	Concluding Note	96
Five	Case Conceptualization as a Strategy for Tailoring Treatment	99
	Case Conceptualization	100
	The Centrality of Pattern Analysis in the Clinical Formulation	107
	Clinical Illustrations	110
	Summary	118
Six	Tailoring Treatment: The Impact of Culture	121
	The Values Underlying Family Life	122
	Culturally Based Views of Family Life: The Impact on Family Therapy	124
	The Experience of Oppression	126
	Cultural Values and Conflict	130
	Cultural Conflict Within the Family: The Impact on Therapy	133

	Strategies for Tailoring Family Therapy	134
	Summary	139
Seven	Tailoring Treatment: Families Under Stress	143
	Families and Addiction	144
	Families' Responses to Illness and Disability	152
	Violence and Abuse	158
	Summary	164
Eight	Tailoring Treatment: Work and Family Concerns	167
	The Relationship of Work Life and Family Life	168
	Common Work–Family Conflicts and Their Consequences	170
	Tailoring Treatment	173
	A Sample Protocol: Matching/Tailoring Treatment with Dual-Career Couples	184
	Case Example of Matching/Tailoring with a Dual-Career Couple	187
	Therapeutic Intervention with the Single, Working Parent	191
	Summary	192
Nine	Treatment Adherence and Relapse Prevention: Ensuring Therapeutic Results	195
	Treatment Adherence	196
	Treatment Adherence Guidelines	197
	What Is Relapse Prevention (RP)?	200
	Why Couples or Families Relapse	203
	Steps to RP	210
	Summary	215
Index		219

FOREWORD

This book could not have been published at a better time: it appears when family therapy faces what may be its greatest challenges, and it offers useful guidelines for how these challenges can be met. With this book, Carlson, Sperry, and Lewis have done the field a great service.

Family therapy is at least as useful today as in any time in its history. Families continue to play a dominant role in creating the secure attachments that are the foundation of satisfying adult relationships, in inculcating and maintaining prosocial values and behavior in children, and in promoting a quality of life that buffers against stress and illness. Yet despite the best efforts of groups like the American Association of Marriage and Family Therapists, and Division 43 of the American Psychological Association, family therapy has declined in importance as an emphasis in training programs and appears with diminishing frequency in clinical settings.

The halcyon period for family therapy was the 1960s through the 1980s, but since then it has suffered because of the combined influence of a number of external and internal factors. Among the external factors are:

- Disproportionately deep cuts in mental health service funding as communities attempted to cope with declining revenues;
- The growing reluctance of insurance companies to reimburse for couple and family service;
- Increased interest in pharmacotherapy;
- Increased understanding of the role of neurobiology in the etiology of behavior;
- Rapid changes in the composition of the nuclear family that make it difficult to put forth a common notion of the family; and

- A dramatic shift toward materialistic values and the pursuit of self-interest (as typified by the spate of televised "survivor" shows) that has contributed to an erosion of interest in the cooperative spirit typified by well-functioning families.

While nominal interest in families persists, resources and commitment to improve them have been evaporating rapidly. But the family therapy enterprise itself has contributed to its own decline, expedited by internal factors such as:

- The long-term emphasis upon the personalities of family therapists who portrayed family therapy as more of an art than a science;
- Fractious conflicts between the emerging "schools" of family therapy;
- Oversimplification of each school's beliefs compounded by the assertion that there are necessary and sufficient conditions to explain and change family behavior;
- A reluctance to replace case reports with more difficult but more convincing group studies of therapeutic outcome; and
- A failure to adapt to the more pragmatic, time-limited forms of practice that are currently in demand.

Correcting for some of these flaws, the authors correctly note the general conclusion of the "common factors" research that attributes as little as 15 percent of the variance in treatment outcome to unique features of the treatment methods used. By following their recommendations, it is hoped that methods can be improved to at least fully utilize, if not raise, this contribution. Chapter 2 offers an invaluable review of the most common approaches to family therapy. A careful review of these methods reveals significant commonalities in technique with all making some effort to identify the family of origin roots of behavior and to promote change in systemic interaction through improved communication and social behavior. Unfortunately, too many of these approaches still include recommend the use of paradox in which therapists disingenuously prescribe symptoms. I believe that by modeling deceptive manipulation and encouraging problematic behavior, the chance of positive change does not outweigh the risk of serious iatrogenic effects. But each approach is a valuable source of metaphors for describing family functioning in ways that can lead to helpful interventions. Chapter 3 offers a review of attempts by others to integrate the best elements drawn from these varied approaches, recognizing that no one theory could possibly explain the vast array of variance found in families.

The author's core contributions are found in chapters 4 and 5. This is where they do a remarkable job of identifying most of the areas of decision-making in family therapy, suggesting guidelines for sound practice but recognizing that specific plans depend entirely upon the clients' assets, liabilities and goals, the therapists' skills, and resources in the community. General therapeutic prescriptions, beyond philosophy, epistemology, values, and general outlines of sound practice, are no longer feasible. In that regard, this is an outstanding guide to the planning of effective intervention using a modern client-driven approach in place of outmoded theory-driven approaches. They begin by offering their model for "matching" clients to optimal treatment modalities and the "tailoring" the approach to fit the couples and families being served. They provide the skills needed to move from the generalizations of theory to the pragmatics of intervention, using case conceptualization to summarize complex information about families into a coherent "map" that guides intervention. The remaining chapters expand the model to include techniques for developing sensitivity to the clients' cultural influences and their response to stress, methods for helping them balance family and work, and means of combating the inevitable tendency to relapse when therapy ends.

Readers might want to consider two areas that the authors could have more fully developed. The first is a framework for deciding when to move between individual, couple, and family intervention. As dynamic systems, families can be changed when the behavior of any of their members act differently. When parents and children are seen together, typically at the instigation of the parents, one unavoidable message to the children is that the parents cannot manage the family on their own. Therefore following one or more assessment interviews in which the children are accorded an opportunity to express their views and therapists can study the patterns of interaction within the family, it is often expedient to initiate systemic change by intervening with either or both parents, seeing only the children, or including extended family members or even other families. This aspect of case structuring is one of the more important decisions made by family therapists.

The other area in which greater attention would be useful is the empirical evaluation of the effects of family therapy. Careful evaluation of the validity of the theoretical underpinning of family therapy is essential. For example, the "double bind" theory of communication paradoxes was used to explain schizophrenogenesis and many other maladaptive dimensions of family and small group behavior. While an intuitively appealing idea, however, it was not supported by a number of careful investigations (Schuham, 1967). It is also possible that some of the interventions methods that seem to have self-evident validity may likewise not live up to expectations. If family therapy is to withstand the requirement that it empirically substantiate its claims. Group designs address general outcomes (e.g., Carroll & Doherty, 2003; Baucom, Shoham, Mueser, Daiuto, & Stickle, 1998; Hazelrigg, Cooper, Borduin, 1987; Prince & Jacobaon, 1995; Shadish, Ragsdale, Glaser, & Montgomery, 1995; and Snell-Johns, Mendez, & Smith, 2004). It is also possible for therapists to evaluate the effectiveness of their work with specific couples and families through the use of non-intrusive goal-attainment scaling (Stuart, 1992) or single-subject designs (Lucyshyn, Albin, & Nixon, 1997). Measuring the results that we achieve will go a long way toward helping us refine our methods and gain acknowledgement of our results in the general community.

In general, clinicians will find this book to be an incomparable guide to effective practice, and family therapy educators will find it to be an invaluably thoughtful review of the wide-ranging theories that underpin treatment methods.

Richard B. Stuart
Program Director,
Respecialization in Clinical Psychology,
The Fielding Graduate Institute
and
Clinical Professor Emeritus, Department of Psychiatry,
University of Washington

References

Baucom, D. H., Shoham, V., Mueser, K. T., Daiuto, A. D., & Stickle, T. R. (1998). Empirically supported couple and family interventions for marital distress and adult mental health problems. *Journal of Consulting and Clinical Psychology, 66*, 53–88.

Carroll, J. S., & Doherty, W. J. (2003). Evaluating the effectiveness of premarital prevention programs: A meta-analytic review of outcome research. *Family Relations, 52*, 105-118.

Hazelrigg, M. D., Cooper, H. M., & Borduin, C. M. (1987). Evaluating the effectiveness of family therapies: An integrative review and analysis. *Psychological Bulletin, 101*, 428–442.

Lucyshyn, J., Albin, R., & Nixon, C. (1997). Embedding comprehensive behavioral support in family ecology: An experimental single case analysis. *Journal of Consulting and Clinical Psychology, 65*, 241–251.

Prince, S., & Jacobaon, N. S. (1995). A review and evaluation of marital and family therapies for affective disorders. *Journal of Marital and Family Therapy, 21*, 377–401.

Schuham, A. I. (1967). The double-bind hypothesis a decade later. *Psychological Bulletin, 68*, 409–416.

Shadish, W., Ragsdale, K., Glaser, R., & Montgomery, L. (1995). The efficacy and effectiveness of marital and family therapy A perspective from meta-analysis. *Journal of Marriage and the Family, 21,* 345–360.

Snell-Johns, J., Mendez, J. L., & Smith, B. H. (2004). Evidence-based solutions for overcoming access barriers, decreasing attrition, and promoting change with underserved families. *Journal of Family Psychology, 18,* 19–35.

Stuart, R. B. (2002). Integrative therapy for couples. In J. Carlson & D. Kjos (Eds.) *Theories and strategies of family therapy* (pp. 317–352). Boston: Allyn & Bacon.

PREFACE

Most of us in the therapy world have received in-depth training that included a single-model approach to therapy. This approach became our framework, or window, for observing, assisting, and providing assistance to those with problems. Each different approach seemed to advocate that its view was superior to others and should be used even in the face of data that seemed to confirm that it didn't work. More and more therapists are realizing the folly of investing in only one window of understanding. They realize the necessity of being able to operate in different manners depending on the couple or family.

We believe that this book will be useful to counselors and therapists both in training and in practice. In *Family Therapy Techniques,* we present the challenges of a diverse population and describe practical strategies for assessing families, developing tailored treatment plans, and maintaining treatment adherence to prevent relapse.

Traditionally, counselors and therapists have lacked the ability to use the vast amounts of data families can provide; thus, they often end up working on only a small aspect of the family picture. This situation reminds us of the story of the blind inhabitants of Ghor who tried to learn about the elephant that had been brought to their town—a mysterious creature they had never seen and could not see (in R. E. Ornstein, *The Psychology of Consciousness*, New York: Viking, 1972, p. 143):

> The populace became anxious to learn about the elephant, and some sightless from among this blind community ran like fools to find it. Since they did not know even the form or shape of the elephant, they groped sightlessly, gathering information by touching some part of it. Each thought that he knew something, because he could feel a part .. . .

Each had felt one part of the many. Each had perceived it wrongly. No mind knew all; knowledge is not the companion of the blind. All imagined something, something incorrect.

Like the blind men in this story, therapists often assess couples and families on the basis of limited knowledge. However, to understand not only the individual aspects of a family but also the family as a whole in its environment, therapists need to conduct a comprehensive and thorough assessment of the situation. Such an assessment allows the therapist to tailor treatment to fit each individual family, thus ensuring treatment efficacy. Without comprehensive and accurate assessments, therapists tend to treat all families in the same fashion according to the theory of family therapy to which they subscribe.

In addition, once treatment has taken place, many counselors feel that they have done their job. However, without implementing sound treatment adherence/relapse prevention strategies, all gains are frequently lost.

Although we are aware that family therapy methods cannot be changed overnight, we believe this book can provide a beginning as well as a basis for future study. In this vein, we are reminded of Aldous Huxley's statement in the foreword to *Brave New World Revisited* (New York: Harper & Row, 1958):

However elegant and memorable, brevity can never, in the nature of things, do justice to all the facts of a complex situation. On such a theme one can be brief only by omission and simplification. Omission and simplification help us to understand — but help us, in many cases, to understand the wrong thing; for our comprehension may be only of the abbreviator's neatly formulated notions, not of the vast, ramifying reality from which these notions have been so arbitrarily abstracted.

But life is short and information endless: nobody has time for everything. In practice we are generally forced to choose between an unduly brief exposition and no exposition at all. Abbreviation is a necessary evil, and the abbreviator's business is to make the best of a job which, though intrinsically bad, is still better than nothing. He must learn to simplify, but not to the point of falsification. He must learn to concentrate upon the essentials of a situation, but without ignoring too many of reality's qualifying side issues. In this way he may be able to tell, not indeed the whole truth (for the whole truth about almost any important subject is incompatible with brevity), considerably more than the dangerous quarter-truths and half-truths which have always been the current coin of thought.

Chapter 1 helps the reader understand the new reality of professional family therapy practice by highlighting the many changes that have occurred and must be considered when developing effective treatment. Chapter 2 presents the theories of family therapy—specifically the goals, treatment process, and techniques of the various theories. This information is essential background knowledge in order to tailor treatment effectively. Chapters 3 and 4 describe how to integrate the concepts of the various models presented in chapter 2. Chapters 5, 6, 7, and 8 describe how to tailor treatment to each family. Different models are considered, as a clear, clinical protocol is developed. Issues of gender, culture, addiction, disability, abuse, and work are highlighted. Chapter 9 concludes the book by presenting the fundamental concepts of treatment adherence and relapse prevention. When these concepts are not duly considered, initial treatment success often ends in long-term treatment failure.

We had a great deal of help in preparing this manuscript. Special thanks to Candace Ward Howell and Laurie Johnson for their valuable assistance.

Jon Carlson
Len Sperry
Judith A. Lewis

1

FAMILY THERAPY
IN THE 21ST CENTURY

NEW STRATEGIES FOR A CHANGING ENVIRONMENT

The field of family therapy has grown rapidly, and many approaches and models of treatment have been created. Although the strategies have had many significant differences, the family has been viewed as a two-parent nuclear family system. Only recently have the importance of race, ethnicity, class, and family variations (single-parent, chosen, or stepfamily) been addressed.

The early pioneers seemed to be focused solely on the family system and its structure. The individual family members were not acknowledged, and their feelings were discounted. The pioneers also ignored the impact that larger issues such as school, work, religion, and so on have on families.

With the advent of postmodernism, all of this has changed. All truths become relative and we began to realize that there is no one reality. Actually, there are no realities or points of view (Maddigan & Law, 1998) that we can all agree on.

The role of theory has changed. Theories no longer try to explain objective reality but instead provide us with alternative explanations. Rather than one "right" or "best" approach, many useful ones exist.

The role of therapy has changed to help cocreate new realities for families that are more satisfying. Therapists need to sample the various

1

theories and use the concepts and methods that will help the family, creating new explanations and meaning for them, with a shift away from behavioral change.

Therapists recognize the importance of seeing the transgenerational nature of family problems, and Carl Rogers's (1961) ideas that people can discover their own solutions have been adopted. Therapists who collaborate with their patients, rather than advise them, have realized the importance of *questions* to change beliefs and patterns, rather than forcing behavioral change.

Gender, ethnicity, race, class, and education have all become important lenses to look through when examining a family and its therapy. Because family therapy is such a young discipline, one may be surprised to realize that the time for a paradigm shift has arrived so soon. In fact, however, much of the conventional wisdom that guided practices in the past has lost its value in this era of rapid change. The transformation of family life can be expected to continue, making it unlikely that therapies constrained by orthodoxy will be viable in the 21st century.

In response to an evolving environmental context, the soul and spirit of what we have known as family are changing at the deepest level as the social context of family life has been altered. As we will discuss, so have the professional and economic contexts within which therapy takes place. These changes will lead irrevocably toward a revolution in the practice of family therapy.

THE NEW REALITIES OF FAMILY LIFE

The practice of couple and family therapy has traditionally been built on the unexamined assumption that a model of appropriate family life exists. Unfortunately, the notion of a "normal" family not only is impractical but also may be harmful. As Bernardes points out, people whose lives fail to fit the popularized model of the family often view themselves at fault. "The guilt and shame of these victims is the direct consequence of our own refusal, thus far, to recognize our responsibility in portraying the image of the normal nuclear family that has become such a popular yardstick against which ordinary people measure personal success and failure" (1993, p. 48). In actuality, if the conventional nuclear family of therapeutic myth ever existed, it would represent the reality of an ever-declining minority of the population (Coontz, 1992). What are the new realities of family life?

The Question of Hierarchy

One concept of family life that remained unquestioned in the past is the assumption that a hierarchical structure is necessarily a good thing. In a classic interview (West & Bubenzer, 1993), Cloe Madanes expressed doubt about the utility of the hierarchy:

> You have to enter the family from wherever you can and to think that you want to reconstitute a hierarchy with parents in charge of the children often doesn't work. I think that this coincides with the general disillusionment about hierarchical institutions in this country. There has been a loss of respect for all the organizations that function like a pyramid. I'm thinking more of the family like a fish net with multiple interwoven threads. (p. 104)

Because a hierarchical structure provides a vehicle for the oppression of women, questioning the validity of the hierarchy becomes especially important when we consider gender roles. Hare-Mustin and Maracek (1988) observed that "a therapist may 'unpack' the metaphor of 'family harmony' and expose the hierarchy by pointing out that accord within the family often is achieved through women's acquiescence and accommodation" (p. 461). Riche (1991) also pointed out the changes taking place in family hierarchies:

> Of course, changes in family structure and composition have been taking place for many years, even within families that appear on the surface to adhere to tradition.
> Even the traditional family unit has seen fundamental changes. Not long ago, husbands brought home the bacon and wives cooked it. Today, only 22% of married-couple households contain a male breadwinner and a female homemaker, a dramatic decline from 61% in 1960. (Riche, 1991, p. 44)

For the most part, women have entered the workforce because their families needed additional income or because they were their families' sole support. If social, economic, and political policies begin to be guided by reality rather than by outmoded prototypes, families can receive the kind of environmental support that can keep them functioning effectively. The best interest of the family will take precedence over the need to generate more income.

Believing that a hierarchy is the only appropriate model for families may not only interfere with a sensible view of gender roles but also with a realistic picture of children's lives. In raising questions about hierarchical structures, Cloe Madanes pointed out that therapists often find themselves working with families in which the children are stronger and healthier than the parents (West & Bubenzer, 1993). Certainly, the lives of children today represent unknown territory to previous generations.

Today's children are living a childhood of firsts. They are the first day care generation, the first truly multicultural generation, and the first to grow up in the electronic bubble, the environment defined by computers and new forms of television. They are the first post-sexual revolution generation, the first generation for which nature is more abstraction than reality, and the first to grow up in new kinds of dispersed deconcentrated cities, not quite urban, rural, or suburban. The combination of these forces has produced a dynamic process. Childhood today is defined by the expansion of experience and the contraction of positive adult contact (Louv, 1990, p. 5).

Ironically, family structures now may be characterized by less intense contact between children and their parents but also by prolonged interaction. Young adults are remaining with their parents longer. In 1960, 43% of 20- to 24-year-olds were living with their parents; by 1988, 55% were living in their childhood homes (Glick, 2001).

Relationships among the generations are also being complicated by the lengthening life span of Americans. Many elderly people who have outlived other family members are existing without a support system of caregivers. If current patterns hold, we will soon have as many as five generations living at one time, with children constituting only one of these generations. The stereotypes of aging must be recognized and abandoned as older adults become healthier (Sperry & Carlson, 1991). Although the idea of a two-paycheck couple is not anything new, the idea of a dual-career couple may be. The "career" designation indicates the partners' pursuit of goal-directed work choices that often bear the seeds of intrapersonal and interpersonal conflict. Overwork and overload are common complaints in most relationships, and these phenomena are compounded in the dual-career couple. Because socially enforced gender stereotypes still abound, the greater burden continues to fall on the woman in the relationship. Only with the appearance of the companionate marriage model have therapists begun to imagine relationships wherein both partners can have goals of equal importance.

Variations of the career-driven couple include the commuting couple, the military couple, the executive couple, and the family-business couple. Each of these models occurs within a new social context that must be assessed and understood by family therapists. At the same time, therapists need to be aware of a trend that seems to run counter to the blurring of boundaries between work and family life. More and more people are "downshifting."

In the past decade, many people embraced the notion of a fast track as the surest path to success. Today, members of a new breed of career trendsetters, "downshifters," are taking control of their careers, rather than allowing their careers to control them. These people are not drop-outs. They are not giving up the intellectual, emotional, and financial rewards of professional success. Instead, they are learning to limit their careers so that they can devote more time to their families, their communities, and their own needs beyond work. Many Americans will work hard at "downward mobility" in the future.

Multicultural Factors

Many of the assumptions we make about family life represent "culturally embedded meanings that have been disguised as universal truths" (Lewis, 1993, p. 338). However, in the 21st century, the United States will emerge as a nation with great ethnic diversity. It is projected that one third of the population will consist of people of color, with the highest concentration of "minority" families being of Hispanic origin, followed by African Americans, Asians, and Native Americans. Models of marital quality and healthy family life will have to involve a new awareness that incorporates ideas from these diverse cultures. The truly effective family therapists will be those who have learned to appreciate diverse worldviews, rather than make judgments based on the dominant culture.

Therapists will also need to examine the effects of the social context on ethnically diverse groups. Research will be needed on resiliency and health among families in varying ethnic groups, as well as on the impact of social policy and programs on cultural values, the role of communal ties in family preservation and survival, and the processes of family adaptation to cross-cultural change.

RESPONSES TO CHANGE

Faced with all these trends and changes, people tend to align themselves with either the pessimists or the optimists. The pessimists believe that changes in the American family are destructive and prevent the family from carrying out its functions of child-rearing and the provision of stability in adult life. The optimists, in contrast, view the family as an institution that is not declining but rather is showing its flexibility and resilience. This group believes that traditional family structures are too male-dominated and conformity-oriented to allow for growth and thus are no longer appropriate.

Regardless of their position, however, most people still reside within a family. According to Doherty (1992),

> The world is now more oriented to individual options, particularly for women, and the family has changed accordingly. From this point of view, the main problems faced by contemporary families can be traced to the failure of society to accept that the "Leave It to Beaver" family is a dinosaur and to provide adequate support for the variety of post-Beaver families that now dominate the landscape. (pp. 32–34)

In addition to the pessimistic and optimistic views just discussed, a third orientation is emerging. This orientation agrees with the pessimistic view, says Doherty, in that the family is in trouble and a transformation of values is needed. However, it also agrees with the optimistic view in that changes in family structure are inevitable and here to stay, and that both old and new family forms should receive more community support.

Doherty believes that families at the beginning of the 20th century were *institutional families* whose chief value was *responsibility*. In the mid-1920s, the focus of marriage and family shifted so that the chief value became *satisfaction*. Now we have moved to the pluralistic family that has a chief value of *flexibility*, but that can also address the needs for responsibility and satisfaction. According to Doherty (1992),

> This completes a century-long trek toward liberation of the individual, particularly women and children, from the oppressive features of the traditional family. The pluralistic family offers individuals freedom to create the family forms that fit their changing needs over life's course with little stigma about failing to conform to a single family structure and value system. (p. 35)

THE FALSE HOPE OF DIVORCE

Once, couples were together until "death do us part," but now it is much more likely that a marriage will end in divorce, which is considered almost commonplace. Numerous accounts have been made on the negative impact of divorce on all family members (Braver, 2003), and recent research supports that the use of divorce as a solution to dissatisfaction and unhappiness is questionable. The research illustrates the following:

- Unhappily married adults who divorced or separated were no happier, on average, than unhappily married adults who stayed together.
- Divorce did not reduce symptoms of depression for unhappily married adults, raise their self-esteem, or increase their sense of mastery on the average compared to unhappily married spouses who stayed married.
- The vast majority of divorce (74%) happened to adults who had been happily married five years previously.
- Unhappy marriages were less common than unhappy spouses.
- Staying married did not typically trap unhappy spouses in violent relationships.
- Two out of three unhappily married adults who avoided divorce or separation ended up happily married five years later.
- Many currently married spouses have had extended periods of marital unhappiness, often for quite serious reasons, including alcoholism, infidelity, verbal abuse, emotional neglect, depression, illness, and work reversals (Waite, Browning, Doherty, Gallagher, Luo, & Stanley, 2002).

Counselors and therapists need to help couples get through the "bumps in the road of life" without using divorce as the solution.

THE NEW REALITIES OF PROFESSIONAL PRACTICE

Just as the realities of family life have changed, so have the conditions within which family therapists practice. Client populations have changed, and family problems have become more complex. At the same time, therapists now find themselves dealing with an ever-changing set of constraints that affects their work.

Therapists' training has always tended to prepare them for working with verbal and sophisticated clients who are able to enter into positive therapeutic relationships with little prodding. Now, however, previously underserved populations have finally found their way into treatment. Since service has become accessible, and even mandated, marriage and family therapists have begun to see very different kinds of families. People with little education, low pretreatment levels of functioning, and multiple life problems are being seen by therapists who have not been trained or compelled to treat them (Garfield & Bergen, 1986).

No longer can we assume that our clients will be voluntary, socio-economically advantaged, well educated, or functional. Mental health services at one time were sought primarily by people who wanted to change their lives. Now treatment is often court-ordered and mandated. In comparison with their self-motivated counterparts, compulsory clients require alternative methods of treatment, assessment, and intervention (Huber, 1992).

The problems being addressed in family therapy have increased in number and complexity as the client population has become more heterogeneous. The increasing rates of drug abuse, suicide, alcoholism, divorce, teenage pregnancy, and violence are rooted in high-risk families. These multiproblem systems require solutions that go beyond palliative interventions to include public policy modifications and preventive strategies.

Just as therapists are addressing some of their most daunting challenges, they must also face the need to adapt to changes in the treatment environment. With managed care has come the pressure to be precise, efficient, and accountable. In the past, therapists and their highly motivated clients could control the course of treatment independently. Now survival in the managed-care environment requires each treatment provider to emphasize careful assessment, to deliver treatments that have been tailored to the assessment, to use brief, empirically supported modalities, and to accept external review.

The need for transformation seems to be both abrupt and painful to many people. Discussing the current plight of traditionally trained therapists, Wylie (1995) points out:

> Their teachers and mentors and role models were the secular gurus who did not so much show them what to do as pass down . . . a body of knowledge and practice, a way of life, that seemed stable as the ages. . . . Degree in hand, the fledgling therapist could count on spending the next 25, 35, 50 years doing what the field's elders had always done—seeing individual or both sides determined, getting paid for doing it in the general confidence that once vacated, no appointment hour would remain long unfilled. Oh, those dear, dead days. (p.22)

Research on the outcome of psychotherapy, marriage, and family therapy has identified four factors that account for change (Blow & Sprenkle, 2001; Lambert, 2003):

- **Client/extratherapeutic factors**. These factors are what the client contributes to making a change. They include the client's characteristics, such as inner strength, religious faith, and goal directedness, as well as things outside of the client's control, such as social support and good fortune. Forty percent of the change is attributed to these factors.
- **Relationship factors**. These variables are what occur between the therapist and client. They include warmth, respect, empathy, and authenticity. Thirty percent of the change is attributed to these factors.
- **Model/technique factors**. These variables are specific to the different theories of therapy and are employed to intervene in the client's life. Fifteen percent of the change is attributed to these factors.
- **Placebo, hope, and expectancy factors**. These variables are attributed to the simple fact that the client is in therapy. Fifteen percent of the change is attributed to these factors.

Exceptional research is being conducted and reported in the major professional journals, such as *Family Process, The Journal of Marriage and Family Therapy, The Journal of Family Psychology, The Family Journal,* and *The Psychotherapy Networker*. Family therapists will need to be aware of the many changes taking place in the profession. The following are some of the most important ones:

- **The importance of the Human Genome Project, DNA, and one's genetics**. The implications are many as families have more and more data about who they are and will be. Research is now being conducted to determine the impact of genes on behavior and relationships (Plomin, Defries, Craig, & McGuffin, 2003). The impact of DNA predictive testing on the family and the psychosocial consequences of testing will require thoughtful and careful interventions (Sobel & Cowan, 2003; Patenaude, 2002).
- **Brain and physiological research**. This information will shed light on what we are capable of becoming. Studies will also show what happens to our bodies during the joys and frustrations of family life (Atkinson, 1999).
- **Spirituality**. An increase in spirituality will have a significant role for families. Therapists will not only need to assess this area but also be comfortable working in this domain.
- **Shamanism and "old age" healing rituals and strategies**. These alternatives to therapy emphasize change without psychological understanding, intervention without taxonomic diagnosis, liberation

without narrative cause, and wisdom without generalized knowledge (Butler, 1998; Kottler, Carlson, & Keeney, 2004).

- **Coaching.** This has been one of the major modes of intervention in family therapy. As this movement grows, more and more people will be seeking coaching services. The goal of coaching is to help clients define themselves proactively in relationship to others in their families without emotionally cutting them off or compromising (McGolderick & Carter, 2001; Naughton, 2002). This will hopefully lead to the client being able to be different and still connected to his or her family. Coaching is a more active, outcome-related form of therapy.

- **Motivational interviewing and the focus on strength building.** Motivational interviewing (Miller & Rollnick, 2002) is a therapeutic approach designed to help people increase their intrinsic motivation to work toward change. It is especially helpful for individuals and couples that have not considered or are somewhat ambivalent about change.

- **Aging.** The world population is growing older each year. Treatment strategies need to be developed to work with the unique developmental needs of the aging. Traditional strategies should be used mainly for clients in early stages of development.

- **Smart marriages and marriage trends/psychoeducation.** The skills needed to have an effective and satisfying marriage have been identified and training programs have been developed (Carlson & Dinkmeyer, 2003; Berger & Hannah, 2002.) Many of today's relationship problems can be addressed with training and not treatment.

- **Happiness/optimism.** Now, completing its first century, psychology has studied the negative and what is wrong with people (Seligman, 2002) This new approach is based on the premise that people can be taught to feel good and happy. Extensive research is being conducted that will provide guidelines and a clearer picture of what healthy living is all about (Aspinwall & Staudinger, 2003).

- **Attachment.** The study of the impact of early attachment patterns on adult relationships has reemerged (Wood, 2002: Erdman & Caffery, 2003) Attachment theory has an evolutionary and biological basis, and places the mother-child bond at the center of an evolutionary bio-behavioral system. These relationships endure throughout a life span.

THE NEW PRACTICE OF FAMILY THERAPY

Today's families are most notable in terms of their variety and diversity. No single structure or set of interactional patterns can be identified as right or healthy for all families. If any one generalization can be made about a healthy family, it is that the family can accomplish its own goals, as well as those of its individual members. Family therapy, then, must focus on helping each client system to be successful on its own terms.

An effective treatment is most likely to occur when the family therapist has a solid grounding across diverse theoretical approaches, has acquired a broad repertoire of intervention techniques linked to theory, engages in comprehensive assessment of the family system, and chooses intervention strategies tailored to that individual family. This general strategy obviously requires important changes in the therapist's approach. Even such sacred cows as the genogram will have to be modified to accommodate blended and nonbiological families. Clearly, the family therapist of the future will work from a new set of guiding principles, including the following:

- **Family therapists will be sensitive to the broader contexts within which families function.** Family therapists have always understood the impact of systems on individuals. In the future, this perspective will be widened, making therapists cognizant of the fact that they can help families most effectively if they recognize the effect of the social, cultural, and economic milieu. Therapists must understand people's life situations, including their resources, problems, and how these problems are embedded within the larger social systems. Among the larger systems that will be addressed through innovative strategies is the workplace, which has a major effect on most families and has remained largely untapped as a source of data for the therapeutic process. Therapists will also need to follow the mandate of Doherty and Carroll (2002) by realizing that therapists are citizens and have a responsibility to work toward family-centered community building.
- **Family therapists will *tailor* treatment to the special needs of each family.** The new realities of both family life and the treatment milieu must direct us toward a tailored treatment. Given the increasing heterogeneity of families, little possibility exists that a generalized package of treatment strategies could be appropriate even for one therapist's clientele. At the same time, the managed-care

environment tends to emphasize the desirability of limiting services to what the specific client needs. If treatment tailoring is based on a comprehensive assessment that clarifies the family's needs and resources, this approach can be both right and practical.

- **Family therapists will use ingenuity and flexibility in the design of brief interventions.** What is right in terms of client needs and what is practical in terms of economic feasibility can be combined through the use of flexible treatment formats. Carlson and Sperry (2000) suggested that a "once-and-for-all cure" achieved through time-unlimited therapy is not necessarily the most appropriate goal for most clients. A more realistic approach might involve the provision of brief interventions as needed through the life cycle of the individual, couple, or family. The success of therapy can also be enhanced through attention to developing the family's own resources for maintaining positive changes over time.

- **Family therapists will celebrate the cultural diversity that characterizes the families they serve.** Given the increasing diversity among families, the most effective therapists will be the ones who are best able to learn from their clients. Culturally based values guide individuals in the definitions and meanings they place on family life. When therapists are willing to explore these meanings with their clients, they are better able to assess family needs and choose promising interventions. When therapists remain unaware of cultural differences, they run the risk of pathologizing behaviors that are acceptable in the family's cultural context (Ng, 2003).

- **Family therapists will be aware of issues related to gender role socialization.** Our review of current and projected alterations in family life has highlighted the changes in how gender roles are perceived. In the past, family therapists sometimes believed they could ignore this issue in the interests of objectivity. Now more clinicians realize that the stance of neutrality tends to support the status quo of inequality. Harriet Lerner pointed out that "a feminist perspective has been enlarging and has helped me to look more objectively at theories that I was taught were neutral and inclusive but that were, in fact, partial, distorted, and insulting to women and other marginal groups" (Lewis & Engle, 1994, p. 373). She further stated, "It's always the case that dominant thinking is confused with what is real and true"(p. 373).

- **Psychoeducation will become more important.** So many of the problems that couples and families face are a result of a lack of skills. Family members want to get along with one another in a healthy fashion but often behave in ways that keep the problems going. Therapists will need to use psychoeducation to help families and couples learn the skills necessary for a satisfying family life (Carlson & Dinkmeyer, 2003; Carlson & Love, 2002; Gottman, Driver, & Tabares, 2003). Ultimately, the key to successful therapy may be the therapist's ability to accept the wide variety of truths on which a healthy family life can be based.

SUMMARY

As family therapists search for the strategies that will ensure effectiveness into the 21st century, they will need to face some new realities. Family life will involve a breakdown of hierarchies, an increase in the number and variety of family forms, and a focus on multiculturalism. The professional practice of family therapy will also change, as therapists continue to work with a more heterogeneous group of clients.

What effects will all of these changes have on family therapists? New principles will guide their work as they learn to recognize the contexts families function within, to tailor treatment that meets the unique needs of specific families, to design flexible strategies, to celebrate diversity, and to develop gender sensitivity.

References

Aspinwall, L.G., & Staudinger, U. M. (2003). *A psychology of human strengths: Fundamental questions and future directions for a positive psychology*. Washington, DC: American Psychological Association.

Atkinson, B. (1999). The emotional imperative: psychotherapists cannot afford to ignore the privacy of the limbic system. *Family Therapy Networker, 23*(4), 22–33.

Berger, R., & Hannah, M. (2002). *Preventive approaches in couples therapy*. New York: Brunner Routledge.

Bernardes, J. (1993). Responsibilities in studying postmodern families. *Journal of Family Issues, 14*(1), 35–49.

Blow, A. J., & Sprenkle, D. H. (2001). Common factors across theories of marriage and family therapy: A modified Delphi study. *Journal of Marital and Family Therapy, 27*(3), 385–401.

Braver, S. L. (2003). The "news" about divorce for family psychologists. *The Family Psychologist, 19*(2), 4–8.

Butler, K. (1998). Beyond the rational: Shamens, scientists and therapists join a quest for mating. *Family Therapy Networker, 22*(5), 24–37.

Carlson, J., & Dinkmeyer, D. (2003). *Time for a better marriage*. San Luis Obispo: Impact Publishers.

Carlson, J., & Love, P. (2002). *Living love*. Phoenix: Zeig, Tucker & Theisen.

Carlson, J., & Sperry, L. (2000). *Brief therapy with individuals and couples*. Phoenix: Zeig, Tucker & Theisen.

Coontz, S. (1992). *The way we never were: American families and the nostalgia trap*. New York: HarperCollins.

Doherty, W. J. (1992, May/June). Private lives, public values. *Psychology Today*, 32–82.

Doherty, W. J., & Carroll, J. S. (2002). The citizen therapist and family-centered community building: Introduction to a new section of the journal. *The Family Process, 41*(4), 561–568.

Erdman, P., & Caffery, T. (2003). *Attachment and family systems*. New York: Brunner Routledge.

Garfield, S. L., & Bergen, A. E. (Eds.). (1986). *Handbook of psychotherapy and behavior change*. New York: John Wiley.

Glick, P. C. (2001). Marriage and family trends. In D. H. Olson & M. K. Hanson (Eds.), *Preparing families for the future*. Minneapolis: National Council on Family Relations. (Original work published in 1990).

Gottman, J. M., Driver, J., & Tabares, A. (2003). Building the sound marital hours: An empirically derived couple therapy. In A. S. Gurman & N. S. Jacobson (Eds.), *Clinical handbook of couples therapy* (3rd Ed.). (pp. 373–399). New York: Guilford.

Hare-Mustin, R. T., & Mavracek, J. (1988). The meaning of difference: Gender theory, postmodernism, and psychology. *American Psychologist, 43*, 455–464.

Huber, C. (1992). Compulsory family counseling. *Topics in Family Psychology and Counseling, 1*(2), 1–81.

Kottler, J., Carlson, J., & Keeney, B. (2004). *The American shaman: An odyssey of global healing traditions*. New York: Brunner Routledge.

Lambert, M. J. (2003). Psychotherapy outcome research: Implications for integrative and eclectic therapists. In J. C. Norcross & M. R. Goldfried (Eds.), *Handbook of psychotherapy integration*. New York: Oxford University Press.

Lewis, J. A.(1993). Farewell to motherhood and apple pie: Families in the post-modern era. *The Family Journal, 1*, 337–338.

Lewis, J. A., & Engle, J. (1994). Harriet Lerner: A conversation. *The Family Journal, 2*, 373–377.

Louv, R. (1990). *Childhood's future: Listening to the American family*. Boston: Houghton Mifflin.

Maddigan, S., & Law, I. (1998). *PRAXIS: Situating discourse, feminism, and politics in narrative therapies*. Vancouver: Yaletown Family Therapy Press.

McGolderick, M., & Carter, B. (2001). Advances in coaching: Family therapy with one person. *Journal of Marital and Family Therapy, 27*(3), 281–300.

Miller, W. R., & Rollnick, S. (2002). *Motivational interviewing: Preparing people for change* (2nd Ed.). New York: Guilford Press.

Naughton, J. (2002). The coaching boon. *Family Therapy Networker, 26*(4), 24–33.

Ng, K. S. (2003). *Global perspectives in family therapy*. New York: Brunner Routledge.

Patenaude, A. F. (2002). Genetic issues. In J. Carlson (Ed.), *Behavioral health and health counseling videotape series*. Washington, DC: American Psychological Association.

Plomin, R., Defries, J. C., Craig, I. W., & McGuffin, P. (2003). *Behavioral genetics in the postgenomic era*. Washington, DC: American Psychological Association.

Riche, M. F. (1991, March). The future of the family. *American Demographics*, 44–46.

Rogers, C. (1961). *On becoming a person*. Boston: Houghton Mifflin.

Seligman, M. E. P. (2002). *Authentic happiness: Using the new positive psychology to realize your potential for lasting fulfillment*. New York: Free Press.

Sobel, S., & Cowan, C. B. (2003). Ambiguous loss and disenfranchised grief: The impact of DNA predictive testing on the family as a system. *Family Process, 42*(1), 47–57.

Sperry, L., & Carlson, J. (1991). The work-centered couple. *The Family Psychologist, 7*(4), 19–21.

Waite, L. J., Browning, D., Doherty, W. J., Gallagher, M., Luo, Y., & Stanley, S. M. (2002). *Does divorce make people happy?* New York: Institute for American Values.

West, J. D., & Bubenzer, D. L. (1993). Interview with Cloe Madanes: Reflections on family therapy. *The Family Journal, 1*, 98–106.

Wood, B. (2002). Attachment and family systems. *Family Process, 41*(3).

Wylie, M. S. (1995). The new visionaries. *The Family Therapy Networker, 19*(5), 21–29, 32–35.

2

THEORIES OF
FAMILY THERAPY

GOALS, TREATMENT PROCESS, AND TECHNIQUES

Therapists must be able to explain family treatment in a manner that makes sense to the family. For example, we are often presented with families with a problem or dysfunction that is easy to describe, yet the family cannot or does not seem to find any meaning in the explanation or treatment that we first provide. It is therefore necessary to use alternative explanations. The many alternative theories of family therapy have well-developed rationales, strategies, and proponents. Each theory regards the family and explains its functioning in a somewhat different fashion. Some theories clearly explain certain phenomena but are vague about others.

In spite of their differences, however, family therapy theories are similar in that they are all interpersonal models. These models are distinct from the traditional intrapsychic, or individual, models. Both types of models (interpersonal and intrapsychic) are based on very different philosophical assumptions and therefore have distinct methods of conceptualization and technique. They are both valuable and effective, given the appropriate context. Most professional therapists have been trained in the intrapsychic model and may have difficulty switching to an interpersonal, systemic paradigm (Kaplan, 2003).

17

Family therapy approaches are based on a family-systems model of therapy and have the following common tenets:

- The whole is greater than the sum of its parts.
- Individual parts of a system can be understood only within the context of the whole system. Since human behavior arises within a social system, it can be understood only within this context.
- Notions of circular, simultaneous, and reciprocal cause and effect replace the traditional models of linear cause and effect.
- Change in one part of a social system (for example, an individual family member) will affect all other parts of that system (for instance, the entire family).
- Systems have a tendency to seek homeostasis, or equilibrium. This balance-seeking function serves to maintain stability and sometimes prevents change.
- When a family is out of balance, or equilibrium, feedback mechanisms attempt to bring the family back into balance.
- The methods used to restore equilibrium (for example, the identified attempts of a patient to solve problems) can become problems themselves.
- Interventions from an interpersonal/family-systems perspective focus on relationships within the entire family system, rather than on one individual in the family (that is, on the identified patient) (Walsh & McGraw, 1996).

As was reported in chapter 1, the common factors associated with a change in therapy (Lambert, 2003), 15% of the outcome of therapy can be attributed to specific techniques and strategies. By tailoring the strategies to each client and circumstance, the therapist must also look carefully at the client's strengths and assets (40% of the outcome). A tailored strategy can occur only if it is preceded by a positive relationship (30% of the outcome). As this occurs, hope or the placebo effect is triggered (15% of the outcome).

The purpose of this chapter is to provide a brief description of some of the main traditional family therapy theories—their goals, treatment processes, and techniques. Additionally, intrapersonal theories (that is, behavioral and object relations) that also address family work are included, because many of their goals, treatment processes, and techniques may be used by the family therapist. We hope the reader will develop an in-depth knowledge of each of these theories by reading or viewing the corresponding additional resources. Therapists must have a broad knowledge base to know when and how to use these techniques.

Treatment cannot be tailored unless the therapist understands the full range of strategies and their epistemology (its theoretical underpinnings). As Gehart and Tuttle (2003) state,

> One's epistemology provides the "lens" through which one interprets the theories one integrates. For example, a "therapeutic letter" will be viewed and utilized quite differently depending on one's epistemology. A modernist therapist would view a therapeutic letter as a vehicle for expressing emotion to reduce distress and symptoms, whereas a systemic therapist might view the letter as a form of positive or negative feedback, and a postmodernist would view the letter as a means of creating space for alternative descriptions and voices. Therefore the same intervention has very different uses depending on one's epistemological assumptions. (p. 160)

ADLER

According to Alfred Adler, all behavior is purposive and interactive. Both individuals and social systems are holistic, and individuals seek significance by the manner of their behavior in social systems. The basic social system is the family, and it is from the family that individuals learn how to belong and interact. Problems, or dysfunctions, in families result from discouragement or a lack of acceptance within the family. The treatment process stresses education to promote growth and change. The therapist addresses the interactions within the family system and changes the interpersonal system. Family dynamics (Walsh & McGraw, 1996) include a wide variety of concepts related to the interplay of structural and functional components in a family system. They include the following:

- **Power**: The lines of movement through which the family and each of its members strive toward goals. Mechanisms in the family through which power is channeled include decision making, manipulation, and negotiation.
- **Boundaries and intimacy**: The degree of physical and emotional closeness and inclusion or exclusion among family members.
- **Coalitions**: Two or more people joined together for mutual support or to oppose one or more other individuals. These arrangements may take the form of open alliances or hidden collusions.
- **Roles**: Reciprocal characteristic patterns of social behavior that members of a social system expect from one another.

- **Rules**: Implicit or explicit guidelines that determine what behavior is acceptable or not acceptable in a family. Rules are related to a family value system and may vary with different roles in the family. Natural or logical consequences provide corrective feedback.
- **Complementarity and differences**: Dissimilar roles in a family that may be integrated by a process of cooperative reciprocity. Individual differences among members of a system can lead to an interaction of theses and antitheses, and ultimately result in a new synthesis.
- **Similarities**: Qualities of a family, including a shared vocabulary and a common perception of experience, that enhance family cohesiveness and identity.
- **Myths**: A family's subjective representational model of reality. Rules and roles in a family arise from the family's myths.
- **Patterns of communication**: Verbal and nonverbal communications that form the basis of interactions in a family. Faulty communication due to double messages, withholding information, or overgeneralizing can lead to misunderstandings and problems in the system (pp. 104–105).

Goals

The general goal of Adlerian family therapy is to promote changes in both individuals and the family as a whole. The specific goals differ with each family; however, the basic ones are as follows:

- To promote a new understanding and insight about purposes, goals, and behavior
- To enhance skills and knowledge in areas such as communication, problem solving, and conflict resolution
- To increase social interest and positive connections with others
- To encourage the commitment to ongoing growth and change

According to Sherman and Dinkmeyer (1987), the goals of family therapy may be attained by changes at several levels:

- In perceptions, beliefs, values, and goals
- In play, structure, and organization
- In social interest, feelings, and participation
- In skills and behavior
- In the use of power

Treatment Process

The treatment process of Adlerian family therapy is organized into four phases. In the first phase, the therapist gains access to the family and uses joining and structuring to set the stage for the remainder of the therapeutic process. The second phase is devoted to assessment. In this phase, information is gathered, and tentative hypotheses about the family dynamics are formulated. During the third phase, the family gains an increased understanding of their problems, develops their awareness, and commits to reorientation. In the fourth phase, the changes achieved in therapy are solidified, and the therapist begins to disengage from the family system and develop a process of relapse prevention.

Techniques

According to Grunwald and McAbee (1985), the key techniques of Adlerian therapy are as follows:

- **Family constellation**: Information is obtained about the birth order of all family members; siblings; the relationships to and between parents; the family climate; additional parental models; physical, academic, sexual/gender, and social development in childhood; and life meanings during childhood. The role of the adult is often formed by his or her birth order and the influence of the personalities of siblings and parents.
- **Early recollections**: Each family member is asked to share eight memories from early childhood. The description of these memories is analyzed according to theme and developmental maturity. Often family members construct memories, but they are still helpful in identifying the unconscious psychological goals of the person and the ideal self.
- **Typical day**: Parents or other family members are asked to detail events in a complete typical day.
- **Encouragement**: Techniques are used that convey respect and equality, and that support understanding, having faith in family members, asking for help, using logical consequences, honesty, the right to make decisions, setting goals, the right to give encouragement, consistency, and the use of encouraging words.
- **Paradoxical intention**: A therapist assigns the presenting problem or symptom as a homework assignment.

- **Use of family council**: Family meetings are held on a regular basis in which all family members participate in the discussion of issues so that each person's views are taken into consideration when making decisions.
- **Use of logical or natural consequences**: Parents are taught how to use natural consequences with their children without arguing or criticizing them. For example, a child who is late for dinner may not eat until the next meal.
- **Confrontation**: The therapist points out mistaken personal logic.

Additional techniques are intended to promote improved communication. All family members are requested to adhere to communication guidelines:

- Speak for yourself and do not suggest what others may think or feel.
- Do not scapegoat or blame.
- Listen and be empathetic.
- Continue to build improved communication in the family (Dinkmeyer & Dinkmeyer, 1991).

Further Resources

Bitter, J., Carlson, J., & Kjos, D. (1999). *Family therapy with the experts: Adlerian family therapy* [Video]. Boston: Allyn & Bacon.

Bitter, J., Roberts, A., & Sonstegard, M. A. (2002). Alderian family therapy. In J. Carlson & D. Kjos, *Theories and strategies of family therapy* Boston: Allyn & Bacon.

Carlson, J. (2003). *Brief integrative Adlerian couples therapy* [Video]. Microtraining, 25 Burdette Ave., Framingham, MA 01702.

Carlson, J., & Dinkmeyer, D. (2003). *Time for a better marriage*. Atascadero, CA: Impact Publishers.

Carlson, J., & Kjos, D. (1998). *Psychotherapy with the experts: Adlerian therapy* [Video]. Boston: Allyn & Bacon.

Carlson, J., & Slavik, S. (Eds.). (1997). *Techniques of Adlerian psychology*. Washington, DC: Taylor & Francis.

Dinkmeyer, D., McKay, G. D., & Dinkmeyer, D., Jr. (2002). *STEP: Parents' handbook*. Circle Pines, MN: American Guidance Service.

Sherman, R., & Dinkmeyer, D. (1987). *Systems of family therapy: An Adlerian integration*. New York: Brunner/Mazel.

BOWEN/INTERGENERATIONAL

Bowen and his followers see the family as an emotionally interdependent unit. A change in one part of the family system will evoke changes in other parts and in the family as a whole. Behavioral patterns are created over time and are frequently repeated for several generations. Each family exerts pressure (that is, homeostasis) on others to force the conformity of each member's behavior. The family creates the emotional climate and behaviors that members will duplicate outside the family setting.

Goals

In the Bowenian model, therapists have treatment goals for themselves that are crucial to the family's attainment of their therapy goals. According to Kerr and Bowen (1988), the primary goals are (a) to reduce the anxiety of the family, allowing family members to improve their ability to function independently and to reduce their symptomatic behaviors, and (b) to increase each family member's basic level of differentiation, enabling each person to respond more effectively to emotionally intense situations. Symptom reduction and decreased anxiety can occur relatively quickly in treatment. Making improvements in the basic level of differentiation is a long-term process that can take many years. The main goal, however, is to assist one or more members of the family to move to a greater level of self-differentiation.

Treatment Process

If the therapist is able to refrain from being triangulated, or being emotionally involved with the family, and the family is able to interact in an atmosphere of low anxiety and reactivity, Bowen believed that progress would occur. Bowen's theory contains two main variables: the degree of anxiety and the degree of self-integration. Most organisms can adapt to acute anxiety of a short duration; however, chronic anxiety over long periods of time can lead to a differentiation of self and to physical illness, emotional symptoms, or social delinquency. This anxiety is also infectious and can spread to other members of the family. People can seem normal at one level of anxiety, but they will become ill or abnormal at more intense levels. The therapist may work with a marital couple, the entire family, or just one individual from the family. The configuration of individuals seen by the therapist may change as treatment progresses. According to Bowen (1985), progress in therapy depends on the therapist's ability to relate meaningfully to the family without becoming emotionally entangled (p. 312).

Bowen listed the five main functions of the therapist in the family treatment process as follows:

- Define and clarify the relationship between spouses (that is, develop and use a genogram, which is a diagram representing at least three generations of a family that is used to organize information and provide a means for tracking progress during therapy).

- Keep one's self detriangled, or emotionally neutral, from the family.
- Teach the functioning of emotional systems using the tenets of the model.
- Demonstrate differentiation by managing one's self during the course of therapy.
- Resolve cutoffs (Papero, 1991, p. 61).

Techniques

- **Talk to the therapist, not to each other**: This is done to keep emotional reactivity and anxiety in the sessions low.
- **Person-to-person relationship**: The therapist establishes a relationship with each person that allows him or her to share personal thoughts and feelings directly with the therapist while his or her partner and/or other family members observe. In this way, the spouses begin to develop a person-to-person relationship in their marriage, rather than creating an emotional divorce. Each person learns to focus on self, rather than talking or gossiping about a third person.
- **Asking frequent factual questions**: This technique serves to focus on thinking and intellectual processes. The thinking of family members is externalized so that members of the family system can hear one another's perspectives.
- **Emotional neutrality**: The therapist remains emotionally neutral and avoids taking sides, thus remaining detriangled from the family. The therapist also maintains neutrality in the sessions through the use of modeling, nonverbal behavior, and the appropriate use of humor (Bowen, 1985).
- **Genograms**: A genogram is a diagram representing the process and structure of at least three generations of a family. Genograms are used to organize family information and provide a means for tracking a family's progress in therapy.
- **Detriangling**: This refers to the process of remaining objective in response to the family. The therapist must be able to share his or her own thoughts and feelings without becoming offensive or putting anyone's views down. The therapist must also remain calm in response to reactions by other family members.

Further Resources

Guerin, K., & Guerin, P. (2002). Bowenian family therapy. In J. Carlson & D. Kjos, *Theories and strategies of family therapy*. Boston: Allyn & Bacon.

Guernin, P., Carlson, J., & Kjos, D. (1998). *Family therapy with the experts: Bowenian therapy* [Video]. Boston: Allyn & Bacon.

Guerin, P. J., Fogarty, T. F., Fay, L. F., & Kautto, J. G. (1996). *Working with relationship triangles: The one-two-three of psychotherapy*. New York: Guilford.

Kerr, M. E., & Bowen, M. (1988). *Family evaluation: An approach based on Bowen theory*. New York: W. W. Norton.

McGolderick, M., Gerson, R., & Shellenberger, S. (1999). *Genograms: Assessment and intervention*. New York: Norton.

Papero, D. V. (1991). *Bowen family systems theory*. Boston: Allyn & Bacon.

SATIR/COMMUNICATION

The hallmark of Virginia Satir's work is increasing the self-esteem of individuals in a family in order to change the interpersonal system. She found a direct correlation between self-esteem and communication, with low self-esteem being associated with poor communication. In her work, the family is viewed as a holistic system. Roles have a major effect on the effectiveness of family functioning by influencing rules, communication processes, and responses to stress. When family members become aware of what they are experiencing in the present, they can grow, both as individuals and as a family.

Goals

Satir's therapeutical goal is increased maturity. Her main aim is to integrate the growth of each family member with the integrity and health of the family as a whole. Specifically, the objective is (a) to assist the family to gain hope, creating ideas of what the future can be like; (b) to strengthen the coping process and family members' coping skills; (c) to make it clear to all that individuals can make choices and take responsibility for the outcomes of those choices; and (d) to promote good health in the individuals and in the family (Satir & Baldwin, 1983). Specifically, Satir focuses on releasing and redirecting blocked energy by facilitating the development of increased self-esteem, improved communication skills, and more tolerant rules. The outcome of family therapy in general terms was stated quite clearly by Satir (1983) as follows:

Treatment is completed:

- When family members can complete transactions, check and ask for feedback
- When they can correctly interpret hostility
- When they can see how others see them
- When one member can tell another how he/she manifests him/herself
- When one member can tell another what he/she hopes, fears, and expects from him/her
- When family members can disagree
- When they can make choices
- When they can learn through practice
- When they can free themselves from harmful effects of past models
- When they can give a clear message—that is, be congruent in their behavior with a minimum of difference between feelings and communication and with a minimum of hidden messages (p. 176)

Treatment Process

The treatment process is consistent with the treatment goals in that the family must undergo a process of facilitating effective communication and building self-esteem in a rational context. Satir and Bitter (1991) indicated that as therapy becomes more successful, the anxiety levels decrease significantly, and the family learns how to see change as an expected part of family life. The five stages of treatment are as follows:

- Establish trust with the family. Develop an assessment and treatment plan early to gain the confidence of the family. Satir referred to this as making contact.
- Develop awareness through experience. The therapist helps the family develop new awareness about their functioning by asking specific questions or by using specific techniques. This Satir called chaos.
- Create new understandings in family members through a new or increased awareness of their family dynamics.
- Have family members express and apply these new understandings through different behaviors during the session.
- Have family members use the new behaviors outside the therapeutic environment, what Satir referred to as integration.

Techniques

This approach is known for its many creative techniques. Some of the best known are as follows:

- **Family-life fact chronology**: A holistic family history is made, extending from the birth of the oldest grandparents to the present.
- **Family maps**: Visual representations similar to genograms are created of the family structure over three generations. In Satir's use of this technique, three family maps are drawn: the mother's family of origin, the father's family of origin, and the current family.
- **Ropes**: Ropes representing relationships with other family members are tied to the waists of each member until each has as many ropes as there are family members. The other ends of the ropes are tied to each of the other family members. All the family members become aware of how they are connected and how tension is created in the ropes. Often entanglements occur. This provides a concrete representation of the family dynamics.
- **Metaphor**: A word used to represent an idea and the idea itself are discussed by analogy. For example, Satir would use the word "pod" as a metaphor for a person's self-esteem and then ask how full a person's pod was at a given time.
- **Touch**: Satir used touch with family members, shaking hands with each person at the beginning of therapy. However, she was careful not to violate the boundaries of individuals, because some people consider touch to be a violation.
- **Sculpture**: A family member is asked to describe his or her relationship to one or more family members using bodily positions and gestures to represent degrees of closeness and communication patterns. When movement is added, the family sculpture becomes a stress ballet. All entities that affect the family dynamics, including pets, extended family, and friends, are symbolically brought into the sculpture through the use of role-playing and fantasy.
- **Drama**: Family members are asked to act out a scene in the life of the family or an individual. These reenactments of significant events in the family history again provide an opportunity for a new perspective and for more insight.
- **Family reconstruction**: Similar to drama, family reconstruction involves the reenactment of events from the family history based on information derived from the family-life fact chronology or the family maps.

- **Reframing:** The therapist creates a shift in the perceptions of family members. He or she decreases the threat of blame by accentuating the ideas of puzzlement and good intentions.
- **Humor:** Humor can be used to promote contact between the therapist and the family, as well as among family members. It can mitigate intensity, clarify exaggerated dynamics, and encourage movement in a way that decreases defensive action. Satir would use a light touch of humor to keep a relaxed atmosphere for learning.
- **Verbalizing presuppositions:** The therapist overtly states presuppositions evident in a family's behavior. For example, Satir would verbalize the hope and expectation for change a family manifests by virtue of their involvement in therapy.
- **Denominalization:** This involves obtaining specific behavioral descriptions for words such as "love" and "respect," and discovering exactly what must be done for someone to perceive that he or she is receiving love and respect. The clarified answer is often related to the individual's primary sensory-base representational system (that is, visual, auditory, or kinesthetic).
- **Anchoring:** This refers to a learned association between a stimulus and a response or between one response and another. This technique serves to bring feelings to the level of interpersonal physical experience.
- **Multiple family therapy:** Numerous unrelated families are brought together for joint family sessions.
- **Communication stances:** Satir would ask family members to participate in an exercise in which each person takes a certain stance to represent a personality: placater, blamer, computer, distracter, and congruent person. Family members share feelings associated with using various stances and with responding as recipients to stances. In this way, family members increase their awareness of effective communication and learn how to become congruent.
- **"I" statements:** Satir would encourage family members to own their feelings. Often people use passive forms such as "it is confusing." Satir would model the active form, "I am confused," in family therapy and develop exercises in which family members would practice using such "I" statements.

Further Resources

McLendon, J., Carlson, J., & Kjos, D. (1998). *Family therapy with the experts: Satir therapy (video)*. Boston: Allyn & Bacon.

McLendon, J. A., & Davis, B. (2002). The Satir system. In J. Carlson & D. Kjos, *Theories and strategies of family therapy*. Boston: Allyn and Bacon.

Satir, V. (1972). *Peoplemaking*. Palo Alto, CA: Science & Behavior Books.

Satir, V., Baxmen, J., Gerber, J., & Gomori, M. (1991). *The Satir model: Family therapy and beyond*. Palo Alto, CA: Science & Behavior Books.

Satir, V. M. (1983). *Conjoint family therapy* (3rd ed.). Palo Alto, CA: Science & Behavior Books.

Satir, V. M. (1988). *The new peoplemaking*. Palo Alto, CA: Science & Behavior Books.

Satir, V. M., & Baldwin, M. (1983). *Satir: Step by step*. Palo Alto, CA: Science & Behavior Books.

EXPERIENTIAL

Carl Whitaker used an atheoretical and practical approach to families. He emphasized experiencing and expressing emotions in the here and now, promoting natural growth in families, and recognizing the struggle between autonomy and interpersonal belonging within the family group. Using a metaphor, Whitaker and Bumberry (1988) compared symbolic–experiential family therapy to telephone lines, water pipes, and gas mains of a city—the infrastructure. The impulses and symbols that flow through the infrastructure affect the surface life of the city in a pervasive way. By participating in symbolic–experiential family therapy sessions, family members become comfortable with their impulses and can integrate them into everyday life. In these sessions, the therapist will need to focus on the discussion of these impulses and symbols, and the family will need to make decisions about how they will live. Life involves decision and struggle, and the therapist cannot make these decisions for the clients: They will need to do it themselves.

Goals

The goals of family therapy are to simultaneously increase each family member's perception of belonging to the family and his or her freedom to be a separate individual (Whitaker & Keith, 1981). To accomplish this overall goal of increased belonging and individuation, therapists attempt to do the following:

- Expand the symptoms, escalating interpersonal stress
- Develop a sense of family nationalism
- Improve relationships with past generations of the extended family
- Increase contact with the community and its members, in particular the ethnic and culture group
- Understand expectations regarding the family and family boundaries

- Increase the separation between generations
- Encourage the family and its members to learn to play
- Provide a model of a continuous joining, separating, and rejoining
- Confront the myth of individuality
- Encourage family members to be themselves

Treatment Process

Because creativity is emphasized, therapy sessions are unpredictable. Often the relationship between parents is one of the primary targets of the work. Whitaker and Bumberry (1988) maintained that men are raised to relate to objects, such as cars, computers, and activities, not to intimacy and close relationships as women are. The therapists show that relationships are bilateral. Each person can change the relationship by what is done and said. By withdrawing and assuming that a relationship is only unilateral, the spouse sentences the relationship to deterioration. By involvement and hard work, relationships can improve.

Techniques

Some of the major techniques are as follows:

- **Joining**: The therapist makes contact with each family member, beginning with the most distant, typically the father. If the therapist forms a relationship with the father, the family usually stays in therapy.
- **Homework**: The only assignment is to refrain from discussing therapy and relationships between sessions and to stop being therapists to one another.
- **Use of self**: One of the main techniques of symbolic–experiential therapy is the therapists' "use of self," in which the therapists share their own personal stories with the family. However, therapists should never betray themselves by getting lost in the family's problems.
- **Additional techniques**: According to Thomas (1992), the following techniques are often used:
  - Redefining symptoms as attempts to grow
  - Encouraging family members to talk about fantasy alternatives (such as how one spouse might kill the other)
  - Converting an intrapersonal problem to interpersonal stress by the use of fantasy (such as asking what the other family members might do if one family member committed suicide; the

therapist initiates the fantasy and asks the suicide-prone individual to complete it)

- Increasing and exaggerating the pain of a family member
- Playing with children in the interview
- Uusing feelings to confront people (such as telling parents to "bug off" when they interrupt the play between the therapist and one of the children)
- Sharing spontaneous, primary process suggestions as they arise (having people talk to rather than about each other)
- Playing with family roles (encouraging family members to reverse roles)
- Seeing love and hate not as opposites but as linked feelings (pp. 1226–227)

Further Resources

Napier, A., & Whitaker, C. A. (1978). *The family crucible.* New York: Harper & Row.

Napier, G. (1998). *Family therapy with the experts: Experiential therapy.* Boston: Allyn & Bacon.

Simon, R. (1985). Take it or leave it: An interview with Carl Whitaker. *The Family Therapy Networker, 9*(5), 27–37, 70–75.

Snow, K. (2002). Experiential family therapy. In J. Carlson & D. Kjos, *Theories and strategies of family therapy.* Boston: Allyn & Bacon.

Whitaker, C. A., & Bumberry, W. M. (1988). *Dancing with the family: A symbolic-experiential approach.* New York: Brunner/Mazel.

MILAN

The Milan group became fascinated by Bateson's (1972) concept of cybernetic circularity (the idea that the family system was constantly evolving). They developed an interview method of circular questioning to scan for differences and to tap the pattern of circularity used by each family. The therapist would remain neutral in an effort to assess the map or belief system of the family. When families appeared stuck, it was because of epistemological errors, or outdated belief systems. The therapist's goals were to develop a hypothesis from the data obtained in the interview and provide the families with new ideas that would allow them to change their belief systems.

This systemic school of family therapy takes its name from the cybernetic systems theory on which Bateson based his work. The information theory and the theory of games of which Bateson often wrote are important in this approach. Accordingly, human beings in reciprocal interactions through time are becoming each other; on viewing the river, one is the river. People are neither good nor evil. The family is always changing its members, who remain connected with one another, influencing one another continuously over time.

The Milan group would be considered the purest application of Bateson's systems work in that every technique or practice represents a particular application of his systemic theory. Presenting problems are recognized as serving a function in the family system. Patterns of interaction are passed on through generations; therefore, the history of the family is important in cognitive processes. Ideas, beliefs, perceptions, and fantasies are addressed, along with behaviors.

Goals

Change is seen as a random, discontinuous process, and therapists have no way to predict the creative, alternative ways families will find to evolve. By changing the thinking patterns and cognitive maps, it's possible to stimulate the family to find its own way of solving its problems. An overriding goal for the therapy team is to have the family discover, interrupt, and eventually change the rules of their game. The family may create a solution to its problem that is different from the therapist's goal. The parental couple is encouraged to regain the skills that will enhance its leadership.

Treatment Process

During treatment, the therapist must remain neutral. Frequently, the therapeutic process involves more than one therapist. The Milan system treatment process uses extended breaks between sessions, often one month or more, to allow prescriptions to affect the family fully.

Techniques

The strategies and techniques need to be used to gain deeper understanding:

- **Telephone chart**: This is an assessment tool developed by the Milan group. Information is obtained from the family over the telephone before they make an appointment. During this interview, the Milan group talks with the family member requesting treatment for at least 15 to 30 minutes. This is done to obtain information necessary to generate a hypothesis before the therapy team meets with the family and to decide whom the family should invite to the first session.

- **Circular questioning**: The role that the symptom is playing and has played in the family system is assessed using circular questions asking each family member to comment on or speculate about other family members' beliefs, feelings, and behavior. The therapist uses circular questions to learn the reactions of family members and determine their perceptions of the problem.
- **Hypothesizing**: A hypothesis is an educated assessment of a family's thinking patterns and myths that are holding it back. Hypothesizing is a process whereby the therapy team speculates, in advance of the family session, about what might be responsible for causing the family's problems. The therapists therefore come to each session prepared with hypotheses to be tested. This prevents the family from imposing its faulty problem definition on the therapy session and thereby preventing solutions.
- **Positive connotations**: The attribution of positive motives for an individual's or a family's symptomatic behavior patterns is critical to success in the Milan model. (Different terms used to describe a similar process in other models include reframing, noble ascription, and positive attribution.)
- **Prescriptions**: Prescriptions are paradoxical interventions whereby the family or certain family members are directed to perform the symptomatic behavior, thereby demonstrating that the symptom is under voluntary control. If the directive is resisted, the family gives up the troubling symptom.
- **Split-team intervention**: This is a type of prescription whereby the family is told that the therapy team has different opinions or ideas regarding a particular family dynamic. This process allows the family game to be uncovered, gives the therapist in the session leverage, and allows the family to find its own resolution.
- **Ritual and ceremony**: These are prescription methods whereby family members put into action a series of behaviors designed to alter the family game. The therapists spell out the specifics of the prescription in minute detail. This is the type of prescription that directs the family members to change their behavior under certain circumstances. Thus, the therapist hopes to change the cognitive map, or meaning of the behavior.
- **Counterparadox**: This technique is used to instill a therapeutic double bind in a family system to undo a preexisting family double bind message. For example, a common counterparadox is to inform the family that even though the therapists are change agents, they do not want to alter what seems to be a workable homeostatic balance in the family and consequently prescribe no change for the time being (Selvini-Palazzoli, Boscolo, Cecchin, & Prada, 1978).

Further Resources

Bateson, G. (1972). *Steps to an ecology of mind*. New York: E. P. Dutton.

Boscolo, L., Cecchin, G., Hoffman, L., & Penn, P. (1987). *Milan systemic family therapy: Conversations in theory and practice*. New York: Basic Books.

Prata, G. (1990). *A systemic harpoon into family games: Preventive interventions*. New York: Brunner Routledge.

Selvini-Palazzoli, M., Boscolo, L., Cecchin, G. F., & Prada, G. (1978). *Paradox and counterparadox: A new model and therapy of the family in schizophrenic transaction*. New York: Aronson.

Selvini-Palazzoli, M., Cirillo, S., Selvini, M., & Sorrention, A. M. (1989). *Family games: General models of psychotic processes in the family*. New York: W. W. Norton.

Simon, R. (1987, September/October). Good-bye paradox, hello invariant prescription: An interview with Mara Selvini-Palazzoli. *The Family Therapy Networker*, 17–33.

CONSTRUCTIVIST/NARRATIVE

This model of family therapy, based on constructivism, examines how individuals can reauthor their lives in a way that externalizes the concern that brought them to therapy. Therapists assist families to create new stories by asking them to explain unique outcomes (that is, situations in which the family has been successful and attained its goals or found solutions). The process of developing new stories creates a sense of personal urgency for family members that enables them to better manage future struggles. This therapeutic process also promotes an appreciation of the subjective nature of human histories. Constructivist family therapy contradicts the typically held position that the family system causes the problem; instead, it believes that the problem promotes the formation of the family's belief system (that is, the family system evolves around it).

Goals

This approach is still in the process of being developed, but many theorists, such as Anderson and Goolishian (1988), and White and Epston (1990), use portions of this approach. The overall focus is to develop new meanings or stories about our lives and our roles in life. Problems are seen as the stories that people have agreed to tell themselves. Constructivist/narrative therapists believe that stories of misery and personal failure are not so much approximations of the truth as they are life constructions made up of stories, metaphors, and the like (Gergen, 1991). Narrative therapists are less interested in objective claims and more so in the social utility that the stories have in explaining one's life. The goal of constructivist therapy is to reconstruct new stories or develop alternative stories in order to promote changes in behavior.

Treatment Process

The process of therapy can take the form of Anderson and Goolishian's (1988) model of seeing themselves as learners and conducting therapy from a position of not knowing. This is not to say that the therapist lacks knowledge or is without therapeutic skills, but rather he or she does not begin with any preconceived ideas about what should change. The family and the therapist work together to cocreate stories different from those previously held. The therapy takes its shape from the emergent qualities of the conversations it inspires. White and Epston (1990), in contrast, have specific stories they want families to adopt. Such stories highlight the family's past, present, and future, putting people and the family, not the problems, in charge. White and Epston also use externalization to help the family see themselves as separate from the problems that brought them into treatment.

Techniques

The following are some of the major techniques and strategies:

- **Externalizing**: In this process, families achieve a nonpathological view of the problem, one in which no one is to blame. The family members are offered an empowering opportunity to develop a new narrative that provides an alternative account of their lives.
- **Deconstruction**: This process unravels the history of the problem that has shaped the family members' lives.
- **Reconstruction/reauthoring**: This is the process by which a new story is developed.
- **Letters**: Following therapy, letters are written to the family that summarize the sessions, invite reluctant members to attend future sessions, and address the future. This serves the purpose of extending conversations while encouraging family members to record or map out their own futures.
- **Unique outcomes**: In this process, the family is asked to identify exceptional events, actions, or thoughts that contradict their dominant problem-saturated story and to develop alternative stories in which the problem does not defeat them or even exist.
- **Reflecting team**: One or more times during the therapy session, a group of other professionals (the reflecting team) who have been observing the session speak to the family and therapist so that they, in turn, may become observers of the process they have been a part of. The team members talk about the family conversation

they have just observed. This allows family members to shift between an inner and outer dialogue process and develop new perspectives on the same event, which often leads to a therapeutic breakthrough.

- **Questions:** Many of the questions used by Michael White (1990) are designed to elicit specific responses. They help people to realize (a) they are separate from the problem, (b) they have power over the problem, and (c) they are not who they thought they were. The questions allows the family to reach empowering conclusions.

Further Resources

Bubenzer, D. L, & West, J. D. (1993). Kenneth J. Gergen: Social construction, families, and therapy. *The Family Journal, 1*(2), 177–187.

Bubenzer, D. L., West, J. D., & Boughner, S. R. (1994). Michael White and the narrative perspective in therapy. *The Family Journal, 2*(1), 71–83.

Freedman, J., & Combs, G. (1996). *Narrative therapy: The social construction of preferred reality.* New York: Norton.

Maddigan, S., Carlson, J., & Kjos, D. (1998). *Family therapy with the experts: Narrative therapy* [Video]. Boston: Allyn & Bacon.

Monk, G., Winslade, J., Crockett, K., & Epston, D. (Eds.). (1997). *Narrative therapy in practice: The archaeology of hope.* San Francisco: Jossey–Bass.

O'Hanlon, B. (1994, November/December). The third wave. *The Family Therapy Networker,* 19–29.

West, J., & Bubenzer, D. (2002). Narrative family therapy. In J. Carlson & D. Kjos, *Theories and strategies of family therapy.* Boston: Allyn & Bacon.

West, J. D., Bubenzer, D. L., McQuistion, R. R., & Cox, J. A. (1995). Harlene Anderson: A conversation on language systems in therapy and training. *The Family Journal, 3*(2), 164–175.

Wylie, M. S. (1994, November/December). Panning for gold. *The Family Therapy Networker,* 40–48.

SOLUTION-FOCUSED

The philosophy behind the solution-focused model is based on the idea that change is constant and inevitable. The emphasis in therapy is on what is possible and changeable, rather than what is impossible. This model focuses on taking small steps to initiate change, and as the process progresses, changes occur. According to this model, deShazer (1985), for example, states that the solutions people are using are the problem, not the presenting problems themselves. Therefore, the focus is on solutions and competencies, rather than on problems. In this model, meanings are negotiable. The goal of therapy, therefore, is to choose meanings that will lead to change.

Goals

The goals of this type of brief therapy are to alter the worldview of the family in subtle ways and to change family members' behavior so that a solution to the problem evolves and the problem is resolved. The primary goal is addressing the family's presenting concern. The formation of a family's goals is a crucial component of the solution-focused model and begins in the first session. The goals should be specific, measurable, attainable, and challenging.

Treatment Process

The general treatment process allows for variation and still follows a fairly structured course. In the initial session, introductions are made, a structure is imposed, and a statement of the complaint is elicited; then specific information is collected from each family member. A discussion ensues about what goes on when the family is not experiencing the problems described in their complaint. Once the therapist gains sufficient background information, he or she may use "the miracle question," which asks the family how things would be different if a miracle occurred and the problem were solved. This encourages the family to think about change. Next the therapist develops compliments and tasks, which prepare the family to be responsive to homework tasks.

Techniques

The following strategies and techniques are used:

- **Deconstructing**: This refers to creating a doubt in the family's frame of reference regarding the complaint, which creates a need and an expectation for change, making the consideration of new behaviors possible.
- **Clue**: A clue is an intervention that mirrors the behavioral responses of the family. If the family operates using double binds or paradoxes, then an intervention would be a counterparadox. If the family behaves in a straightforward manner and takes direction well, the prescription of a task to be completed would constitute the clue.
- **Confusion**: Each family member is asked in detail about family differences, especially as they relate to goals in therapy, and the therapist admits confusion without reaching any resolution of the differences.

- **Past successes:** The therapist compliments the client on particular past successes but does not directly link these to the resolution of the present problem.
- **Skeleton keys:** These formal interventions or stock prescriptions can be used with many different types of problems:
  - **Write/read/burn:** On odd-numbered days of the month, the client is to spend 1 hour writing about all the bad and good times that he or she experienced with the ex-spouse, for example. On even days of the month, the client spends 1 hour reading what has been written and then burns it.
  - **Structured fight:** To decide the order of a fight, toss a coin. The winner complains for 10 straight minutes. Then the other person gets a turn for 10 minutes. Ten minutes of silence are maintained before the coin is tossed for a second round.
  - **Do something different:** The therapist directs the client to do something different related to the specific problem between the current session and the next session (agree not to mention the problem; when you are angry, smile).
  - **Overcoming the urge:** Clients who are tempted to eat too much or to return to drinking alcohol or taking drugs are directed by the therapist to observe whatever they are doing when they overcome the desire to indulge.
  - **Intervention before the initial session:** Clients are asked to pay attention to whatever is occurring in their lives—in marriage, family, or relationships—that they would like to have continue so that they can describe it in detail at the initial session (deShazer, 1985).
- **Miracle question:** Ask the family how things would be different if a miracle occurred and the problem were solved. This question encourages the family to think about change and exactly what would happen if it occurred.
- **Scaling:** The therapist has the family provide numerical ratings regarding the state of affairs in the family. On a scale from 1 to 10, with 1 being as bad as it could be and 10 being as good as it could be, where do they rate the situation now? Ongoing scaling in sessions presupposes change and provides feedback on differences among family members.

Further Resources

Berg, I. K., & Miller, S. (1992). *Working with the problem drinker: A solution-focused approach.* New York: W. W. Norton.

Berg, I. K., & Steiner, T. (2003). *Children's solution work.* New York: Norton.

Bubenzer, D. L., & West, J. D. (1993). William Hudson O'Hanlon: On seeking possibilities and solutions in therapy. *The Family Journal, 1*(4), 365–379.

DeJong, P., & Berg, I. K. (2000). *Interviewing for solutions* (2nd ed.). Pacific Grove, CA: Brooks Cole.

deShazer, S. (1982). *Patterns of brief family therapy: An ecosystemic approach.* New York: Guilford Press.

deShazer, S. (1985). *Keys to solutions in brief therapy.* New York: W. W. Norton.

deShazer, S. (1988). *Clues: Investigating solutions in brief therapy.* New York: W. W. Norton.

deShazer, S. (1991). *Putting differences to work.* New York: W. W. Norton.

deShazer, S. (1994). *Words were originally magic.* New York: W. W. Norton.

Miller, S., & Berg, I. K. (1995). *The miracle method.* New York: W. W. Norton.

O'Hanlon, B., Carlson, J., & Kjos, D. (1998). *Family therapy with the experts: Solution-oriented therapy* [Video]. Boston: Allyn & Bacon.

O'Hanlon, S., & O'Hanlon, B. (2002). Solution-oriented therapy with families. In J. Carlson & D. Kjos, *Theories and strategies of family therapy.* Boston: Allyn & Bacon.

STRATEGIC

The strategic family therapy model is based on the idea that families are rule-governed systems and can be understood best in this context. Furthermore, the presenting problem serves a function in the family that must be recognized. Symptoms are system-maintained and system-maintaining, and destructive ongoing cycles of interaction prevent the family or couple from achieving its basic purposes. Developmental stages in the family life cycle warrant consideration because halted development can lead to problems later. In strategic family therapy, the focus is on the present; an insight into the cause of the problem is less important than effecting a change in behavior or functioning.

Goals

Naturally, the goal of treatment is to solve the family's presenting problem, but the problem is defined as a sequence of behaviors among family members within a social context. It is the therapist's responsibility to plan interventions that resolve the problem within the social context of the clients. A secondary goal of treatment is to help the family members move to the next phase of the family life cycle, as well as their own individual life cycles. For example, the stage of a young adult's leaving home can be a particularly difficult one for him or her and for the rest of the family.

Treatment Process

The therapeutic process is practical, brief, and conducted by the therapist. The objective is to interrupt behavioral sequences to promote goal attainment. According to Haley (1987), therapy has five stages:

- **Social stage**: The therapist talks to each person, asking his or her name and obtaining a response, similar to a hostess or a host encouraging guests to feel comfortable. The therapist looks at the seating arrangement the family has chosen, mentally drawing tentative hypotheses, and matches the mood of the family to vocal tone and gestures.
- **Problem stage**: The therapist asks formal questions about the problem.
- **Interaction stage**: The therapist asks family members to talk with one another about the problem and observes who talks to whom, who remains silent, and who interrupts whom, but he or she does not share any tentative hypotheses with the family.
- **Goal-setting stage**: The therapist finds out what changes are expected by family members as a result of therapy, specifying these in clear behavioral terms.
- **Task-setting stage**: The therapist gives the family a directive. This may be practiced in the session, but it is more often a homework assignment to be completed between sessions. An appointment for the next session is set during this stage, and the therapist specifies which family members are to return.

Problem-solving therapy follows these stages until the presenting problem and any other problems are resolved.

Techniques

Several of the important techniques are as follows:

- **Directives**: In strategic therapy, the predominant technique is the use of directives, also occasionally called prescriptions. Directives are orders the therapist gives, either directly or indirectly, hoping for either compliance or its opposite, rebellion. The goal is to help people change their behavior, thereby changing their subjective reality. Directives serve three basic functions in therapy: (a) to promote a behavior change and new subjective experiences for family members, (b) to intensify the therapist–client relationship through the use of tasks, and (c) to gather useful information about the family by noting the family's responses to the directives.
- **Paradoxical directives**: The therapist assigns tasks in which success is based on the family defying instructions or following them to an extreme point and ultimately recoiling, thus producing

change. Typically, these tasks are assigned when the therapist has reason to believe the family will resist straightforward directives.

- **Reframing**: This is also referred to as relabeling, positive interpretation, positive connotation, and reattribution. In this intervention, the therapist offers a different view of the presenting problem that enables the family members to think and behave differently within the next context.
- **Prescribing the symptom**: In this paradoxical intervention, the client is directed to perform the symptomatic behavior.
- **Pretend techniques**: These are paradoxical interventions in which the clients are directed to pretend to be experiencing the problem behavior. For example, a father who fears having a heart attack is told to pretend he is having one during the therapy session. Because the behavior is the result of pretending, it may be classified as voluntary and unreal.
- **Restraining changes**: In these paradoxical interventions, the therapist attempts to discourage the family from moving too fast. He or she may even deny the possibility of change.
- **Ordeals**: The therapist issues a directive that tells the client to do something that is more severe than having the symptoms of the problematic behavior. Typically, the directive refers to something that is good for the person. For example, a woman who feels anxious is required to exercise for several minutes.
- **Metaphor for tasks**: These are directives that involve activities or conversations that symbolically relate to the presenting problem and thereby indirectly facilitate change.
- **Devil's pact**: This is a task to which the family must commit before the therapist discloses it. The family is advised that the task is extremely demanding, and therefore the family must decide whether or not they really want to resolve their problems.

Further Resources

Carlson, J. (2002). Strategic family therapy. In J. Carlson & D. Kjos, *Theories and strategies of family therapy*. Boston: Allyn & Bacon.

Coyne, J., Carlson, J., & Kjos, D. (1998). *Family therapy with the experts: Strategic therapy* [Video]. Boston: Allyn & Bacon.

Haley, J. (1963). *Strategies of psychotherapy*. New York: Grune & Stratton.

Haley, J. (1973). *Uncommon therapy: The psychiatric techniques of Milton H. Erickson, M.D.* New York: W. W. Norton.

Haley, J. (1984). *Ordeal therapy: Unusual ways to change behavior*. San Francisco: Jossey–Bass.

Haley, J. (1987). *Problem solving therapy* (2nd ed.). San Francisco: Jossey–Bass.

Haley, J., & Richeport–Haley, M. (2004). *The art of strategic therapy*. New York: Brunner Routledge.

Madanes, C. (1981). *Strategic family therapy*. San Francisco: Jossey–Bass.

Madanes, C. (1984). *Behind the one-way mirror: Advances in the practice of strategic therapy*. San Francisco: Jossey–Bass.

Simon, R. (1986, September/October). Behind the one-way kaleidoscope. *The Family Therapy Networker*, 19–29, 64–67.

West, J. D., & Bubenzer, D. L. (1993). Cloe Madanes: Reflections on family therapy. *The Family Journal*, 1(1), 98–106.

STRUCTURAL

Structural family therapy focuses attention on the present and the future. According to this theory, the history of the family is manifest in the present, and therefore it is accessible through interventions in the here and now. Humans are viewed as social creatures and must be viewed holistically within the context of their social systems. Environmental factors are given priority over hereditary factors. The reciprocal nature of systemic causality (that is, the situation whereby an individual's behavior influences and is influenced by his or her social system) is acknowledged.

An emphasis is also placed on process over content. The family structure is seen as being composed of sets of family transactions. Transactions determine how family members relate; they can be verbal or nonverbal, known or unknown. Transactions also regulate behavior in two ways: (a) a power hierarchy exists that dictates authority and decision making in a family, and (b) mutual expectations formed by negotiations over time are determined and fulfilled by individuals in a family.

The components of the family structure that exist to carry out various family tasks are called subsystems. Subsystems can be formed on the basis of generation, interest, or a specific family function. It is possible for family members to belong to several subsystems at the same time. The most important subsystems are the adult, parental, and sibling subsystems. Subsystem boundaries are constructed by a set of rules that define who participates in the subsystem and how individuals participate. The nature of the boundaries has a significant effect on the functioning of the subsystem as well as the entire family unit. The three types of boundaries lie on a continuum: (a) rigid boundaries, (b) clear boundaries, and (c) diffuse boundaries.

The rules of the family provide the structure by which operations can occur that meet the needs of the family as a whole. Substructures within the family system interact according to the rules that serve as boundaries between the subsystems. Internal and external stressors necessitate an adaptation of the family structure to maintain homeostasis. In addition, the developmental process creates a predictable stressor for most family systems.

Goals

The overriding goal of structural family therapy is to solve problems in the family and to change the underlying systemic structure. By bringing about changes in the structure of the family, one can solve the presenting problems. Structural family therapy emphasizes action over insight. In particular, action occurs in the session. By restructuring family transactions directly in the session, one effects change in the family structure, and through homework assignments, families continue to change through action.

Treatment Process

Minuchin (1974) saw treatment as a structural change that modifies the family's functioning so it can better perform necessary tasks. Once the therapist has initiated change, new processes will be maintained by the family's self-regulating mechanisms. Because the family is a dynamic system in continual movement, the steps in the therapeutic process may overlap and recycle. The typical steps in the treatment process of structural family therapy are as follows:

1.) **Joining and accommodating**: The therapist adjusts to the communication style and perceptions of family members to join with the system. The goal in this stage is to establish an effective therapeutic relationship with the family.
2.) **Structural diagnosis**: This refers to the continuous process of observation, hypothesis testing, and reformulation relevant to the family's structure and transactions. The goal in this stage is to provide a framework of information relevant to the problem in the family system, which is amenable to structural intervention.
3.) **Restructuring**: The therapist uses therapeutic interventions that bring about change through a modification in the family structure. The goal in this stage is the development of a family structure capable of appropriately dealing with future stressful situations.

Techniques

The following are some of the strategies and techniques:

• **Joining**: The primary goal of joining or accommodating techniques is to establish an effective therapeutic relationship. This involves acting out the predominant mood of the family. To accomplish this end, three restructuring functions occur:

- **Maintenance**: Supporting specific behaviors and verbalizations to increase the strength and independence of individual subsystems and alliances
- **Tracking**: Using clarification, amplification, and approval of family communication to reinforce individuals and subsystems
- **Mimesis**: Adopting the family's communication style and conforming to its affective range (for example, if the family frequently uses expletives, the therapist adopts this mode of speaking)
- **Restructuring**: This is a process of changing the structure of the family. It can be accomplished through enactments, delineating the boundaries, unbalancing (by forming a coalition with some family members against another family member), and complementarity. Walsh and McGraw (1996) listed the following as restructuring techniques used by Minuchin:
  - **Enactment**: Having family members recreate an interaction. The interaction may be relatively innocuous or may relate directly to the presenting problem. Enactments are used to diagnose family structure, increase intensity, and restructure family systems.
  - **Actualizing family transactional patterns**: Stimulating naturalistic family interactions so the therapist can observe the typical transaction. This may be achieved by directing the family to have a conversation or by the therapist refusing to answer a question.
  - **Marking boundaries**: Strengthening diffuse boundaries and increasing the permeability of rigid boundaries to enhance healthy subsystem interaction. This can be accomplished by helping the family members to set new rules, renegotiate old rules, and establish specific functions for each subsystem.
  - **Escalating stress**: Heightening tension in a family to force members to accept restructuring. This can be achieved by encouraging conflict when it occurs, joining alliances against other family members, and blocking dysfunctional transactional patterns that serve to decrease stress in a system.
  - **Assigning tasks**: Assigning specific tasks for individuals or subsystems to be accomplished in the session and at home.
  - **Utilizing symptoms**: Altering the function that a symptom serves in the family system by encouraging, deemphasizing, or relabeling the symptom. This might also remove the secondary gain that may be inherent in the symptomatology.

- **Paradoxical injunction**: Imposing a directive that places the client in a therapeutic double bind that promotes change, regardless of client compliance with the directive. This technique is typically used when resistance to the directive is anticipated.
- **Manipulate mood in the family**: Modeling an exaggerated reflection of a frequently manifested mood in the family. For example, if yelling is frequently used in the family, to create a volatile mood the therapist may yell even louder.
- **Support, education, and guidance**: Providing direct instruction to the family to behave differently.
- **Reframing**: In reframing, a positive connotation is given to a negative behavior. For example, a mother may yell at her son to do his homework. The yelling on the part of the mother is reframed as concern about her son. Reframing is an important interpersonal skill; it shows that every behavior has advantages and disadvantages. By accepting the behavior, the person will often decrease the behavior.
- **Relabeling**: If blaming is typical of a family in treatment, an adjective that is positive in connotation is substituted for an adjective that is negative in connotation. For example, if the wife screams at the husband that he is controlling, the therapist relabels by saying the husband is overburdened.
- **The family lunch**: Minuchin, Roseman, and Baker (1978) developed a technique for working with anorexic families in which the therapist actually eats with the family and enacts the parents attempting to force the anorectic person to eat.

Further Resources

Aponte, H. J. (1994). *Bread and spirit: Therapy with the new poor: Diversity of race, culture and values*. New York: Norton.

Aponte, H., Carlson, J., & Kjos, D. (1998). *Family therapy with the experts: Structural family therapy* [Video]. Boston: Allyn & Bacon.

Aponte, H. J., & DiCesare, E. J. (2002). Structural family therapy. In J. Carlson & D. Kjos, *Theories and strategies of family therapy*. Boston: Allyn & Bacon.

Minuchin, S. (1974). *Families and family therapy*. Cambridge, MA: Harvard University Press.

Minuchin, S., & Fishman, C. H. (1981). *Family therapy techniques*. Cambridge, MA: Harvard University Press.

Minuchin, S., & Nichols, M. P. (1993). *Family healing*. New York: Free Press.

Minuchin, S., Roseman, B., & Baker, L. (1978). *Psychosomatic families: Anorexia nervosa in context*. Cambridge, MA: Harvard University Press.

Simon, R. (1984). Stranger in a strange land: An interview with Salvador Minuchin. *The Family Therapy Networker, 8*(6), 21–31, 66–68.

West, J. D., & Bubenzer, D. L. (1993). Salvador Minuchin: Practitioner and theoretician. *The Family Journal, 1*(3), 277–282.

BEHAVIORAL AND COGNITIVE-BEHAVIORAL

Behavioral and cognitive–behavioral family therapists believe that families and couples are influenced solely by their environments. Behavioral patterns are learned, so therefore dysfunctional behaviors can be replaced by more adaptive ones. In marriage and family therapy, therapists and the family can specify behavioral goals, assess present patterns, and develop new patterns. Cognitive–behavioral therapists have gone beyond a focus on just observable actions to include the words people say to themselves and others. They have developed specific techniques for confronting irrational ideas espoused by family members.

Behavioral and cognitive–behavioral approaches are also linear. They address the thoughts and behaviors of individuals who pursue goals in logical ways. The family is not viewed as a separate system with properties of its own (Thomas, 1992, p. 312).

Goals

The goals of cognitive–behavioral therapy are as follows:

- Assess present patterns and teach families how to assess behavioral interactions and/or thoughts.
- Teach new adaptive patterns such as communication skills, problem resolution, competencies, behavioral exchange, contracting, negotiation of rules and roles, and management of conflict.
- Weaken or decrease maladaptive behavior.
- Create and maintain reinforcement patterns that create a collaborative reciprocity.

Treatment Process

The therapeutic process involves a clear analysis and assessment of the family's functioning. The cognitive–behavioral therapist uses assessment before initiating therapy, during the initial session, throughout the therapy process, at termination, and often in follow-up many months after therapy is terminated. The therapist functions as an educator and role model to teach the family how to assess their own relationships, implement the strategies of behavioral/cognitive change, and to use their own resources to strengthen their relationships. This is essentially a teacher and learner model.

Techniques

Some of the major techniques are as follows:

- **Completing inventories and presenting ground rules**: This technique is used at the beginning as well as throughout the treatment process. An assessment is made of the treatment expectations as well as what is going on in the present relationship. The developmental history is of a secondary nature and is only of interest as it affects the present.
- **Caring days**: Here each spouse is asked to describe the exact behavior his or her partner should show in order for the spouse to know his or her partner cares. For example, each spouse is required to clearly state, "I feel loved when you. . . . " The rules stipulate that the requested behaviors be small and exhibited at least daily. The behaviors also must not have been the cause of recent conflicts, are not chores, are positive, and are specific (Stuart, 1980).
- **Communication skills training**: Behavioral and cognitive-behavioral therapists teach couples to listen, to make constructive requests using "I" statements, to give positive feedback complimenting a spouse on a particular positive behavior immediately after it occurs, and to use clarification and questions to discuss nonverbal and verbal behaviors.
- **Contracting**: Using a win–win approach, families are encouraged to negotiate a holistic contract. Each family member is required to make requests of the others for specific positive behaviors. Other family members rephrase the request and ask for clarification of meaning. After reaching a consensus, they record their request in contract form and sign it.
- **Decision-making skills**: Each person identifies those areas where they exercise power and those areas where they ideally would like to exercise power. The family then negotiates who will control what area, under what conditions, and in what situations. Families may use a "powergram," a strategy that asks family members to discuss those areas that each member controls alone, those that each controls after consulting others, and those that are controlled equally.
- **Conflict management skills**: Here discussions are confined to the present, rather than expanding to related incidents or issues from the past. The stages of conflict include trigger, reflex, fatigue, commitment, reconsolidation, and rapprochement.

- **Maintenance of therapeutic outcome**: This process includes the following components:
  - Explaining the rationale for each intervention and the principles of relationship change
  - Modeling techniques during the therapy that the clients themselves can apply in their relationship in the future
  - Teaching family members how to assess interaction and change the relationships so that they can continue these processes after termination
  - Helping families to anticipate predictable relapses
  - Identifying support in the environment by encouraging the family to spend 1 hour a month assessing the family relationship, rewarding one another for the gains that have been made, and making new requests for additional desirable behaviors
  - Equipping the family with reminders of ways the family has successfully handled problems in the past, such as a written summary of the interventions used and the changes made by each person after the completion of an experiential "what-if" exercise
- **Cognitive restructuring**: Family members are encouraged to become observers of their own interpretations of family events and to develop skills to test the validity of these interpretations through collecting and processing data (Epstein, Schlesinger, & Dryden, 1988).

Further Resources

Beck, A. T. (1988). *Love is never enough*. New York: Harper & Row.

Epstein, N., Schlesinger, S. E., & Dryden, W. (Eds.). (1988). *Cognitive-behavioral therapy with families*. New York: Brunner/Mazel.

Freeman, A. (Ed.). (1983). *Cognitive therapy with couples and groups*. New York: Plenum.

Stuart, R. (1980). *Helping couples change: A social learning approach to marital therapy*. New York: Guilford Press.

Stuart, R., Carlson, J., & Kjos, D. (1998). *Family therapy with the experts: Behavioral family therapy* [Video]. Boston: Allyn & Bacon.

Stuart, R. (2002). Integrative therapy for couples. In J. Carlson & D. Kjos, *Theories and strategies of family therapy*. Boston: Allyn & Bacon.

OBJECT RELATIONS

The essence of object–relations theory is quite simple: We relate to people in the present partly on the basis of expectations formed by an earlier experience. This theory is based on Freudian theory and the later work of theorists such as Kohut, Mahler, Fairbairn, and Winnicott. The theory conceptualizes current relationship difficulties as originating in early parent–child interactions. This model attempts to bridge intrapsychic and interpersonal approaches by using object–relations concepts such as individual development, projection, and ego identity within a relations context. The general goal of this model is to provide a therapeutic environment in which the family can understand and resolve unconscious issues that are problematic to current family functioning.

Goals

The goal of object–relations family therapy is to make the clients conscious of the unconscious patterns established in the family of origin. This is done through interpreting patterns of transference and countertransference, which leads to an increased awareness and an elimination of blocks.

Treatment Process

Stages of object–relations therapy involve:

- Establishment of a therapeutic contract
- Development of therapeutic alliance
- Working through defenses and resistances; family members' object relations from the family of origin are played out and talked about, leading to an increased understanding of any interlocking pathologies
- Termination issues dealing with loss and separation

Techniques

Object–relations therapists are a diverse group that shares the idea that internal images derived from significant relationships in the past produce faulty, unsatisfying, or distorted dealings with people in the present. This approach is characterized by four basic techniques:

- **Listening**: The therapist resists the pressure to do something and maintains an analytic neutrality, which promotes an atmosphere of listening and understanding. No demands are placed on the family to change.
- **Empathy**: The analyst works very hard at understanding the world from the family's point of view.

- **Interpretation**: Interpretations are used to clarify hidden and confusing aspects of experience.
- **Maintaining analytical neutrality**: The therapist suspends involvement with the outcome and maintains an atmosphere of analytic exploration.

Further Resources

Erdman, P., & Caffery, T. (2003). *Attachment and family systems: Conceptual, empirical and therapeutic relatedness*. New York: Brunner Routledge.

Framo, J. (1992). *Family of origin therapy: An intergenerational approach*. New York: Brunner/Mazel.

Scharff, D. E., & Scharff, J. S. (1987). *Object relations family therapy*. Northvale, NJ: Jason Aronson.

Scharff, J., Carlson, J., & Kjos, D. (1998). *Family therapy with the experts: Object relations therapy* [Video]. Boston: Allyn & Bacon.

Scharff, J. S., & Scharff, D. E. (2002). Object relations therapy. In J. Carlson & D. Kjos, *Theories and strategies of family therapy*. Boston: Allyn & Bacon.

Slipp, S. (1984). *Object relations: A dynamic bridge between individual and family treatment*. New York: Jason Aronson.

Slipp, S. (1988). *The technique and practice of object relations family therapy*. Northvale, NJ: Jason Aronson.

SUMMARY

This chapter has presented the main traditional approaches to family therapy. Each was presented in terms of a brief description of approach, goals, therapeutic process, and techniques. Readers can refer to this overview to develop a general intervention plan before developing a more tailored plan. The remaining chapters of the book describe the process of tailoring therapy plans to meet individual family needs.

References

Anderson, H., & Goolishian, H. (1988). Human systems as linguistic systems: Preliminary and evolving ideas about the implications for clinical theory. *Family Process, 27*, 371–393.

Bateson, G. (1972). *The steps to an ecology of mind*. New York: E. P. Dutton.

Bowen, M. (1985). *Family therapy and clinical practice*. New York: Jason Aronson.

deShazer, S. (1985). *Keys to the solution in brief therapy*. New York: W. W. Norton.

Dinkmeyer, D., & Dinkmeyer, J. (1991). Adlerian family therapy. In A. M. Home & J. L. Passmore (Eds.), *Family counseling and therapy*. Itasca, IL: F. E. Peacock.

Epstein, N., Schlesinger, S. E., & Dryden, W. (1988). Concepts and methods of cognitive–behavioral family treatment. In N. Epstein, S. E. Schlesinger, & W. Dryden (Eds.), *Cognitive behavioral therapy with families* (pp. 5–48). New York: Brunner/Mazel.

Gehart, D. R., & Tuttle, A. R. (2003). *Theory-based treatment planning for marriage and family therapists*. Pacific Grove, CA: Brooks Cole.

Gergen, K. J. (1991). *The saturated self: Dilemmas of identity in contemporary life*. New York: Basic Books.

Grunwald, B. B., & McAbee, H. V. (1985). *Guiding the family: Practical counseling techniques*. Muncie, IN: Accelerated Development.

Haley, J. (1987). *Problem solving therapy*. (2nd ed.). San Francisco: Jossey–Bass.

Kaplan, D. M. (2003). *Family counseling for all counselors*. Greensboro, NC: CAPS Publications.

Kerr, M. E., & Bowen, M. (1988). *Family evaluation: An approach based on Bowen 's theory*. New York: W. W. Norton.

Lambert, M. J. (2003). Psychotherapy outcome research: Implications for integrative and eclectic therapists. In J. C. Norcross & M. R. Goldfried (Eds.), *Handbook of psychotherapy integration*. New York: Oxford University Press.

Minuchin, S. (1974). *Families and family therapy*. Cambridge, MA: Harvard University Press.

Minuchin, S., Roseman, B., & Baker, L. (1978). *Psychosomatic families: Anorexia nervosa in context*. Cambridge, MA: Harvard University Press.

Papero, D. V. (1991). The Bowen theory. In A. M. Home & J. L. Passmor (Eds.), *Family counseling and therapy*. Itasca, IL: F. E. Peacock.

Satir, V. (1983). *Conjoint family therapy* (3rd ed.). Palo Alto, CA: Science & Behavior Books.

Satir, V., & Baldwin, M. (1983). *Satir step by step: A guide to creating change in families*. Palo Alto, CA: Science & Behavior Books.

Satir, V., & Bitter, J. R. (1991). Human validation process model. In A. M. Home & J. L. Passmore (Eds.), *Family counseling and therapy* (2nd ed.). Itasca, IL: F. E. Peacock.

Selvini-Palazzoli, M., Boscolo, L., Cecchin, G. F., & Prada, G. (1978). *Paradox and counterparadox: A new model and therapy of the family in schizophrenic transaction*. New York: Aronson.

Sherman, R., & Dinkmeyer, D. (1987). *Systems of family therapy: An Adlerian integration*. New York: Brunner/Mazel.

Stuart, R. (1980). *Helping couples change: A social learning approach to marital therapy*. New York: Guilford Press.

Thomas, M. D. (1992). *An introduction to marital and family therapy*. New York: Charles Merrill.

Walsh, W. M., & McGraw, J. A. (1996). *Essentials of family therapy: A therapist's guide to eight approaches*. Denver: Love Publishing Company.

Whitaker, C. A., & Bumberry, W. M. (1988). *Dancing with the family: A symbolic-experiential approach*. New York: Brunner/Mazel.

Whitaker, C. A., & Keith, D. V. (1981). Symbolic–experiential family therapy. In A. S. Gurman & D. P. Kniskern (Eds.), *Handbook of family therapy* (pp. 187–225). New York: Brunner/Mazel.

White, M., & Epston, D. (1990). *Narrative means to therapeutic ends*. New York: W. W. Norton.

3

INTEGRATIVE TREATMENT
WITH COUPLES AND FAMILIES

THE BASIS FOR TREATMENT EFFICACY

In each treatment session, the therapist is confronted with a barrage of information: verbal and nonverbal behavior, intrapsychic and interpersonal processes, transactional patterns, attitudes, and more. The multitude of processes that occur in the individual, the subsystem, the family, and the therapeutic system are so complex and multidimensional that no one could possibly attend to all or even most of them. Neither is it possible for any therapist to reflect on all these perceptions, to perfectly formulate them, and to decide on the best possible intervention plan and strategies. Therefore, the therapist limits his or her observations, reflections, and interventions to a reasonable and manageable number of variables and selectively decides on which processes, patterns of behavior, and structure to focus. These decisions are often determined by the therapist's own life history, personality, philosophy, and professional training. Many possible paths are available.

An important aspect of professional training is the theory or theories of family therapy that the therapist espouses. These theories serve to organize clinical information, concepts, and experiences in a way that limits reality to a limited number of concepts and processes that then allows plausible effect and goal–means–results thinking and conclusions to be made (Textor, 1988; Gehart & Tuttle, 2003). In short, the adopted theories greatly influence what the therapist perceives, formulates, and reports or describes, and then he or she intervenes. Thus, because of this selectivity factor, each theory of family therapy is necessarily limited and one-sided. Because no theory can explain and predict all the behavioral patterns and intrapsychic and interpersonal processes a therapist may observe, similarly no theory or approach is suited for the treatment of all behavioral, intrapsychic, and interpersonal problems.

Most introductory family therapy texts detail various theories, schools, and approaches to family therapy, some of which were highlighted in chapter 2. Some of these approaches have engendered considerable support, but the loyalty of supporters tends to be based more on evangelical fervor than scientific rigor. Historically, the early development of each individual therapy approach seems to have gone through an evangelical phase in which the new approach is viewed as transcending the mistakes of previous therapy systems and seeming to possess unlimited therapeutic potential. Proselytizing about the new approach to converts actually begins with workshops, publications, independent training institutes, and then university training programs. Psychoanalysis went through such an era between 1900 and 1930, whereas the mid-1950s to the early 1970s were the evangelical years of behavior therapy.

INTEGRATION

Since 1970 we have witnessed evangelical fervor in the field of couples and family therapy. Too often the proponents of the psychoanalytic, systems, and behavioral family therapy models have espoused purism and denounced attempts toward eclecticism and integration. Haley (1987) was one of the strongest opponents of integration. He believed that those who espouse integration are essentially unable and unwilling to understand the unique nature of family therapy. Thankfully, this evangelical era in family therapy has passed, and the expectation that family therapists must adhere to a particular model of family therapy is lessening. More and more therapists are concluding that no single theory or set of interventions can be applied to all cases. The shifting therapeutic scene and the increasing number of nontraditional families presenting for therapy have hastened this conclusion. The question now is, how can the insights of different theories and approaches be combined and systematically integrated to yield a more comprehensive and useful theory to guide therapeutic work with today's family?

The past decade has been replete with published accounts of ingenious and successful efforts at integrating the concepts and techniques of the traditional models of family therapy. However, these efforts at integration are often hampered by conceptual and terminological confusion. The following section attempts to clarify such concepts and terminology.

The term integration is similar to, but still different from, the related concepts of eclecticism, tailoring, and matching. Eclecticism refers to a philosophy of treatment in which the clinician selects concepts and treatment methods from a variety of theoretical sources. This approach also contains an element of pragmatism. In other words, eclectic clinicians practice the way they do because they have found that such an approach works. Integration refers to a treatment philosophy in which the clinician incorporates and combines discrete parts of theories and treatment processes. The purpose of theory integration is the construction of a more useful model that maximizes the therapist's understanding and ability to intervene effectively in changing a specific family system (Norcross & Goldfried, 2003).

Integrators are eclectics, but not all eclectics are integrators. Both eclectic and integrative positions are basically clinician-centered, which is to say that the clinician develops a particular way of personalizing therapeutic concepts and techniques to meet his or her own needs for therapeutic effectiveness, intellectual syntheses, or whatever is necessary. In contrast, tailoring refers to the philosophy of basing treatment decisions on what is best for the client or system. Gordon Paul's (1987) classic formulation describes the focus of tailoring: "What treatment, by whom, is the most effective for this individual or couple with that specific problem and under which set of circumstances?"(p. 111). Essentially, tailoring is basically a client or couple-centered orientation to treatment planning and intervention. Furthermore, tailoring can be distinguished from matching. Technically, *matching* means assigning a client, whether a couple or family, to a specific clinician or treatment modality most likely to increase therapeutic efficacy. *Tailoring* means specifically adapting treatment methods to client needs once matching has occurred. Nevertheless, the two terms are often used interchangeably.

Another way of thinking about integration is in terms of the "process" of integration—how integration takes places—and the "content" of integration—what is being integrated (Case & Robinson, 1990). The family therapy literature describes the content of integration in at least four distinct ways: (a) combining individual and family therapy, (b) developing a specific method of treatment that combines elements from different family therapy schools, (c) creating metatheoretical models, and (d) matching family therapy models with family style or level of functioning.

The process of integration can involve a number of strategies. Colapinto (1984) described three such strategies: (a) the recipe book approach, based on the belief that a particular problem dictates a particular method; (b) the spontaneous approach, based on the clinician's intuitive judgment about what might work best at a given time; and (c) the model-building approach, whereby the clinician chooses a unifying conceptual core as a central organizing principle supplemented by specific techniques or ideas from other approaches.

In 1986, Norcross estimated that approximately 40% of psychotherapists classify themselves as favoring an integrative orientation among professional disciplines, 40% of counseling psychologists, 35% of clinical psychologists in independent practice, 42% of behavioral therapists, and 54% of clinical social workers. No data seem to be available to indicate the percentage of family therapists who primarily identify themselves as operating from an integrative perspective.

Norcross found no differences, except for clinical experience, between those espousing an eclectic perspective and those adopting a noneclectic perspective. Clinicians espousing integration tended to be older and more experienced than their nonintegrative counterparts. Robertson (1979) identified six factors that appear to facilitate the adoption of an integrative viewpoint. The first is a lack of pressure in training and professional environments to bend to a doctrinal position. This includes the absence of charismatic figures to emulate. The second factor is the length of clinical experience. As therapists gain experience with a heterogeneous client population and a wide variety of problems, they tend to reject a single theory or model approach. The third factor involves the extent to which their practice of psychotherapy is perceived as a career versus a vocation or job. Robertson believed that integrators are more likely to represent the former position. The last three factors are personality variables. Integrators have an obsessive/compulsive desire to synthesize all the interventions in the therapeutic universe. They have maverick temperaments, allowing them to move beyond their therapeutic model of origin. Finally, integrators possess a skeptical attitude toward the status quo.

According to Lebow (2003), most family therapy in the 21st century is practiced with integrative methods. He found several strengths of integrative approaches: They are able to explain behavior in a more comprehensive fashion, provide greater treatment flexibility, apply to a broader population base, match the treatment to the unique needs of the client, use the major benefits of the approaches, to be more objective in the selection of strategies for change, and to readily adopt new efficacious techniques. These strengths are very well suited, and the challenges for the future in couples and family therapy include the following (Sexton, Weeks, & Robbins, 2003):

- Avoid the enticing comfort of simplicity—embrace the ambiguity of complexity.
- Embrace the era of evidence and accountability.
- Rediscover the "relationship" in family and couples therapy.
- Identify and incorporate the common mechanics of successful change.
- Expand evidence-based models of practice that are clinically responsive and systematic.
- Integrate diversity and culture into the call of theory, research, and practice.
- Disseminate effective models into the world.

The shortcomings of the various family therapy approaches have prompted the search for more comprehensive and integrative theories of family therapy—the topic of this chapter. The next section will present six of the models of integrative treatment that seem to address these future challenges. The following chart highlights some of the major theoretical influences of each of the six models:

Transtheoretical	Psychoanalysis
	Gestalt
	Cognitive
	Experiential
	Existential
	Behavioral
	Person-Centered
	Family Systems
Integrated Problem-Centered Therapy (IPCT)	Family Systems
	Behavioral
	Psychodynamic
	Gestalt
	Self-Psychology
	Sex Therapy
	Biobehavioral

Integrative Behavioral Couples Therapy (IBCT)	Behavioral Strategic Person-Centered Emotion-Focused
Emotionally Focused Couples Therapy (EFCT)	Experiential Humanistic Gestalt Family Systems Person-Centered Attachment Theory
Olsen's Integrative	Cognitive Family Systems Object Relations Structural Family Therapy Multigenerational Family Therapy
Snyder's Pluralistic	Structural Family Therapy Cognitive Behavioral Insight Schema Therapy Attachment Theory Interpersonal Role Therapy Developmental Theory

TRANSTHEORETICAL THERAPY

Most theories focus on why people do *not* change, rather than on how people do change. They also do not provide models for how insights and ideas from diverse therapies might be integrated into their approach to change. The transtheoretical approach sets out to consciously construct a model of therapy and change that draws from major theories.

Processes of Change

The following are the 10 processes of self-change that have received the most empirical support to date (Prochaska & DiClemete, 2003):

- Consciousness raising
- Dramatic relief
- Self-reevaluation
- Environmental reevaluation

- Self-liberation
- Social liberation
- Counterconditioning
- Stimulus control
- Reinforcement management
- Helping relationship

This is an eclectic set. Consciousness raising has roots in the psycho-analytic tradition; dramatic relief or catharsis has roots in the Gestalt tradition; self-reevaluation and environmental reevaluation have roots in the cognitive and experiential traditions; self-liberation and social liberation have roots in the existential tradition; counterconditioning, stimulus control, and reinforcement management have roots in the be-havioral tradition; and the helping relationship has roots in the person-centered tradition.

Prochaska and his colleagues realized that most systems of psycho-therapy use only two or three of these processes. They believed that to be helpful an approach was needed that could use all 10 processes of change.

Stages of Change

The appropriate use of change processes involves the stages of change through which people progress (Prochaska & DiClemente, 1982). Change unfolds over a series of six stages: precontemplation, contem-plation, preparation, action, maintenance, and termination. Each stage of the change process calls for different skills.

Levels of Change

The levels of change represent a hierarchical organization of five dis-tinct but interrelated levels of psychological problems that can be ad-dressed in psychotherapy. Although the therapist can isolate certain symptoms and syndromes, they occur in the context of complicated, in-terrelated levels of human functioning:

- Symptom–situational problems
- Maladaptive cognitions
- Current interpersonal conflicts
- Family–systems conflicts
- Intrapersonal conflicts

Historically, systems of psychotherapy attribute psychological problems to one or two levels and intervene there. For example, behavior therapists deal with symptom–situational problems, cognitive therapists on maladaptive cognitions, family therapists on the systems level, and analytic therapists on intrapersonal conflicts. It is important that the client and therapist agree at what level of change they attribute the problem to and are willing to work together.

Interventions

The types of interventions that are used depend on an accurate assessment of the stages, the processes, and the levels of change. Specific instruments have been developed that can be used to assess each stage, level, and process of change (Prochaska & DiClemente, 2003).

Among the stages of change, individuals apply change processes the least during precontemplation. Precontemplators process less information about their problems, spend less time and energy reevaluating themselves, experience fewer emotional reactions to the negative aspects of their problems, are less open with significant others about their problems, and do little to shift their attention or their environment in the direction of overcoming their problems. In therapy, these clients are labeled resistant.

Consciousness raising and dramatic relief help to increase awareness and the emotional release that relates to problems. Clients in contemplation are most open to consciousness-raising interventions and bibliotherapy. As they become more aware of themselves and the nature of their problems, they are willing to evaluate themselves both cognitively and effectively. The evaluation is both of self and the impact on the environment.

Movement from precontemplation to contemplation and movement through the contemplation stage involves the use of cognitive, affective, and evaluative processes of change. To better prepare individuals for action, changes are required in how they think and feel about their problem behaviors and how they value their problematic lifestyle.

In the preparation stage, clients are on the verge of taking action and need to set goals and priorities. They often need to develop an action plan for new behaviors and find that counterconditioning and stimulus control are useful in reducing the problem behaviors. As action proceeds, the therapist works as a consultant or coach to help clients fine-tune their life change. Supportive counseling can also be helpful as times of change also produce uncertainty. Knowing that another person cares helps to reduce some of the predictable stress of change.

Successful maintenance involves assessing the conditions under which one is vulnerable to relapse to the previous ineffective behaviors. Strategies to prevent relapse are then implemented:

> As therapy progresses through the stages at the symptom/situational level, particular processes are applied at each stage. Therapy can shift to a deeper level, if necessary and progress through the stages by applying the particular processes relevant to each stage. This *shifting levels* approach is one strategy for applying transtheoretical therapy. Another is the *key level* strategy, in which one particular level is assessed as relevant for a particular patient with a particular problem. With this strategy, therapy focuses on only one key level and progress involves movement through the stages by applying appropriate processes at each stage. A third approach is the *maximum impact* strategy, which involves impacting on all the relevant levels at once, such as consciousness raising for the situational, cognitive, interpersonal, family of origin, and intrapersonal determinants of the problem. Interventions can be created to affect clients at multiple levels of a problem to produce a maximum impact for change in a synergistic rather than sequential fashion. (Prachaska & DiClemente, 2003)

The transtheoretical approach integrates processes of change from leading theories of therapy. Effective interventions involve matching change processes to the client's current stage of change. Research is supportive of using this approach with a wide population level, including those who are not interested in change at this time.

INTEGRATIVE PROBLEM-CENTERED APPROACH

Integrative Problem-Centered Therapy (IPCT) is a psychotherapeutic framework that integrates family, individual, and biological therapies (Pinsof, 2003). This approach views therapy as human problem solving. People seek psychotherapy because they have one or more psychosocial problems that they cannot resolve by themselves. Often by the time they have sought treatment, they have made several unsuccessful attempts at solving the problem on their own. The IPCT therapist teaches patients new problem-solving skills in regard to the particular class of problems for which they want help. The overall goal is to teach them skills so that they will be empowered to solve future problems on their own.

IPCT is based on three central hypotheses (Pinsof, 2003):

- No single psychotherapy approach can treat the myriad problems confronting contemporary therapists.
- Every psychotherapy has its domain of expertise—that is, certain types of problems or patients respond best.
- Different approaches can be related to one another in a cost-effective fashion to reduce treatment failure.

This approach addresses the question, what do you do when your approach does not work? The question may further be divided into short- and long-term results. IPCT organizes treatment approaches sequentially so that the next one picks up the failures of the previous one. Therapists are urged to begin treatment with the simplest, most direct, and least expensive treatment strategies and then progress toward more complex, indirect, and expensive models. Treatment concludes when the presenting problems have been resolved.

Pinsof (2003) attributed the development of this approach to his 40-year journey of professional training and personal experience. He integrated systems, behavioral, psychodynamic, Gestalt, self-psychology, sex therapy, and biological therapy. The major theoretical constructs embody three core concepts: interactive constructivism, systems theory, and differential causality.

Problem Focus

The *presenting problem* is the client's definition for which he or she is seeking help. Other issues that the therapist might believe need to be worked on can be considered only if they are linked to the presenting problem or an evolution of the presenting problem. The IPCT therapist focuses on the other side of the presenting problem or the solution or goal. Therapy occurs in episodes, with each being organized around a different presenting problem or set of problems. This is viewed as similar to the way people use medical care. Medical personnel are contacted on a problem-by-problem basis.

The actual focus of IPCT is on the problem cycle, which consists of two types of sequences. The first, the *problem sequence*, is the sequence of events in which the presenting problem usually emerges or gets worse. It involves three phases: the events that precede the problem, the problem's emergence, and the events that follow. The second type, the *alternative adaptive sequence*, constitutes the adaptive alternative to the problem sequence. The goal of therapy is to replace the problem sequence with the alternative adaptive sequence.

The patient system consists of all the people who are or may be involved in maintaining the presenting problem. The patient system is greater than the family, and each problem has a unique patient system. Therapy is the interaction of the patient system with the therapy system. The therapist system involves all the people who are providing therapy to the patient system.

The last and most important problem-related concept is the problem maintenance system (PMS). The PMS consists of all the factors or constraints within the patient system that prevent solving the problem (Breunlin,1999). Pinsof (2003) formulates the PMS as consisting of six levels:

- Social organization constraints (behavioral)
- Biological constraints (biobehavioral)
- Meaning: cognitive and emotional constraints (experiential)
- Family of origin constraints (transgenerational)
- Object relations constraints (psychodynamic)
- Narcissistic constraints (self-psychological)

Each presenting problem will have its own unique PMS. A major implication of this concept is that clinical psychology and psychiatry's attempt to match treatments to disorders will never work (Pinsof, 2003). It is not the superficial aspects of the presenting problem or symptom that determine the requirements of treatment but the unique set of constraints in which the problem is embedded.

Intervention and Assessment

Assessment and intervention are viewed as inseparable and coexistent in this model. It is impossible to know the nature of any particular problem maintenance structure before actually working on it. The PMS will reveal itself through therapy, and even then one cannot ever know the PMS completely. A diagnosis can never be definite, but it can be adequate to make a meaningful change.

The IPCT therapist conducts assessments and interventions on various modalities and approaches. The modalities are the direct intervention contexts (i.e., family, couple, or individual) and the approaches are the orientations (i.e., behavioral, biobehavioral, experiential, transgenerational, psychodynamic, or self-psychological). Specifying which orientations and direct contexts to use at which point in therapy is one of the most important aspects of IPCT.

INTEGRATIVE BEHAVIORAL COUPLES THERAPY (IBCT)

Integrative Behavioral Couples Therapy (IBCT) is a derivative of Behavioral Couples Therapy and was developed by Andrew Christenson and Neil Jacobsen (Christensen, Jacobson, & Babcock, 1995; Jacobsen & Christensen, 1996; Doss, Jones, & Christensen, 2003; Dimidjian, Martell, & Christensen, 2003). This approach was created to address some of the criticisms of traditional behavior therapy: low commitment, older age, emotional disengagement, traditional or conventional outlook, and divergent goals. According to Jacobsen and Christensen (1996), "these five factors relate to the partner's capacity for accommodation, compromise, and collaboration" (p. 10). Traditionally, behavior therapy taught couples the skills needed for change. It was assumed that, if couples used these skills, the loving behaviors created would create loving feelings. This tended to work in specific situations but did not always generalize to the overall feelings toward one another.

IBCT then created what is called emotional acceptance. This approach integrates the acceptance of one another with change strategies. Change techniques are designed to remove a negative behavior or reduce the frequency of negatives, such as criticism. Acceptance techniques are designed to change the way one experiences negative behaviors and emotions. This might involve teaching understanding and empathy. When spouses are more accepting, their partners are often more willing to change; when they change, their behavior becomes easier to accept. This is not the same as resignation or surrender. These strategies are designed to help both partners realize how they are caught in a mutual trap brought about by their interaction patterns or individual histories or both. IBCT realizes that many conflicts cannot be resolved and that the best we can hope for is a mutual acceptance that we are different.

The IBCT approach is rooted in behavioral therapy but also contains some of the tolerance interventions of strategic therapy and the empathic joining of client-centered and emotionally focused therapies. This approach focuses as much on the recipient of behavior as it does on the agent of behavior. The relationship context can change as a result of not only one partner's altering the frequency or intensity of the behavior but also from the other partner's receiving the behavior differently.

The treatment goals of IBCT are to help each partner better understand and accept the other as an individual, and to develop a collaboration where each partner is willing to make the changes necessary to improve the quality and satisfaction of the relationship. These treatment goals are guided by the formulation that occurs in the assessment phase.

IBCT formulates each problem in three parts: a theme, a polarization process, and a mutual trap. The *theme* is a brief summary of the main underlying issue in the couple's relationship. This can take many forms, such as closeness/distance, rigid/flexible, and saving/spending. Themes express the difference (not similarities) in the couple. The *polarization* process occurs as one partner repeatedly attempts to change the other. Couples feel hopeless and frustrated with this process, which is never resolved and leads to the *mutual trap*. Both feel stuck and unable to change.

Assessment

IBCT begins with a thorough assessment of the couple. This assessment consists of an initial conjoint session, one session with each partner individually, and specific questionnaires. This phase of therapy is designed to answer six questions:

1.) How distressed is this couple?
2.) How committed is this couple to continuing the relationship?
3.) What are the divisive issues?
4.) Why are these issues so sensitive for them?
5.) What are the relationship's strengths that encourage them to keep trying?
6.) What can treatment (couples therapy or other intervention) do to help them?

Once the assessment is completed, a feedback session occurs. The therapist describes the couple's level of satisfaction, the couple's formulation (their problematic issues, how they deal with those issues, and why those issues seem so difficult for them), their strengths, and finally the process of therapy.

Therapist's Role

The IBCT therapist operates in different roles depending on the context of the therapy. Usually, however, the therapist is active and directive. Sometimes the therapist may be a teacher or coach and help the couple learn or improve existing skills. At other times, the therapist may need to be a compassionate listener or the interpreter of the function the behavior is having on the relationship. The highest priority is to maintain the focus on the couple's formulation.

Techniques

The techniques of IBCT fall into three categories: acceptance, tolerance, and change. Two strategies can promote acceptance: namely empathic joining and unified detachment. These strategies attempt to provide a couple with a new experience of the present problem; these techniques aim to help the partners turn their problems into vehicles for greater intimacy. In contrast, tolerance interventions allow partners to let go of their efforts to change each other, without aspiring to the somewhat greater goal of empathic joining and unified detachment. Tolerance is promoted through pointing out the positive features of negative behavior, practicing negative behavior in the therapy session, faking negative behavior between sessions, and self-care (Jacobsen & Christensen, 1996). Finally, change techniques are used to directly promote change in a partner's behavior and consist largely of behavior exchange and communication–problem-solving training.

EMOTIONALLY FOCUSED COUPLES THERAPY (EFCT)

Emotionally Focused Couple Therapy (EFCT) is an integration of an experiential/Gestalt approach with an interactional–family systems approach. It is also a constructivist approach in that it focuses on the ongoing construction of present experience and an attachment approach in that it focuses on the nature of relationships. The approach was developed by Leslie Greenberg and Susan Johnson (1988). The theory is essentially a synthesis of systemic and experiential approaches.

Key Principles

The key principles of EFCT can be summarized as follows (Johnson, 1996; Johnson & Denton, 2003; Greenberg & Johnson, 1988):

- A collaborative alliance offers the couple the security needed to explore their relationship. The therapist serves as a process consultant to the relationship.
- Emotion is primary in organizing attachment behaviors and determining how self and other are experienced in intimate relationships.
- The attachment needs and desires of partners are essentially healthy and adaptive. It is the way such needs are enacted in a context or their perceived insecurity that creates problems.

- Problems are maintained by the ways in which interactions are organized and by the dominant emotional experience of each partner in the relationship.
- Change occurs not through insight into the past, catharsis, or negotiation, but through new emotional experience in the present context of emotional–salient interactions.
- In couples therapy, the actual client is the relationship between partners.

The Process of Change

The process of change has been organized into nine treatment steps. The first four steps involve assessment and the deescalation of problematic interactional cycles. The middle three steps emphasize the creation of specific change events, where interactional positions shift and new bonding events occur. The last two steps of therapy address the consolidation of change and the integration of these changes in to the everyday life of the couple (Johnson & Denton, 2003).

Stage One: Cycle Deescalation
1.) Identify the relational conflict issues between the partners.
2.) Identify the negative interaction cycle where these issues are expressed.
3.) Access the unacknowledged emotions underlying the interactional position each partner takes in this cycle.
4.) Reframe the problem in terms of the cycle, accompanying underlying emotions, and attachment needs.

Stage Two: Changing Interactional Positions
5.) Promote each partner's identification with disowned attachment needs and aspects of self. Such attachment needs may include the need for reassurance and comfort. Aspects of self that are not identified may include a sense of shame or unworthiness.
6.) Promote acceptance by each partner of the other partner's experience.
7.) Facilitate the expression of needs and wants to restructure the interaction based on new understandings, and create bonding events.

Stage Three: Consolidation and Integration
8.) Facilitate the emergence of new solutions to old problems.
9.) Consolidate new positions and cycles of attachment behavior.

Overview of Interventions

The first task is creating an alliance. The second task is to facilitate the identification, expression, and restructuring of emotional responses. The therapist focuses on the destructive emotions (i.e., anger or fear) that play a central role in the couple's cycle of negative interaction. In the third task, the restructuring of interactions, the therapist begins by tracking the negative cycle that constrains and narrows the partners' responses to each other. The therapist uses structural–systemic techniques such as reframing and coaching new relationship events. Problems are reframed in terms of cycles and attachment needs and fears.

The timing and delivery of the interventions are as important as the interventions themselves. The process of therapy evolves with the couple and therapist attuning to each other, as well as the therapist matching interventions to each partner's style (Johnson & Whiffen, 1999).

OLSEN'S INTEGRATIVE FAMILY THERAPY

David C. Olsen (1999) provided an integrative approach to couples and family therapy based on seven family therapy theories. This is a treatment-friendly approach that combines core concepts from different kinds of therapy, including cognitive, family life cycle, interactional–communications, multigenerational, object relations, problem solving, and structural family therapy theories.

This approach is based upon three implicit assumptions. The first is that assessment and intervention are intimately related, and that effective, integrative treatment requires an in-depth, integrative assessment. The second is that an effective assessment is a sequential activity that begins at the first level and only proceeds to the next level if there has not been a sufficient resolution of the family's problem at that level. The third is that an in-depth, systemic assessment of each level will suggest specific intervention goals and strategies for that level.

Although labeled as "integrative," this approach appears to be more about inclusion and incorporation than integration. It incorporates and sequentially orders selected concepts from major family therapy theories, rather than transforming them into higher-order constructs as do other integrative approaches. Nevertheless, this approach has considerable face validity for trainees trying to understand how specific theories relate to one another. Furthermore, it offers clinicians a specific, easy-to-follow protocol for structuring the process of treatment in the beginning stage of therapy with couples and families.

Integrative Assessment

In this approach, a couple or family's problem is assessed from a broad, multilevel perspective rather than a narrow, single theoretical perspective. Olsen argued that the core concepts of family therapy theories provide a clinically useful basis for a holistic and integrative assessment that is conceptualized in terms of six levels of assessment. The first level involves an assessment of the family's capacity for problem solving, while the second level involves an assessment of the family's structure and interactional issues. Assessment at level three involves cognitive issues, level four involves family-of-origin issues, and level five looks at individual development issues. The assessment of any family or couple begins with the most basic level of functioning, problem solving, and then proceeds to subsequent levels of assessment.

Problem-Solving Assessment

A basic assessment of presenting problems and concerns is conducted in the initial interview. The inquiry results in a preliminary definition of the problem that the couple accepts. This is followed by an assessment of the couple's or family's capacity for problem solving. It involves ascertaining the style by which they solve or attempt to solve problems together, and whether their impasse with the presenting problem is new or long-standing. It may be that they have limited problem-solving skills and need training in order to move forward.

Interactional Assessment

The next step is to assess their interactional cycles and their effect on problem solving. Several aspects of their interactions are assessed, including symmetrical and complementary interactional sequences, as well as the degree of "fit" between family members and how these sequences disrupt or maintain homeostasis.

Structural Assessment

Because structural problems can also block problem-solving abilities, the structure of the family is assessed next. These include the various subsystems, that is, spousal, executive, and sibling, as well as the presence and extent of triangulation, alliances, and boundaries within and between generations.

Cognitive Assessment

Structural or interactional interventions may be adequate to produce the necessary changes in a couple or family. But when a family or couple is locked in a relational pattern, it may be necessary to assess the underlying beliefs that maintain the counterproductive pattern. This assessment targets how these underlying beliefs distort interactions as well as how the beliefs are mutually reinforcing.

Family-of-Origin Assessment

Belief systems frequently have their roots in family-of-origin material. These beliefs emerge as individuals create their own family, particularly amidst anxiety and ongoing stress. This assessment might include eliciting each partner's internalized representations of significant parental figures, unconscious factors in mate selection, and how conscious contacts and expectations are formed between partners. The presence of triangles, family rules, and the role each partner plays in their family of origin is noted.

Individual Developmental Assessment

A final level of assessment endeavors to understand how individuals have internalized family-of-origin issues. The focus centers on the developmental process of each marital partner, the extent of projective identification, his or her personality style, and how each handles separation, individuation, and identity formation.

Utilizing this integrative assessment approach, the clinician can assess a couple or family on several levels. This sequential assessment approach should provide the clinician with a useful conceptual overview of the issues to be addressed in couples or family therapy. It becomes the foundation on which the clinician develops an integrative treatment plan. Figure 3.1 illustrates this assessment approach.

INTEGRATIVE TREATMENT

In this integrative approach, an assessment provides a map that forms the basis of the treatment plan. Thus, treatment planning starts at the simplest, most basic level, that is, problem solving, and moves sequentially through a number of treatment levels depending on how multilayered the couple or family's problem is.

The initial step in developing a treatment plan is to focus, with the family or couple, on problem-solving skills in reference to their

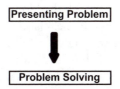

Presenting Problem

Problem Solving

What are the problem-solving abilities of the couple or family?

Structural Issues

What does the family structure look like?

Interactional Issues

Communication skills
Interactional dance patterns
Ability to metacommunicate
Problem-solving skills
How is anger and conflict handled?

Cognitive Issues

How do beliefs distort interactions?
How are beliefs mutually reinforcing?

Family-of-Origin Issues

How do family-of-origin issues impact belief systems?
Degree of differentiation for the couple
Key triangles
Roles
Family rules

Individual Assessment

Projective identification
Level of functioning
Developmental issues
Other individual issues; abuse, etc.

Figure 3.1 Model of integrative assessment

presenting problems. Unlike an assessment that proceeds in a linear fashion, treatment intervention proceeds through the levels in a circular fashion. For example, as couples are able to isolate specific problematic belief systems, they will move back to problem-solving skills as a way of changing beliefs. Furthermore, as they engage in family-of-origin work, they will move backward through the levels and not only increase their understanding of how their core beliefs were formed in childhood, they will revisit their problem-solving skills to find ways of changing beliefs or communication patterns. In short, although an assessment is more sequential, treatment is more circular. Treatment moves through various levels but always returns to problem solving and improved communication. Nevertheless, treatment need not cover all these levels, because the family ultimately determines the extent and nature of treatment. For some families, work at the problem-solving and structural levels may be sufficient, and treatment terminated. Other families may need to go further.

As treatment concludes, the couple or family will have become more aware of their interactional style, structure, and cognitive beliefs, and, if they continue long enough, more awareness of their family-of-origin material. Presumably, this awareness will be coupled with an increased capacity for problem solving with increased creativity, so that they can manage the normal developmental difficulties of life. Figure 3.2 depicts this integrative treatment approach.

SNYDER'S PLURALISTIC APPROACH TO COUPLES THERAPY

Couples therapists must treat a tremendous diversity of individuals and relationship difficulties. Snyder (1999; Snyder & Schneider, 2003) developed a hierarchical model that structures interventions through an informed pluralistic approach. Special attention is given to affective reconstruction or the interpretation of recurrent maladaptive relationship patterns that have evolved from developmental processes.

A pluralistic model of couple's therapy may be facilitated by viewing the therapeutic tasks along a hierarchy reflecting the couple's overall level of functioning (see Figure 3.3). Couples enter treatment at different stages of functioning and therefore will require different interventions. They also move along the continuum of overall functioning during the course of treatment, which necessitates interventions of increased depth and emotional challenge. The therapeutic tasks of couples therapy are viewed as having six levels of intervention.

Snyder proposed a progression from the most fundamental interventions promoting a collaborative alliance to more challenging interventions that address the developmental sources of relationship distress. The developmental origins of interpersonal themes and their manifestation in a couple's relationship are explored in a process

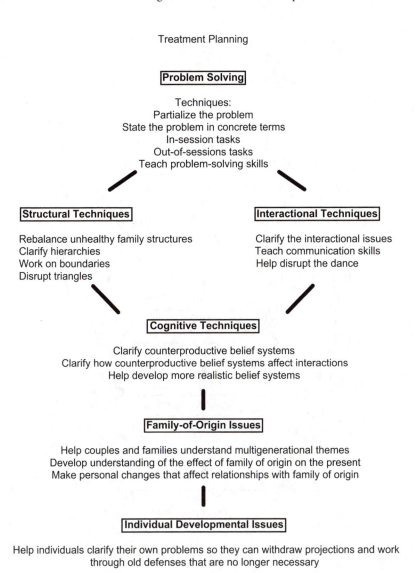

Treatment Planning

Problem Solving

Techniques:
Partialize the problem
State the problem in concrete terms
In-session tasks
Out-of-sessions tasks
Teach problem-solving skills

Structural Techniques

Rebalance unhealthy family structures
Clarify hierarchies
Work on boundaries
Disrupt triangles

Interactional Techniques

Clarify the interactional issues
Teach communication skills
Help disrupt the dance

Cognitive Techniques

Clarify counterproductive belief systems
Clarify how counterproductive belief systems affect interactions
Help develop more realistic belief systems

Family-of-Origin Issues

Help couples and families understand multigenerational themes
Develop understanding of the effect of family of origin on the present
Make personal changes that affect relationships with family of origin

Individual Developmental Issues

Help individuals clarify their own problems so they can withdraw projections and work
through old defenses that are no longer necessary

Figure 3.2 Model of integrative treatment

referred to as *affective reconstruction*. This is similar to promoting insight but emphasizes interpersonal schemas.

Young (1994) conceptualized early maladaptive schemas as enduring themes initially developed in childhood that serve as a template for processing interactions with one's self and the environment. These early

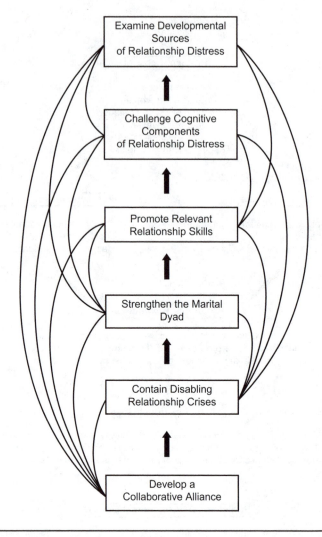

Figure 3.3 A hierarchial model of implementing informed pluralism

maladaptive schemas are viewed as originating from dysfunctional experiences with parents, siblings, and peers during the first few years of life. Young described 15 common maladaptive schemas across four general domains:

- **Autonomy**. With schemas addressing specific issues of dependence, self-subjugation, vulnerability to harm, and fears of losing self-control.

- **Connectedness.** With schemas regarding issues of emotional deprivation, abandonment, mistrust, and social isolation.
- **Worthiness.** With schemas concerning specific issues of one's own defectiveness, social undesirability, incompetence, guilt, and shame.
- **Expectations and limits.** Including schemas concerning unrelenting standards for self or, conversely, an exaggerated sense of entitlement.

The therapist needs to help couples identify their core relationship themes, link the themes to current conflicts, and then promote alternate relationship behaviors.

According to Snyder (1994),

> affective reconstruction strives to bring about critical changes in how individuals view themselves, their partner, and their relationship. In examining recurrent maladaptive relationship themes, both partners gain increased understanding of their own emotional reactivity and exaggerated patterns of interacting that contribute to their own unhappiness. Increases in partners' self-understanding can lead to diminished confusion and anxiety about their own subjective relationship experiences. Moreover, insight into developmental influences contributing to current difficulties often facilitates an optimism regarding the potential for self-change and restores hope for greater emotional fulfillment in the relationship. (p. 357)

ADDITIONAL MODELS

Several other models use integration. Each has a comprehensive theory and a research base to support its use. Among the more prominent are the following:

- **Functional family therapy** (Alexander & Sexton, 2002; Sexton & Alexander, 2003)
- **Metaframeworks** (Breunlin & MacKune–Karrer, 2002; Breunlin, Schwartz, & MacKune–Karrer, 1997)
- **Internal family systems** (Schwartz, 1995; Mann & Schwartz, 2002)
- **Multi-systemic** (Sheidow, Henggeler, & Schoenwald, 2003)

CONCLUDING NOTES

How can the insights of different theories and approaches be combined and systematically integrated to yield a comprehensive and useful guide for therapeutic work with families? In answer to this question, several models and approaches to integration have been reviewed in this chapter. This review suggests that individual theories or models of family therapy are necessarily limited with regard to assessment, formulation, and intervention (Mikesell, Lusterman, & McDaniels, 1995). Specifically, the assessment process will, of necessity, be multidimensional and comprehensive. Furthermore, matching and tailoring interventions require a comprehensive, integrative assessment. This theme will be continued in the following chapter on tailoring treatment.

References

Alexander, J. F., & Sexton, T. L. (2002). Functional family therapy: A model for treating high-risk, acting-out youth. In J. Lebow (Ed.), *Comprehensive handbook of psychotherapy IV: Integrative/eclectic.* New York: John Wiley.

Breunlin, D. C. (1999). Toward a theory of constraints. *Journal of Marital and Family Therapy, 25,* 365–382.

Breunlin, D. C., & MacKune–Karrer, B. (2002). Metaframeworks. In J. Lebow (Ed.), *Comprehensive handbook of psychotherapy: Volume 4 integrative/eclectic.* New York: John Wiley.

Breunlin, D. C., Schwartz, R. C., & MacKune–Karrer, B. (1997). *Metaframeworks: Transcending the models of family therapy.* San Francisco: Jossey–Bass.

Case, E., & Robinson, N. (1990). Toward integration: The changing world of family therapy. *American Journal of Family Therapy, 18*(2), 153–160.

Christensen, A., Jacobson, N. S., & Babcock, J.C. (1995). Integrative behavioral couples therapy. In N. S. Jacobsen & A. S. Gurman (Eds.), *Clinical handbook of couple therapy* (pp. 31–64). New York: Guilford.

Colapinto, J. (1984). On model integration and model integrity. *Journal of Strategic and Systemic Therapies, 4,* 38–42.

Dimidian, S., Martell, C. R., & Christensen, A. (2003). Integrative behavioral couple therapy. In A. S. Gurman & N. S. Jacobson (Eds.), *Clinical handbook of couple therapy* (3rd ed.). (pp. 251–277). New York: Guilford.

Doss, B. D., Jones, J. T., & Christensen, A. (2002). Integrative behavioral couples therapy. In J. Lebow (Ed.), *Comprehensive handbook of psychotherapy. Volume 4: integrative/eclectic* (pp. 387–410). New York: John Wiley.

Gehart, D. R., & Tuttle, A. R. (2003). *Theory-based treatment planning for marriage and family therapists.* Pacific Grove, CA: Brooks Cole.

Greenberg, L. S., & Johnson, S. M. (1988). *Emotionally focused therapy for couples.* New York: Guilford.

Haley, J. (1987). The disappearance of the individual. *The Family Therapy Networker, 11,* 39–40.

Jacobson, N. S., & Christensen, A. (1996). *Integrative couple therapy: Promoting acceptance and change.* New York: Norton.

Johnson, S. M. (1996). *The practice of emotionally focused marital therapy: Creating connection.* New York: Guilford.

Johnson, S. M., & Denton, W. (2003). Emotionally focused couple therapy: Creating secure connections. In A. S. Gurman & N. S. Jacobson, *Clinical handbook of couple therapy* (3rd Ed.). (pp. 221–250). New York: Guilford.

Johnson, S. M., & Whiffen, V. (1999). Made to measure: Adapting emotionally focused couple therapy to partners attachment styles. *Clinical Psychology: Science and Practice, 6,* 366–381.

Lebow, J. L.(2003). Integrative approaches to couple and family therapy. In T. L. Sexton, G. R. Weeks, & M. S. Robbins (Eds.), *Handbook of family therapy.* New York: Brunner Routledge.

Mann, B. J., & Schwartz, R. C. (2002). Internal systems theory. In J. Lebow (Ed.), *Comprehensive handbook of psychotherapy: Volume 4 integrative/eclectic.* New York: John Wiley.

Mikesell, R., Lusterman, D., & McDaniels (Eds.). (1995). *Integrating family therapy: Handbook of family psychology and systems theory.* Washington, DC: American Psychological Association.

Norcross, J. (1986). Eclectic psychotherapy: An introduction and overview. In J. Norcross (Ed.), *Handbook of eclectic psychotherapy.* New York: Brunner/Mazel.

Norcross, J., & Goldfried, M. (2003). *Handbook of psychotherapy integration.* New York: Oxford.

Olsen, D. C. (1999). *Integrative family therapy: Creative pastoral care and counseling.* Minneapolis: Fortress Press.

Paul, G. (1987). Strategy of outcome research on psychotherapy. *Journal of Consulting Psychology, 31,* 109–118.

Pinsof, W. (2003). Integrative problem-centered therapy. In J. Lebow (Ed.), *Comprehensive handbook of family therapy.* New York: John Wiley.

Prochaska, J. O., & DiClemente, C. C. (1982). Transtheoretical therapy: Toward a more integrated model of change. *Psychotherapy: Theory, Research and Practice, 19,* 276–278.

Prochaska, J. O., & DiClemente, C. C. (2003). Transtheoretical therapy. In J. Lebow (Ed.), *Comprehensive handbook of psychotherapy: Volume 4 Integrative/eclectic.* New York: John Wiley.

Robertson, M. (1979). Some observations from an eclectic psychotherapist. *Psychotherapy: Theory, Research and Practice, 16,* 18–21.

Schwartz, R. C. (1995). *Internal family systems.* New York: Guilford.

Sexton, T. L., & Alexander, J. F. (2003). Functional family therapy: A mature clinical model for working with at-risk adolescents and their families. In T. L. Sexton, G. R. Weeks, & M. S. Robbins (Eds.), *Handbook of family therapy.* New York: Brunner Routledge.

Sexton, T. L., Weeks, G. R., & Robbins, M. S. (2003). *Handbook of family therapy.* New York: Brunner Routledge.

Sheidow, A. J., Henggeler, S. W., & Schoenwald, S. K. (2003). Multisystemic therapy. In T. L. Sexton, G. R. Weeks, & M. S. Robbins (Eds.), *Handbook of family therapy.* New York: Brunner Routledge.

Snyder, D. K. (1999). Affective reconstruction in the context of a pluralistic approach to couple therapy. *Clinical Psychology: Science and Practice, 6*(4), 348–365.

Snyder, D. K., & Schneider, W. J. (2003). Affective reconstruction: A pluralistic, developmental approach. In A. Gurman & N. Jacobson (Eds.), *Handbook of couples therapy.* New York: Guilford.

Textor, M. (1988). Integrative family therapy. *International Journal of Family Psychiatry, 9*(1), 93–106.

Young, J. E. (1994). *Cognitive therapy for personality disorders: A schema-focused approach* (Rev. ed.). Sarasota, FL: Professional Resource Press.

4

TAILORING TREATMENT FOR COUPLES AND FAMILIES

MODELS AND PROTOCOLS FOR TAILORING AND MATCHING

Tailoring treatment to the specific needs of the client has long been an ideal. As early as 30 years ago, it was hoped that psychotherapy research would focus on "what treatment, by whom, is most effective for this individual with that specific problem and under which set of circumstances" (Paul, 1967, p. 111). To date, some notable progress has taken place in meeting Paul's challenge, but we are just beginning to see the tip of the tailoring iceberg, and there's more to be seen.

What is tailored treatment and what does it have to do with families and couples? Clinicians are asking this question in their quest to provide more effective and cost-efficient treatment. Although tailoring, matching treatment, and differential therapeutics, are prominent in the practice of individual psychotherapy, the same cannot yet be said about couples or family therapy. This chapter will briefly sketch the emerging trend of tailoring treatment in both individual and marital–family therapy. The first section distinguishes tailoring from similar phenomena and delineates some of the resistance to the tailoring trend. The second and main section describes several perspectives on tailoring treatment. The third section describes an assessment and treatment-planning protocol as the basis for tailoring treatment.

TAILORING TERMINOLOGY AND RESISTANCE

As mentioned in the last chapter, tailoring is similar to but still different from the related concept of matching. Worthington (1992) used a sartorial analogy to make the distinction. Matching is choosing an appropriate suit from the rack, whereas tailoring involves custom-fitting the suit to the individual. In other words, in matching, a couple or family is "assigned" to a specific treatment approach based on important client variables. Tailoring involves modifying that treatment approach to "fit" the couple or family so they are most likely to benefit from the treatment. Matching typically precedes tailoring and is accomplished early in the course of treatment, usually during or after the initial evaluation. Tailoring, in contrast, occurs throughout the course of treatment. In some clinics and group practices, matching is often done in case staffing, when cases are assigned to therapists; in private practice, it may involve referral to another therapist. Tailoring usually involves the flexible use of therapeutic strategies and tactics after a particular therapeutic approach has been chosen.

Tailoring has three goals. The first is to enhance the therapeutic relationship. The second is to create an environment in which a couple or family can benefit from therapeutic suggestions and directives. The third is to deal with specific therapeutic impasses such as noncompliance or resistance (Worthington, 1992).

Tailoring is also distinct from integration and integrative approaches. Integrative approaches are basically clinician-centered. Clinicians develop a particular way of personalizing therapeutic concepts and techniques to meet their own needs for therapeutic effectiveness, intellectual synthesis, or whatever is necessary. Tailoring, however, refers to the philosophy of basing treatment decisions on what is best for the client, couple, or family system. Paul's (1967) dictum clearly specifies what the focus of tailoring should be: the particular needs and styles of the individual, couple, or family. Essentially, tailoring is basically a client or couple-centered orientation to treatment planning and intervention.

Individual psychotherapies have been found to be more effective when matched to the client's dispositional needs, presenting problems, and treatment expectations than when a single theory or treatment modality is used without regard to these client features (Beutler & Clarkin, 1990). The literature on tailoring individual treatment is continually expanding. Significant contributions have been made by Beutler (1983); Frances, Clarkin, and Perry (1984); Perry, Frances, and Clarkin (1990); and Beutler and Clarkin (1990) to name a few.

Tailoring the therapy also increases the therapy's effectiveness for couples and families. The basic motivation for tailoring treatment should be the clinician's concern that the couple or family receives the most effective and appropriate treatment. Unfortunately, family therapy clinicians and researchers have been more resistant to the prospective of tailoring than individual psychotherapy clinicians and researchers. This resistance occurs for a number of reasons.

First, marital and family theory and therapy are relatively recent additions to the therapeutic landscape. Most clinicians are just learning, or have recently learned, the theory and skills of this "new" area. Consequently, few have become dissatisfied with the shortcoming of standardized, nontailored treatment. Second, relatively little theorizing has been done about tailoring as witnessed by the near absence of work on tailoring in the family therapy literature. Third, the couple and family therapy movement is still strongly parochial in its belief in the universal applicability of its dominant theories (Worthington, 1989). Consequently, a clinician's allegiance to a dominant theory or approach almost guarantees that treatment will be clinician-centered, rather than client-centered, which is incompatible with the basic principles of tailoring. Finally, education and training in marital and family therapy typically occur within theory-consistent programs that further reinforce a nontailoring view of treatment.

PERSPECTIVES OF TAILORING

Only recently has the process of tailoring been described in marital and family literature (Sperry, 1986). This section overviews tailoring approaches based on (a) the level of family functioning, (b) the level of relational conflict, (c) the individual functioning, (d) the level of readiness, (e) the level of distress, and (f) differential therapeutics.

Tailoring by Level of Family Functioning

Weltner (1985) believed in tailoring treatment to a couple's or family's level of systems functioning. He described four levels of functioning in terms of treatment issues, then proposed a corresponding intervention strategy, and set techniques for each level. The first two levels describe two kinds of underorganized couples or families, the third describes the overorganized couple, and the fourth describes the adequately functioning couple.

Weltner contended that intervention must first address the level of a couple's most basic problem before moving on to a higher-level intervention. He believed that an effective therapist must be sufficiently conversant with the major therapeutic approaches to marital therapy in order to mix and match techniques appropriately to a specific level, rather than unilaterally applying one approach to all couples or families. For level one, the main issue involves the parental capacity to provide basic nurturance and protection. Therefore, the basic treatment strategy is to mobilize available outside support to assist the single parent or the strongest member of the family facing severe stress or illness, including alcoholism. The therapist's role is that of advocate, convener, teacher, and role model. Structural interventions and support are key interventions.

In level two, issues of authority and limits are prominent for the couple and family. Expectations may be unclear or unmet. The basic strategy is to clarify expectations and power issues by means of such techniques as written contracts, the formation of coalitions, and behavioral reinforcers.

Level-three families and couples are more complicated. They have a structure and a style that appear to be functional, yet issues regarding boundaries are prominent. Resistance to change is another hallmark of this type of family or couple. The basic strategy is to create sufficient inner space for a spouse or specific family member and to protect that spouse, family member, or subsystem from overinvolvement. Therapeutic techniques at this level include rebuilding alliances, managing paradoxes, and developing generational boundaries.

Issues for level-four couples and families are usually focused on intimacy and inner conflict. Whereas families and couples at levels one to three are immersed in day-to-day survival issues, level-four couples are able to consider self-actualizing concerns. Making insights is a basic therapeutic strategy, and techniques include marital and family enrichment, Gestalt and experiential marital therapies, or even individual psychodynamically oriented psychotherapy.

Schultz (1984) proposed a similar model of family and couple functioning based more specifically on DSM-III psychopathology. Schultz likewise described four levels. He labeled the first level of family functioning as "psychotic" and matched this with the family transactional approach as developed by Wynne and Singer. The second level is labeled as "immature" and is matched with the structural-system approach, such as Minuchin's. The third level is called "neurotic" and is matched with various strategic methods. Finally, the fourth level is labeled "mature" and is matched with growth-focused approaches, such as Satir's communication approach, the symbolic–experiential approach of Whitaker, or the psychodynamic approaches.

Tailoring by Level of Relational Conflict

Guerin, Fay, Burden, and Kautto (1987) believed that marital conflict differs significantly from one couple to another, not only with respect to specific issues but more importantly with respect to the duration and intensity of the conflict. Accordingly, they tailor treatment to the level of severity (that is, the intensity and duration) of the marital discord. They describe couples in terms of four levels.

The first level involves couples who demonstrate a preclinical or minimal degree of marital conflict. Often this conflict has lasted for less than 6 months, and most often the couples are newlyweds. These couples readily respond to information focusing on how marriages work and do not work, and they are able to apply this information to positively change their relationship for the better. Thus, therapy for this level is primarily a group psychoeducational intervention. Occasionally, a few couples sessions are necessary as an adjunct to the group sessions. This psychoeducational treatment involves six weekly sessions of 1 1/2 hours each. Developed in the Bowenian tradition, the sessions focus on such concepts as multigenerational transmission, triangles, behavior styles, and differentiation, as well as specific common problems that couples are likely to present in the beginning stages of a marriage.

Level two consists of couples who are experiencing significant marital conflicts lasting longer than 6 months. Although their communication patterns remain open and adequate, criticism and projection have increased. When the therapist dissects the conflict-ridden marital process, however, both spouses can generally move to a self-focus within six to eight sessions, after which the intensity of the conflict can be substantially reduced. Therapy in level two provides a structure for the couple that lowers emotional arousal and anxiety, and helps the spouses reestablish self-focus.

Level-three couples present with severe marital conflict. Often the conflict's duration is longer than 6 months, and projection is intense. Anxiety and emotional arousal are high, as are the intensity and polarization of surrounding triangles. Communication is closed with marked conflict. The degree of criticism is high, and blaming is common. Therapy at this level is primarily focused on controlling the couple's reactivity, their tendency to react to each other emotionally without thinking. Even when a positive result is obtained through therapy, a recycling of conflicts inevitably occurs within the ensuing 6 to 8 months. Guerin notes that such recycling is a common phenomena at all levels of marital conflict, but particularly at this stage. When this re-cycling continues to occur, both spouses have probably lost most of their resilience and tend to be unresponsive to further treatment.

Finally, couples at level four are characterized by extremes in all the criteria that Guerin used for a marital evaluation of conflict. Com-munication is closed, information exchange is poor, criticism and blam-ing are very high, and self-disclosure is absent in the relationship. Relationship time and activity together are either minimal or nonexist-ent. The definitive marker for this level is the engagement of an attor-ney by one or both spouses. Such a situation is likely to be more adversarial than conciliatory. In the vast majority of cases, attempts to keep the marriage from dissolving are doomed. Therefore, treatment is aimed at diminishing emotional damage to the spouses, their children, and their extended family. The goal becomes the successful disengage-ment from the relationship. In short, mediation is the treatment of choice.

Guerin and his associates detailed treatment protocols in which spe-cific dynamic, behavioral, and systems interventions are used with cou-ples at different levels of functioning. Assessments of each of the four levels of couple functioning are aided by specific behavioral indices. These indices are criteria likely to ensure that an accurate assessment of the levels of marital discord is made and that appropriately tailored treatment will follow.

Tailoring Based on Individual Functioning

Lazarus (1981; 1985) advocated the matching or tailoring of therapeu-tic techniques to seven specific areas of individual functioning. These areas of functioning are represented by the acronym BASIC-ID: behav-ior, affect, sensory, imagery, cognitive, interpersonal, and biological (identified as D and referring to drugs in particular and physical health in general). The therapist's role is to assess these areas of functioning, develop a problem list, prioritize their importance to the spouses' func-tioning, and direct a focus intervention for each. Lazarus's orientation is an eclectic form of cognitive–behavioral therapy. Research studies at-test to the effectiveness of focused multimodal intervention as com-pared to unimodal intervention (Lazarus, 1981). Lazarus noted that couples constitute the overwhelming majority of referrals to his prac-tice. The BASIC-ID profile provides both couples and therapists with a blueprint map for assessing the individual's, as well as the couple's or family's, current level of functioning and for setting clear objectives for change. This unique methodology aids the therapist in establishing a one-to-one correspondence between diagnosis and treatment. Each item on the problem list is matched or tailored with a specific treatment intervention.

The couple or family is seen together in the initial interview to discuss the main presenting problems. They are then helped to prepare a list of undesirable behaviors that they note in themselves and in their spouse. Then each individual independently fills out a life history questionnaire, which is discussed with the therapist as a subsequent individual session. During this session, a modality profile is constructed. A conjoint session follows to compare the two profiles and tailor the treatment process.

Tailoring Based on Level of Readiness

Adaptive counseling and therapy (ACT) is a developmental and systems model developed by Howard, Nance, and Myers (1987) and adapted by Myers (1992). Basically, ACT requires clinicians to adapt the degree of direction and extent of support they provide client couples or families. Clinician direction and support will vary with the couple's or family's readiness to accomplish the particular therapeutic tasks involved in the therapeutic process.

Myers specified three criteria for the family's "readiness": willingness, ability, and confidence. First, the family's willingness to participate in therapy is assessed. A family that is self-referred would have a higher degree of willingness to participate in treatment than a family that refused voluntary treatment but came because the court ordered them to obtain compulsory counseling. Second, the family's ability to participate is measured by the adequacy of family members' verbal skills for participating in talking therapy. Third, the family's confidence in a positive therapeutic outcome is reflected by the strength of their belief that they can make needed changes in their family relationships.

Four levels of family readiness are noted. The highest level involves high levels of willingness, ability, and confidence, while the lowest level involves the absence of these three criteria. Myers views a family's readiness as a trait contingent on specific tasks, rather than on a fixed global characteristic.

For Myers, the therapist tailors treatment, particularly therapeutic style, on the family's level of readiness. Four therapeutic styles are specified based on the extent of direction and support supplied by the therapist. The styles are telling, teaching, supporting, and delegating. Thus, a therapist would respond in a delegating style to a family with a very high level of readiness. This contrasts with the therapist responding in a telling style to a family with the lowest level of readiness.

Tailoring Based on Level of Distress

Worthington (1989; 1992) described a method for matching treatment based on the family's distress. Because couples and families often seek therapy during times of upheaval owing to normative or non-normative events, Worthington based treatment matching on an assessment of the family's response to the event. Three variables characterize the way a family responds to transitions: (a) the degree of disruption in the family members' schedules, (b) the number of decisions about which the family members disagree, and (c) the degree of ongoing conflict. Worthington used these three variables, dichotomized as high or low, to predict eight categories of a family's response to treatment that can then be matched to six specific treatment strategies. For example, enrichment strategies are matched to families in which the degree of disturbance is small. Crisis-oriented strategies are matched to families experiencing schedule disruption. Experiential strategies can be matched to all situations except for those of high conflict. Psychoeducational strategies are good matches for families experiencing severe disturbances regarding power issues. Structural and process strategies are matched with families with unstable power structures and high conflict. Finally, psychodynamic strategies are matched with families with disturbances in intimacy.

Worthington (1992) recognized that family members may not respond uniformly to life transitions. In such instances, the therapist must be mindful of subsystems and carefully tailor the strategy. Finally, Worthington (1989) carefully indexed the likelihood of success for each of the six therapeutic strategies based on the eight levels or types of family distress.

Tailoring Based on Differential Therapeutics

A somewhat different perspective on tailoring is provided by Perry, Frances, and Clarkin (1990), who believed that all forms of treatment have five inherent factors that should be considered in treatment selection: setting, format, duration and frequency, treatment method, and the need for somatic treatment. Setting refers to where treatment occurs: inpatient, outpatient, partial hospitalization program, and so on. Format is determined according to who directly participates in the treatment: individual, marital, family, or group. Duration and frequency refer to both the length of the session and the frequency in terms of the number of sessions per week or month. The treatment method refers to the type of psychosocial strategies and tactics employed: exploratory, supportive, cognitive–behavioral, or psychoeducational. Somatic treatment refers to prescribed medications, diet and exercise, electroshock therapy, and so forth. A metadecision overrides the previous five factors: the matter of whether the couple or family should be offered treatment or the "no treatment" option. These authors offer specific guidelines for making informed, tailored decisions.

A CLINICAL PROTOCOL FOR MATCHING AND TAILORING TREATMENT

The previous section suggests that although there have been creative clinical innovations and even clinical research efforts to match and tailor treatment, currently no scientifically validated protocol exists for tailoring psychotherapeutic treatment. Until such a validated protocol is available, therapists will continue to use their clinical acumen and best judgment for matching/tailoring treatment. The following protocol has been employed by the authors in their clinical practice, supervision, and teaching. It will be described here and illustrated with clinical case material in subsequent chapters. This matching–tailoring protocol involves four steps:

1.) A comprehensive assessment
2.) The matching of the therapeutic strategy(ies) based on the comprehensive assessment
3.) Tailoring the chosen therapeutic strategy to couple/family needs, circumstances, treatment capacity, and response to therapist and treatment
4.) Implementation, review, and revision of matching–tailoring efforts

Comprehensive Assessment

As mentioned previously, an important value of the integrative approaches to marital and family therapy is that they discourage parochial thinking and shortsightedness. Practically speaking, integrative approaches require more multidimensional than unidimensional assessments, as do matching and tailoring, which also require a comprehensive assessment. A therapist who questions the value of a comprehensive assessment would do well to seriously consider the statistics on treatment failure in family therapy. In *Failures in Family Therapy*, Coleman (1985) noted that 83% of treatment failures could be primarily attributed to inadequate initial assessments.

The following assessment schema is derived from a biopsychosocial assessment model (Sperry, 1989). This comprehensive assessment schema has five basic dimensions. The schema is visually represented as follows:

$$\text{Comprehensive assessment} = \text{situation/severity} + \text{system} + \text{skills} + \text{style/status} + \text{suitability for treatment}$$

These five assessment dimensions and associated factors are listed in Table 4.1 and described on the following pages.

Situation/Severity Situation/severity refers to assessing the symptoms and severity of stressors that the family is experiencing, along with demographic factors and the family's level of functioning.

1. Presenting complaints and problems Families that seek family therapy or are referred for a family evaluation or treatment or both present

Table 4.1 Comprehensive Assessment in the Evaluation of Couples and Families

A. Situation/severity
1.) Presenting complaints and problems
2.) Couple or family demographics: age, number of members, and sociocultural and financial status
3.) Level of family functioning

B. System
4.) Family history, developmental stage, and genogram
5.) The factors of boundaries, power, and intimacy

C. Skills
6.) Self-management skills
7.) Relational skills

D. Style/status
8.) Personality style
9.) Individual psychological and health status

E. Suitability for treatment
10.) Formulations of problem and distress
11.) Expectations for treatment
12.) Readiness and motivation for treatment

with relatively similar concerns: communication; child and adolescent conflicts; sex; finances; physical, sexual, or verbal abuse; or various crises related to the death of a family member, a job, a health problem, and so on. The presenting complaints are not always identical to the problem(s) that distress the family. More often the vagueness of their difficulty, as well as their inability to alleviate their discomfort by themselves, may be part of the presenting complaint (Nichols, 1988).

2. Couple or family demographics: age, number of members, and sociocultural and financial status   Family demographics may exacerbate or buffer the family from internal and external stressors. Generally speaking, an inverse relationship exists between spousal age at time of marriage and the probability of divorce. Those who marry at a very young age have the highest divorce rates, probably because they have not developed sufficient maturity or relational skills or both (Stuart, 1980). Similarly, families with very young children, irrespective of the age of the parents, tend to be more stressed than families with adult children. Family size is usually correlated to family problems and divorce proneness. A U-shaped distribution is noted in which childless couples and those with large families were more likely to divorce than those with families of moderate size (Thornton, 1977).

Economic hardship in large families might explain their proneness to divorce, because financial issues can be a source of considerable family stress. Financially stressed families struggle with a wide variety of issues, including marital instability (Lorenz, Conger, Simon, & Whitbeck, 1991). The recent and current trend of corporate mergers, downsizing, and layoffs has added additional burdens to an increasing number of families, including those from the managerial and professional class that have been virtually immune to job loss, or the fear of job loss, since the end of World War II. When job loss is noted, its psychosocial effect must be fully assessed (Kates, Greiff, & Hagen, 1990).

Family income is more strongly and negatively associated with family conflict and divorce than any other census variable (Levinger, 1976). Too little income or a decrease in income because of job loss or wage cutbacks, relative to the family's expectation and standard of living, is a common precipitant of discord.

Cultural values and socioeconomic status combine to shape the character of a family, particularly the role expectations of its members, and the nuances of daily experience. Cultural values stem from early socialization experiences and are reinforced daily by others in the subculture in which the family resides (Laner, 1978). Social class differences also greatly affect attitudes and behavior. Lower-class families tend to have superficial contacts with more outsiders than do middle-class families, who have deeper contacts with fewer individuals outside their family (Stuart, 1980).

3. Level of family functioning   The level of family functioning should be initially assessed and then monitored throughout the course of treatment. The level of functioning is a key variable in matching a particular therapeutic strategy to a particular family. Earlier in this chapter three methods of assessing level of functioning were described: Weltner (1985) and Schultz (1984) for the entire family, and Guerin et al. (1987) for the couple.

System   System refers to the family's history and developmental stage, as well as the system factors of boundaries, power, and intimacy.

1. Family history, developmental stage, and genogram   It is useful for the therapist to have some understanding of how the family has come to be where it is today. Much of this information can be gathered in the course of constructing a genogram. The therapist may begin the history taking with questions about the parents' births and childhood, especially what their family lives were like as children, how they did at school, and how their lives were after leaving school. Information about their parents and siblings is also noted, as well as how the couple met and courted. The course of the marriage, including information about births of children and the children's development to date, should also be noted.

The family's stage in its life cycle, as well as transition points, usually can be noted at this point in the assessment. McGoldrick and Carter's (1982) family life cycle stages provide a useful model: (a) unattached young adult, (b) the joining of families through marriage, (c) family with young children, (d) family with adolescents, (e) launching children and moving on, and (f) family in later life.

Of course, intergenerational influences affect families. The exploration of each spouse's family of origin and their parent's families of origin in the presence of the family is frequently helpful in clarifying current issues and bringing them into the therapeutic arena. This can be accomplished in several ways. A common method is the use of the genogram, which in this case (McGoldrick & Gerson, 1985) is a visual depiction of the family tree covering at least three generations for both spouses. Important information is reported on the genogram such as names, ages, marital statuses, divorces, separations, and years of death. Typically, the therapist constructs a genogram of one spouse and has the second spouse fill in information and make comments following the initial disclosure of the first spouse. Then the process is reversed, and the second spouse's family of origin is explored with input from the first spouse.

2. The factors of boundaries, power, and intimacy   Berman and Leif (1975) and Fish and Fish (1986) suggested a series of questions that therapists can ask themselves during the evaluation to determine three critical systems factors in families. These questions involve boundaries, power, and intimacy.

Questions regarding boundaries include, who else is considered to be part of the family system? What's being excluded from family relationships and assigned to grandparents, relatives, or others? Who and what events or things are intruding into the family?

Questions of power involve, who is in charge? How do the parents deal with power in their relationship and in relationships with the children?

And finally, questions regarding intimacy include, how near, how far, and how do family members tolerate or respond to the needs and desires of one another for intimate contact and closeness? What is their pattern of vacillation in emotional and geographical distance as family members struggle with their need for closeness?

Answers to these questions provide significant data for the therapist in assessing the family system. Inventories such as the Family Adaptability and Cohesion Evaluation Scale (FACES-III) (Olson, Portner, & Labee, 1985; Olson, Sprenkle, & Russell, 1979) and the Self-Report Family Instrument (SFI) (Beavers, Hampson, & Hulgus, 1985) are also useful in clarifying family system factors.

Skills   Skills refers to the level of self-management and relational skills that family members possess and use within the family. Family members may effectively use a skill such as assertiveness outside the family but not within the family or with a particular family member. Others cannot use a particular skill within or outside the family because they never acquired the skill. The therapist assesses skills and their use directly through the observation of enactments and indirectly through the family members' self-report. Two classes of skills are noted: self-management and relational.

1. Self-management skills   A number of skills are necessary for family members to function effectively as individuals. Deficits in these skills can greatly affect family group functioning. These skills are assertiveness, problem solving, managing money, time management, making conversation, developing friendship, finding and maintaining a job or remaining in and succeeding in school, and other aspects of self-responsibility.

2. Relational skills   At least five skills appear necessary to sustain effective, healthy family functioning: encouragement, congruent communications, empathic listening, conflict resolution, and negotiation and consensus building. Nichols (1988) listed additional skills he believes are necessary for effective couple functioning: caring, commitment, and volunteering. Dinkmeyer and Carlson (1986) listed many of these skills as necessary for a growing marriage relationship as well.

Style/Status   Style/status refers to the individual system dimension. In addition to assessing family system functioning, the therapist should also assess the style and functioning of individual family members. This would include personality style as well as physical and psychological health status.

1. Personality style   Personality style refers to the enduring stylistic pattern of perceiving, responding, and thinking about the world, other people, and one's self. It can be thought of as a continuum with one end characterized by healthy, flexible, and adoptive functioning and the other end by unhealthy, rigid, and maladaptive dysfunctioning. (Extreme dysfunction is referred to as an Axis II personality disorder in DSM-IV.) Each family member manifests a dominant personality style, or disorder, often with traits or features of other styles. Personality styles and disorders can be assessed through clinical observation and developmental history, as well as through standard interview schedules and personality inventories such as the Millon Clinical Multiaxial Inventory II (MCMI-II)

2. Individual psychological and health status   One or both spouses may present for treatment with a psychiatric disorder along with a relational dysfunction. Even while marital and family therapists may prefer to formulate problems systemically, the fact is individual psychopathology exists that affects relational functioning. A handbook on such disorders, entitled *The Disordered Couple*, has recently been published (Carlson & Sperry, 1996).

Accordingly, psychological functioning on Axis I and II should also be assessed. With regard to couples, Stuart (1980) noted that assessing the level of potential depression in both spouses is the most critical factor affecting the process of marital therapy. Treatment will be hindered if a diagnosable psychiatric disorder in a family member is not properly evaluated and considered in the treatment plan (Beavers, 1985).

The importance of assessing physical health factors cannot be over-stressed. Current acute and chronic medical conditions, medication use (both prescription and nonprescription), drug and alcohol use, exercise and diet, sleep patterns, and job stress can greatly affect family functioning. These factors must be assessed (Doherty & Baird, 1987).

Suitability for Treatment   Suitability for treatment refers to the adequacy of the family's explanation or formulation of its problems and dysfunction, as well as their expectations and motivation for treatment. The better the family is suited for treatment, the better the outcome and vice versa (Beutler & Crago, 1987).

1. Formulations of problem and distress   Usually therapists think of developing *the* formulation of the couple's or family's dynamics and problems, which means, of course, their professional explanation of why the family acts and functions the way it does. So why should the therapist be concerned with the family's own formulation? For a number of reasons.

First, all families, particularly parents and older children, have formed an explanation of the family's concerns. These may be singular or plural; that is, family members have different explanations, and their formulations may either be common knowledge or they may never have been disclosed before.

Second, the family's formulation may be considerably different from the therapist's. Because treatment goals and plans are based on formulations, the greater the disparity between the therapist's and family's formulations, the more resistance and noncompliance to the treatment plan can be anticipated. Couples and families will collaborate more easily with a therapist when they have achieved a "meeting of the minds." Thus, the therapist should elicit formulations, share his or her own formulation, and then negotiate an acceptable common formulation (Sperry & Carlson, 1991). This may involve considerable discussion and education of family members on family dynamics. Such a discussion is central to collaboratively focused treatment. If the family insists on projecting or scapegoating their problems onto the identified patient, an outsider, or an outside influence, they probably are not able to assume the kind of responsibility required to engage in the change process and would rank low in suitability for treatment.

Eliciting the couple's or family's formulation begins with asking, "Why do you think your family isn't working so well?" This question should be posed to each member, without discussion, until all have spoken. Common explanations range from, "It's really because of Dad being gone all the time," "It's because we don't have enough money to make ends meet," "We're being punished because of that abortion," to "We just don't know how to communicate or respect one another." The therapist must ask the family members to come up with a formulation they can all accept. The way in which they respond to this task can be diagnostic.

2. Expectations for treatment   The therapist assesses the family or couple's expectations for treatment, beginning with the questions, "What were you hoping would be the result of our work together in therapy?" and "What needs to happen for these results to come about?" Unrealistic expectations, particularly those that involve "magic cures" with little or no commitment and involvement from family members, need to be noted and discussed. The family should be queried on their treatment objectives. Do they want symptom relief only, structural changes, divorce, medication, and so on? It is also useful to assess the family's or couple's previous efforts to make changes in their relationship. The family that has a history of some previous success in making a change is likely to repeat that success and can be so encouraged.

3. Readiness and motivation for treatment   Treatment readiness for couple and family therapy has been described by Myers (1992), who specified three criteria for readiness: (a) the family's willingness to participate in therapeutic tasks, (b) their ability to engage in the tasks of therapy, and (c) their confidence that therapeutic success is possible. She describes four levels of readiness, ranging from high (whereby the family is able, willing, and confident to make a specific change) to low (whereby the family is unable, unwilling, and lacks the confidence to make a specific change). Myers (in press) describes methods for assessing readiness.

In addition to treatment readiness, one must clarify the motivation of family members for change. Usually, one or two family members appear more motivated than others. In individual therapy, the client with high motivation tends to be self-referred, verbalizes a desire to change, has ego–dystonic symptoms, and is responsive to initial therapeutic tasks and intrasession homework. This is counter to the individual with low motivation, who tends to be referred by others, has ego–syntonic symptoms, and shows little desire for change. These same characteristics can be noted in family members. Thus, the therapist will observe family members' verbalizations concerning other family members, themselves, and therapy, noting the degree of congruence between their behavior and their statements. The therapist may ask the family members questions such as "What specifically do you want to be different in this situation?" "What role do you see yourself taking?" and "How willing are you to see this change through?"

Matching a Therapeutic Strategy

Rational decisions about matching specific treatment strategies to couples or families are possible based on the comprehensive assessment. The first three dimensions of that assessment—situation/severity, system, and skills—are the basis for matching. Situation/severity is a particularly useful criterion. It can be operationalized in terms of the family functioning levels as described by Weltner (1985) and Schultz (1984), the distress level as described by Worthington (1989), or the marital conflict level as described by Guerin et al. (1987). For example, a family functioning at level two—an underorganized family—would probably be best matched with a structural intervention, whereas a family functioning at level three—an overorganized and resistant family— would probably be best matched with a more strategic intervention.

The extent to which the family's problems appear to be focused on power as compared to boundary or intimacy issues will also suggest different types of intervention or strategies. Boundary problems appear to be best matched with structural strategies, whereas intimacy problems lend themselves to psychodynamic, psychoeducational, behavioral, and communication approaches. Power problems may be best matched with strategic and cognitive–behavioral strategies.

If skill deficits are the prominent basis for family or couples dysfunctioning, psychoeducational and behavioral strategies offer good matches. Similarly, if a couple is recently married and presents with minimal marital conflict, that is, level one (Guerin et al., 1987), a psychoeducational approach would likely be the best match.

Often, however, couples or families present with a major dysfunction in both the systemic and skills dimensions. In such situations, matching will involve two or more strategies. For example, structural and psychoeducational strategies may be indicated for the family, with prominent boundary problems and skill deficits in assertiveness and conflict resolution. The therapist must then decide whether to sequence or blend and combine these strategies.

Tailoring the Strategy

As noted earlier, tailoring is the process of "fitting" or customizing a particular treatment strategy to a particular individual, couple, or family.

Currently, no standardized or research-based guidelines exist for tailoring. Nevertheless, Worthington (1992) offered some suggestions for making tailoring decisions. First, decide at which level tailoring will occur. Will it be based on client–system values, requests, cultural identity, or some other variables? Second, decide on the decision rules for tailoring. What are the cultural family deficits, characteristics, and strengths? Third, decide what to do if family members differ on important variables. Fourth, predict what will happen if the clinician does or does not consider important issues or factors when tailoring treatment. Fifth, be realistic. Practical considerations must be weighed against ethical mandates and clinical resources. Tailoring decisions can be based on the comprehensive assessment of dimensions of style and the suitability for treatment. The therapist's timing and sequencing of questions, clarifications, reframes, confrontations, or interpretations or both should be based on an understanding of individual family members' personality styles. Clearly, the couple's or family's readiness for treatment (Myers, 1992) must be considered. Accordingly, the therapist can titrate, or modify, the degree of direction and support he or she provides the couple or family based on their level of readiness.

Implementation, Review, and Revision

The last step of the protocol involves continuing the implementation of the matched strategy or strategies along with the continued monitoring of the couple's or family's responses to treatment. Treatment will continually be tailored or fine-tuned based on this ongoing monitoring and assessment.

The preceding pages described the suggested clinical protocol for matching and tailoring the treatment of couples and families. Descriptions of clinical applications of this protocol appear in subsequent chapters. An extended case example involving a chronically conflictual dual-career couple is presented in chapter 7.

CONCLUDING NOTE

This chapter described the theoretical as well as the clinical challenges of individualizing psychotherapeutic treatment for clients. It presented several clinical innovations for matching or tailoring treatment for couples and families. It also provided a clinical protocol for both matching and tailoring treatment based on a comprehensive assessment. The current interest in matching and tailoring treatment reflects not only the economic realities of present times but also the maturing of the family therapy field. The prospects for the future of couple and family therapy continue to grow as more effective treatment is created.

References

Beavers, W. (1985). *Successful marriage: A family systems approach to couples therapy*. New York: W. W. Norton.

Beavers, W., Hampson, R., & Hulgus, Y. (1985). Commentary: The Beavers systems approach to family assessment, *Family Process, 24*, 398–405.

Berman, E., & Lief, H. (1975). Marital therapy from a psychiatric perspective: An overview. *American Journal of Psychiatry, 132*, 582–591.

Beutler, L. B. (1983). *Eclectic psychotherapy: A systemic approach*. New York: Pergamon.

Beutler, L. E., & Clarkin, J. F. (1990). *Systematic treatment selection: Toward targeted therapeutic interventions*. New York: Brunner/Mazel.

Beutler, L., & Crago, M. (1987). Strategies and techniques of prescriptive psychotherapeutic intervention. In R. Hales & A. Frances (Eds.), *Psychiatric updates: APA annual review Vol. 6*. (pp. 331–446). Washington, DC: American Psychiatric Press.

Carlson, J., & Sperry, L. (Eds.). (1996). *The disordered couple*. New York: Brunner/Mazel.

Coleman, S. B. (Ed.). (1985). *Failures in family therapy*. New York: Guilford.

Dinkmeyer, D., & Carison, J. (1986). TIME for a better marriage. *Journal of Psychotherapy and the Family, 2*, 9–28.

Doherty, W., & Baird, M. (Eds.). (1987). *Family-centered medical care: A clinical casebook*. New York: Guilford.

Fish, R., & Fish, L. (1986). Quid pro quo revisited: The basis of marital therapy. *American Journal of Orthopsychiatry, 56*, 371–384.

Frances, A., Clarkin, J. F., & Perry S. (1984). *Differential therapeutics in psychiatry: The art and science of treatment selection*. New York: Brunner/Mazel.

Guerin, P., Fay, L., Burden, S., & Kautto, J. (1987). *The evaluation and treatment of marital conflict: A four-stage approach*. New York: Basic Books.

Howard, G. S., Nance, D. W., & Myers, P. (1987). *Adaptive counseling and therapy: A systematic approach to selecting effective treatments*. San Francisco: Jossey–Bass.

Kates, N., Greiff, B., & Hagen, D. (1990). *The psychosocial impact of job loss*. Washington, DC: American Psychiatric Press.

Laner, M. (1978). Love's labors lost: A theory of marital dissolution. *Family Coordinator, 25*, 175–181.

Lazarus, A. (1981). *The practice of multimodal therapy*. New York: Guilford.

Lazarus, A. (Ed.). (1985). *The practice of multimodal therapy*. New York: McGraw-Hill.

Levinger, G. (1976). In conclusion: Threads in the fabric. *Journal of Social Issues, 32*, 193–207.

Lorenz, F., Conger, R., Simon, R., & Whitbeck, L. (1991). Economic pressure and marital quality. *Journal of Marriage and the Family, 53*, 375–388.

McGoldrick, M., & Carter, E. (1982). The family life cycle. In F. Walsh (Ed.), *Normal family processes* (pp. 221–249). New York: Guilford.

McGoldrick, M., & Gerson, R. (1985). *Genograms in family assessment*. New York: W. W. Norton.

Myers, P. (1992). Using adaptive counseling and therapy to tailor treatment to couples and families. *Topics in Family Psychology and Counseling, 1*(3), 56–70.

Myers, P. (1995). *How therapists ACT: Cases combining major approaches to psychotherapy and the Adaptive Counseling and Therapy model* (pp. 105–128). Washington, DC: Accelerated Development, Inc.,

Nichols, W. (1988). *Marital therapy: An integrative approach*. New York: Guilford.

Olson, D., Portner, J., & Labee, Y. (1985). *FACES-Ill*. St. Paul, MN: Family Social Science.

Olson, D., Sprenkle, D., & Russell, C. (1979). Circumflex model of marital and family systems: I. Cohesion and adaptability dimensions, family types and clinical applications. *Family Process, 18,* 3–28.

Paul, G. (1967). Strategy of outcome research in psychotherapy. *Journal of Consulting Psychology, 31,* 109–118.

Perry, S., Frances, A., & Clarkin, J. (1990). *A DSM-III-R casebook of treatment selection.* New York: Brunner/Mazel.

Schultz, S. (1984). *Family systems therapy: An integration.* New York: Jason Aronson.

Sperry, L. (1986). Contemporary approaches to family therapy: A comparative and meta-analysis. *Individual Psychology, 42,* 591–601.

Sperry, L. (1989). Assessment in marital therapy: A couples-centered biopsychosocial approach. *Individual Psychology, 45,* 446–451.

Sperry, L., & Carlson, J. (1991). *Marital therapy: Integrating theory and technique.* Denver: Love Publishing.

Stuart, R. (1980). *Helping couples change: A social learning approach to marital therapy.* New York: Guilford.

Thornton, A. (1977). Children and marital stability. *Journal of Marriage and the Family, 39,* 531–540.

Weltner, I. (1985). Matchmaking: Choosing the appropriate therapy for families at various levels of pathology. In M. Mirkin & S. Koman (Eds.), *Handbook of adolescent and family therapy* (pp. 237–246). New York: Gardner.

Worthington, E. (1989). Matching family treatment to family stressors. In C. Figely (Ed.), *Treating stress in families* (pp. 44–63). New York: Brunner/Mazel.

Worthington, E. (1992). Strategic matching and tailoring of treatment to couples and families. *Topics in Family Psychology and Counseling, 1*(3), 21–32.

5

CASE CONCEPTUALIZATION AS A STRATEGY FOR TAILORING TREATMENT

Jack is a 13-year-old Caucasian male in a residential treatment program because of his angry outburst and physical threats to his mother and stepfather. After a short course of residential treatment, which included individual and family therapy, Jack's relationship with his family not only did not improve but actually worsened. The treatment staff was baffled. Individual sessions with Jack were planned to focus on anger management skills, while family sessions were to focus initially on Jack's sadness and anger at his parent's divorce and his mother's subsequent remarriage. Although this treatment plan and intervention strategies had been quite successful with many other acting-out adolescents in this residential program, they appeared to be a poor "fit" with Jack and his family. Interestingly, Jack's three siblings were not initially involved in the treatment process. This case scenario, which will be revisited later, serves to illustrates how "standard" treatment plans and interventions that are *not* based on a clinically useful case conceptualization are less likely to achieve expected treatment outcomes because they ignore key dynamics in the case. On the other hand, when these key dynamics are understood and incorporated into a tailored treatment plan, the likelihood of positive treatment outcomes is much greater.

The purpose of this chapter is to illustrate how case conceptualization and particularly the *pattern analysis* strategy can be an effective and powerful tailoring treatment when working with individuals, couples, and families. First, case conceptualization is defined, and its components, as well as its relationship to tailored treatment, are described. Then, the relationship between the client's and the therapist's conceptualizations is noted. Next, some guidelines for developing case conceptualizations are provided. Finally, two case examples illustrate the use of case conceptualization as a strategy for tailoring treatment.

CASE CONCEPTUALIZATION

A case conceptualization is a method and process of summarizing seemingly diverse case information into a brief, coherent statement or "map" that elucidates the client's basic pattern of behavior. The purpose of a well-articulated case conceptualization is to better understand and more effectively treat the client, which refers to an individual, couple, or family. In short, it is a "theory" of a particular case.

Three Components of a Case Conceptualization: Diagnostic, Clinical, and Treatment

Essentially, a case conceptualization consists of three components: a diagnostic formulation, a clinical formulation, and a treatment formulation (Sperry, Blackwell, Gudeman, & Faulkner, 1992). This section describes these components.

A *diagnostic formulation* is a descriptive statement about the nature and severity of the individual's psychiatric presentation. The diagnostic formulation aids the therapist in reaching three sets of diagnostic conclusions: whether the client's presentation is primarily psychotic, characterological, or neurotic; whether the client's presentation is primarily organic or psychogenic in etiology; and whether the client's presentation is so acute and severe it requires immediate intervention. In short, diagnostic formulations are descriptive, phenomenological, and cross-sectional in nature. They answer the "What happened?" question. For all practical purposes, the diagnostic formulation lends itself to being specified with DSM-IV criteria and nosology.

A *clinical formulation*, on the other hand, is more explanatory and longitudinal in nature and attempts to offer a rationale for the development and maintenance of symptoms and dysfunctional life patterns. Just as various theories of human behavior exist, so do various types of clinical formulations: psychoanalytic, Adlerian, cognitive, behavioral, biological, family systems, and biopsychosocial. Clinical formulations answer the "Why did it happen?" question. In short, the clinical formulation articulates and integrates the intrapsychic, interpersonal, and systemic dynamics to provide a clinically meaningful explanation of the client's *pattern* (that is, the predictable style of thinking, feeling, acting, and coping in stressful circumstances) and a statement of the causality of their behavior. Not surprisingly, the clinical formulation is a key component in a case conceptualization and serves to link the diagnostic and treatment formulations.

A *treatment formulation* follows from a diagnostic and clinical formulation and serves as an explicit blueprint governing treatment interventions. Informed by both the answers to the "What happened?" and the "Why did it happen?" question, the answer to the "What can be done about it, and how?" question is the treatment formulation. A well-articulated treatment formulation provides treatment goals, a treatment plan, treatment interventions, and predictions about the course of treatment and its outcomes.

The most clinically useful case conceptualizations are those that emphasize the unique context, needs, and resources that the individual, couple, or family brings to treatment. They are "integrative" case conceptualizations in that they integrate and incorporate these factors in all three formulation dimensions: diagnostic, clinical, and treatment. In line with the contemporary movement toward integration, this chapter will emphasize integrative case formulations.

The Clinical Value of Case Conceptualizations

Whatever one thinks about the value and advisability of diagnosis, particularly DSM-based diagnoses, diagnosis and diagnostic labels are a reality in clinical practice, particularly when third-party payers are concerned. Accordingly, therapist trainees are taught to use diagnostic language and some, if not many, unwittingly assume that a specific and preferred treatment exists for every diagnosis. Advertisers have much to gain by reinforcing this assumption. For example, they expect that those watching television commercials will associate depression (diagnosis) with Paxil or Prozac (treatments) and then ask their physician or therapist for it.

The reality is that no proven connection has been made between a specific diagnosis and a specific treatment, whether it be medication or psychotherapy, or even some combination of both (Nathan & Gorman, 2002). Therapy trainees are often surprised to learn, usually by trial and error, that such an assumed direct connection is spurious. Nevertheless, they may model more experienced therapists or supervisors or follow a clinic's "policy" of specifying a goal and intervention such as anger management (treatment) for clients with angry or violent outbursts (diagnosis). As in the case of Jack that began this chapter, such a treatment plan may be quite effective or quite ineffective. What makes the difference?

The difference is whether the treatment is a "fit" for the client. An effective and well-articulated case conceptualization can maximize the "fit," which is the main clinical value of case conceptualizations.

Case conceptualizations provide clinical value and utility in other ways. First, case conceptualizations can be of an inestimable value by predicting, with some degree of certainty, both the course of treatment and its outcome. Second, a well-articulated conceptualization can suggest therapeutic "traps" that are likely to be encountered in the course of treatment. Third, the client's adherence to the treatment process, whether it be homework assignments, medication compliance, or other recommendations, can be derived from a case conceptualization. Finally, a well-formulated case conceptualization can alert the therapist to the nature and type of transference and countertransference issues that could be encountered by that client. The case examples later in this chapter will illustrate the clinical value of case conceptualizations.

Case Conceptualizations and Tailored Treatment

As noted earlier, a well-articulated case conceptualization can maximize the "fit" between a client's or a client system's issues or symptomatic presentation and the treatment interventions provided. Because a case conceptualization focuses on the vitally important "Why did it happen?" question (clinical formulation), as a prelude to the "What can be done about it?" question (treatment formulation), the case conceptualization inevitably leads to a better tailored treatment than if the treatment formulation was based entirely on the diagnostic formulation. Because the treatment formulation is informed by the client's and client system's unique dynamics and pattern (clinical formulation), presumably the proposed treatment goals and treatment plan will eventuate in the provision of tailored treatment.

Case Conceptualizations: Therapists vs. Clients

Effective therapists are skilled at developing, eliciting, and negotiating case conceptualizations. What do we mean by eliciting case conceptualizations? Therapists-in-treating are surprised to learn that some clients have developed case conceptualizations of their own. Although clients may not consciously be aware of their conceptualizations, these are nevertheless powerfully operative in the treatment process. Effective therapists not only recognize the presence of these conceptualizations but elicit them and then negotiate a common conceptualization with their clients.

What are these client conceptualizations like? They closely resemble the structure of the three formulations we have been describing. First, the client's or client system's description of their presenting problem, including their symptomatic distress and their rating of their impairment in various life areas, is analogous to the therapist's clinical formulation. Similarly, the client's explanatory model of their condition or presenting problem is analogous to the diagnostic formulation. Finally, the client's expectations for treatment is analogous to the therapist's treatment formulation.

Where the client and therapist case conceptualizations usually differ is in content. Although the therapist develops a case conceptualization based on a critical understanding of the scientific basis of human behavior, that is, biological, psychological, and sociocultural, the client's explanation is more likely to be based on a highly personal, idiosyncratic, and uncritical understanding or theory of human behavior. Social psychologists refer to this phenomenon as "naive personality theory."

Why is it important to recognize the client's own case conceptualization? Because the greater it differs from the therapist's conceptualization, the less likely treatment is to be effective and the more likely noncompliance or nonadherence will be present. This can show itself in many ways: Clients may arrive late to sessions or not at all, they may fail to do homework or take medication, or they may prematurely terminate therapy.

For example, imagine that the client's nonelicited explanatory model for panic symptoms and difficulty doing grocery shopping and other household responsibilities is because "of a chemical imbalance in my brain." Imagine also that this client's nonelicited treatment expectation is for Ativan, "because it really worked for a neighbor," but not for talk therapy. Then imagine that his therapist, who is considered a specialist in the behavior therapy of anxiety disorders and is adamantly against the use of tranquilizers like Ativan, comes up with a diagnostic formulation of panic with agoraphobia, a clinical formulation of symptoms being caused by avoidance behavior, and specifies a treatment formulation of exposure therapy. That is, the client will be trained with a gradual exposure to feared stimuli—large stores and other open spaces.

What is likely to happen? Probably the client will directly or indirectly reject the plan for exposure therapy directly by refusing the exposure protocol or by premature termination. He or she may indirectly reject it by making a half-hearted attempt to follow the therapy. Now, if the therapist elicited the client's case conceptualization, the therapist could then provide the client with reasons why Ativan or other medications in that class would only be a short-term treatment with a high addictive potential, and why exposure would be preferable. It may be that after further discussion both agree that a safer and more effective medication like Ativan, which has FDA approval for use with panic and agoraphobia, will be utilized in combination with the behavioral approach.

The effective therapist's task then is to elicit the client's or client system's case conceptualization. This means eliciting the presenting problem, its symptoms, the areas of impaired functioning, the treatment expectations, and particularly the explanatory model. An explanatory model is the client's or client system's *personal explanation* of their problems, symptoms, and impaired functioning. In other words, an explanatory model is akin to the therapist's *professional and scientific explanation* for the client's or client system's problems, symptoms, and impaired functioning.

Effective therapists can reconcile differences between what is often two differing explanations or conceptualizations. Such a reconciliation involves negotiation. This negotiation process begins with the therapist acknowledging the client's explanation and the similarities and differences from the therapist's conceptualization. The ensuing discussion allows the therapist to educate the client about his or her illness and clarify misconceptions about it and the treatment process. Furthermore, a discussion of the client's or client system's expectations for the treatment process and outcome facilitates negotiating a mutually agreeable direction for treatment and a therapeutic relationship based on cooperation. Then the specifics of treatment selection can be discussed.

Diagnostic Formulation Although family therapists may be more comfortable with a systemic model of human behavior than with a pathology or medical model, the reality is that virtually all third-party reimbursement for individual, couples, or family therapy requires a five-axis DSM-IV TR diagnosis (Fauman, 2002). In addition to the convention of providing such a diagnosis, some family therapists have found it valuable to specify a client's Global Assessment of Relational Functioning score (GARF) on Axis V in addition to the Global Assessment of Functioning score (GAF). The GARF can be particularly useful in monitoring intimate relationship functioning (Yingling, Miller, McDonald, & Galwaler, 1998). A culturally sensitive family therapist might also include a cultural dimension to their diagnostic formulation or even add a separate cultural formulation statement. A cultural formulation is a systematic review of cultural factors and dynamics that can have an impact on therapy. This formulation may include a discussion on the cultural identity of the individual, a cultural explanation of the individual's condition, the cultural factors that affect the individual's level of functioning and support system, and the cultural elements that may affect the relationship between the individual and the therapist (GAP, 2002; Sperry et al., 2003).

Clinical Formulation   A clinical formulation is a way of analyzing, interpreting, and explaining the personal and systemic dynamics of a case in light of a specific theoretical perspective or other explanatory rationale. In short, a clinical formulation provides an explanation of why the client or client system developed the particular symptom(s), the degree of impairment and their characteristic personality or systemic pattern, and why this pattern is maintained.

Current theoretical perspectives include the psychodynamic, cognitive–behavioral, Adlerian, biological, social, family systems, biopsychosocial, and integrative perspectives. The following is a brief description of seven contemporary perspectives underlying clinical formulations (Sperry et al., 2003).

> *Biological formulation:* In this perspective, psychopathology is understood to result from psychobiological disequilibrium. Consequently, symptoms are understood as the manifestation of this underlying psychobiological disequilibrium. Treatment then consists of normalizing this disequilibrium or compensating for the effects of this disequilibrium, usually with medications, in the most efficient, effective manner with the fewest side effects.

> *Psychodynamic formulation:* In this perspective, psychopathology is understood to result from intrapsychic conflicts, developmental impasses, or distorted object relations. Consequently, symptoms are understood as the manifestation of unconscious processes and neurotic character structures. Treatment consists of resolving these conflicts, strengthening the ego, and modifying the character structure.

> *Cognitive–behavioral formulation:* In this perspective, psychopathology is learned as a result of aversive events or disordered thinking and faulty cognitive schemas. It is also maintained by reinforcing events. Consequently, symptoms are understood to be the manifestation of maladaptive behavior patterns or disordered thinking and faulty cognitive schemas. Treatment focuses on specific symptoms and maladaptive behaviors or thoughts based on their antecedents and consequences.

Social formulation: This is a broad perspective involving a wide range of factors, including the interpersonal relations, family system dynamics, socioeconomic status, and cultural values and norms. In this perspective, psychopathology is understood to result from maladaptive patterns of marginalization, alienation, poverty, prejudices, boundary violations, power and domination, intimacy conflicts, or social skill deficits. Consequently, symptoms can be a manifestation of one or more of these factors. Treatment can involve several types of interventions, ranging from social skills training to establishing more functional system boundaries and fostering equality, to education and the elimination of poverty and prejudice.

Family systems formulation: In this specialized form of the social formulation perspective, psychopathology is understood to result from dysfunctional patterns of family boundaries, narratives, schemas, power, intimacy, or skill deficits. Consequently, symptoms can be a manifestation of one or more of these factors, and thus one or more of these factors is the focus of therapy. Treatment typically consists of joining, enactment, reframing, restorying, boundary restructuring, strategic techniques such as paradox, skill training, and so on.

Integrative formulation: Perhaps the most commonly utilized integrative clinical formulation is based on the biopsychosocial model. This perspective emphasizes three sets of dimensions: the biological, the psychological—including selected psychodynamic, social, cognitive–behavioral—and the systemic aspects. In this perspective, psychopathology is understood as a complex, holistic response of the individual to stressors as they impact the individual's biological, psychological, and social–cultural vulnerabilities and resources. Consequently, symptoms are understood as the manifestation of the individual's attempt to cope with stressors, given their vulnerabilities and resources. Treatment is directed to the amelioration of symptoms and an increase of the individual's levels of functioning often through a multimodal approach tailored to the individual's needs, expectations, and resources.

Adlerian formulation: Another common integrative clinical formulation is based on Adlerian psychology. In this perspective, psychopathology is understood to result from faulty lifestyle patterns, that is, maladaptive schemas or beliefs of self and others developed within the individual's family as one strives to achieve a sense of belonging and meaning in life. Consequently, the purpose of symptoms is to safeguard the individual's self-esteem in the face of faulty beliefs and failed strivings. Treatment consists of modifying these faulty beliefs and increasing social interest and belonging.

THE CENTRALITY OF PATTERN ANALYSIS IN THE CLINICAL FORMULATION

As noted earlier, a pattern is described as the predictable and consistent style or manner of thinking, feeling, acting, coping, and defending one's self in stressful and nonstressful circumstances (Sperry et al., 1992). Pattern analysis is the process of examining the interrelationship among four elements or factors: precipitating factors, predisposing factors, perpetuating factors, and presentation factors, including relational response factors.

A *precipitant* is a trigger or stressor that activates the pattern. *Presentation* refers to the characteristic and predictable manner in which the client responds to the precipitants. *Perpetuants* are the processes by which a client's pattern is reinforced and confirmed by both the client and the client environment. *Predisposition* refers to all the intrapsychic, interpersonal, and systemic factors, including early life experiences, attachment style, and trauma, that render a client or client system vulnerable to maladaptive functioning. In short, a client's pattern is a predicable style of behavior and functioning that reflects and is reflected in precipitants, presentation, perpetuants, and predisposition.

Although it may appear that predisposing factors such as traumatic events, maladaptive beliefs or schemas, defenses, personality style, or system factors primarily drive one's thoughts, feelings, and actions, we would contend that both individual and systemic dynamics are a function of all four factors and thus should be included in a pattern analysis. Furthermore, we contend that a pattern analysis that includes these factors, along with associated individual and systemic dynamics, is central to developing and articulating a clinically useful clinical formulation.

Developing a Clinical Formulation

Here are some specific guidelines for developing a clinical formulation statement:

- *Begin by analyzing a critical incident resulting in distress or dysfunctional behavior.* Note the nature of the presentation, including individual and relational responses of all those involved. Look for relevant precipitants or triggers, perpetuants, and predisposing factors.

- *Specify relevant biological, psychological, and social–cultural considerations for presentation, precipitants, perpetuants, and predisposing factors.* On a sheet of paper, list any biological, psychological, and social indicators for each of the four factors where applicable. For example, in the case of Jack, a social indicator for precipitant would be his mother's preferential treatment, whereas a social indicator for presentation would be Jack's angry outburst.

- *Analyze and specify the basic pattern of the client.* Look for possible causal relationships among the four factors, starting with precipitants and presentation. For example, when Jack's mother acts provocatively, as when she makes demands that Jack believes are unreasonable or when she gives preferential treatment to Jack's brother (precipitant), Jack is likely to act out with angry words or threats (presentation). Next, look for possible reasons to explain why Jack would act out rather than act in, such as hurting himself or ignoring and downplaying his mother's behavior by making a joke of it. Presumably, Jack perceives that he is being treated unfairly, which could reflect early maladaptive beliefs or schemas that life is unfair and that he must be on guard and aggressively look out for his own needs and safely, lest he be hurt or lose even more in the process (predisposition). Review the seven contemporary perspectives on clinical formulations (described previously) for one that provides a realistic explanation or clinical rationale for the pattern and convincingly links precipitants and presentation.

- *Write a clinical formulation statement.* Strive to develop a formulation statement with high explanatory power, that is, one that best answers the questions "Why did it happen?" and "Why does the client behave or respond in this way?" Then write a formulation statement that realistically and compellingly links the precipitants and presentation.

Treatment Formulation   The treatment formulation provides a blueprint for treatment intervention and expected treatment outcomes (Sperry et al., 1992; Sperry, 2001). It is assumed that the therapist has already elicited the client's treatment expectations. These include the outcomes the client is hoping for, the client's expectations about roles and responsibilities, and the extent of the collaboration between the therapist and client. Ideally, these expectations will be included as part of a general treatment formulation mutually agreed to by the client and therapist. For instance, when the client can now manage the anxiety of leaving home without a panic attack, it is time to terminate therapy because the mutually agreed treatment outcome has been achieved.

After this overall goal/outcome has been agreed upon, it is then possible to formulate a specific treatment plan with targeted treatment goals and specific intervention methods. It goes without saying that specific goals should be realistic and achievable for the client. It should also be added that these specific goals should be manageable for the therapist. Targeted goals are manageable when specific and measurable steps can be specified. Some examples of manageable goals would be talking to one individual at work before the next scheduled session, reducing the number of angry outbursts from four to one per week, and spending 20 minutes every day alone reading or listening to music. Specified in this manner, these manageable goal/steps become the tasks that the therapist and client work on during therapy, and which are assigned between sessions.

Developing a Treatment Formulation

Here are some guidelines for developing an integrative or biopsychosocial treatment formulation statement:

- Specify targeted psychological treatment goals based on the diagnostic and clinical formulations and specify treatment interventions to achieve these goals. Psychological treatment goals are often specified as the opposite of the targeted symptom or skill deficit; that is, when a lack of assertiveness is a targeted symptom, the goal might be specified as "increase assertive communication" and the targeted intervention might be "assertiveness training."
- Specify targeted social treatment goals based on the diagnostic and clinical formulations and specify treatment interventions to achieve these goals. Social treatment goals are often specified as the opposite of the targeted symptom or skill deficit. That is, job stress could be a targeted symptom, so the goal might be specified as "decrease job stress" and the targeted intervention might be "workplace job accommodation."
- Specify targeted biological treatment goals based on the diagnostic and clinical formulations and treatment interventions to achieve these goals. Biological treatment goals are often specified as the opposite of the targeted symptom or skill deficit. When depressive symptoms are the targeted problem, the goal might be specified as "decrease depressive symptoms" and the targeted intervention might be "referral for medication evaluation."

- Write an integrative treatment formulation statement incorporating these goals and interventions. This statement incorporates the psychological and social treatment goals and interventions (as well as the biological goals and interventions, if applicable).

CLINICAL ILLUSTRATIONS

Case 1

As already discussed, Jack is a 13-year-old Caucasian male currently in a residential treatment program that emphasizes behavior modification for acting-out adolescent males. He has been in the program for nearly 7 months, having been placed there by his mother and stepfather due to extreme anger and disrespect toward his parents, including physically threatening his mother on two occasions. The police were called, and it was suggested that Jack might benefit from counseling. Nevertheless, 3 days later, Jack's mother found a church-sponsored residential program that was willing to accept him for treatment. During the first 5 months of treatment, Jack's relationship with his family had somewhat improved but recently had begun to escalate as he became progressively more verbally and physically abusive to his mother and stepfather. This escalation followed his parents' decision to have Jack remain in the program for the duration of the school year, in spite of his progress and eligibility for graduation from the program. The staff response was to refer Jack for individual therapy and insist on family therapy.

Jack was 1 1/2 years old when his parents divorced and 8 when his mother remarried. Jack's siblings include an 18-year-old brother, a 14-month-old stepsister, and a 4-year-old stepbrother. He is unaware of the exact reason his parents divorced, and his mother insists on withholding this information until she believes he is old enough to "really understand it all." Jack maintains weekly phone conversations with his biological father, who has remarried with two children and lives in New York.

Jack notes that he is closest to his mother. His stepfather is very involved in his life, and Jack refers to him as his father unless he is angry with him. During those times, Jack calls his stepfather by his surname, reminding him that he is not his "real" father. His stepfather is performance-driven and will only offer words of praise and affirmation when Jack performs well. Jack reports having several friends in school and several close friends in his neighborhood. He also enjoys spending time with his older brother whom he looks up to. Jack is making good grades in school and enjoys playing football. He reports feeling happy with himself.

Jack indicates that his parents divorce was very difficult for him, and that his basic desire in life is to live with his biological father. His mother continually explains why that is not feasible, which Jack responds to by saying that it is not fair that his parents divorced, not fair that his mother moved away from his father, and not fair that he cannot live with him.

Although Jack appears to be engaged in individual counseling with a focus on anger management training, it seems to have little impact on his behavior. Similarly, family sessions seem to be going nowhere. Similarly, processing the impact of divorce on Jack seems to have little or no impact.

Diagnostic Formulation   A five-axis DSM-IV-TR diagnosis can be specified with an Axis I: Adjustment Disorder with Mixed Disturbances of Mentions and Conduct (309.4), Parent–Child Relational Problems (V61.20), Axis II: No Diagnosis (V71.09), Axis III: None, Axis IV: Family Conflict, Axis V: GAF 62, and GARF 52. A family narrative with a story line of a heroic, constant struggle to maintain family loyalty and cohesion is noted.

Clinical Formulation   Pattern analysis reveals that, when Jack's mother acts provocatively, as when she makes demands Jack believes are unreasonable, he is likely to act out with angry outbursts and possibly physical threats. It appears that Jack acts out because he perceives he is being treated unfairly. Presumably, this reflects his belief that life is unfair and that he must be look out for his own needs.

Thus, when he perceives he is not being treated fairly by his parents, he reacts by becoming disrespectful, angry, and sometimes physically threatening and menacing. He seems convinced that because his mother remarried and moved away from Jack's father that she no longer cares for Jack, demonstrated by the lack of meaningful, positive time she spends with him. His perception is that the only time she gives him any consideration is when she makes what he considers "unreasonable demands" or criticizes him. This serves to reconfirm his belief in the "unfairness" from his mother and stepfather.

Lately, as parental demands and criticism increase, it is not surprising that Jack's anger outbursts have increased in number and intensity. It appears that the manner in which they communicate their expectations and their style of discipline is operative in triggering Jack's outbursts, which then trigger further parental criticism, and the situation escalates. On the other hand, Jack responds appropriately to the expectations and correction offered by teachers and program staff, presumably because their style of communication and discipline is perceived by him to be firm but fair. Remarkably, his outbursts have been selective: including only his mother and stepfather. Interestingly, despite the occasional taunts of older adolescents in school and the residential program, Jack has been able to control his anger, suggestive of the circumscribed nature of his schema and beliefs. That it is situation-specific at the present and has not generalized to all or most situations is a positive prognostic indicator, indeed.

In terms of systemic dynamics, it appears that the family's narrative (White & Epston, 1990), championed largely by the mother, is one of a constant, heroic struggle. In this narrative or story line, family members are achievement-oriented and show their concern for others by defending them against forces perceived as threatening the family's integrity, loyalty, and cohesion. The struggle is everything, even if the cost in relationships is high. The overriding belief of the family is that Jack's mother upholds the standards for achievement and morality, and others must be high achievers, loyal and obedient, or risk exclusion. That is, the father was excluded via divorce and Jack to the residential treatment program.

Treatment Formulation   As noted earlier, the residential treatment team added individual and family therapy when Jack's angry outburst began increasing. Individual sessions focused on anger management skills, and family sessions focused on processing Jack's reaction to his parent's divorce and his mother's subsequent remarriage. It was assumed, incorrectly it now appears, that these treatment targets were appropriate for Jack, largely because these two standard treatment strategies had been quite successful with many other adolescents in the residential program. In hindsight, it appears that Jack's admission into the residential treatment was probably not necessary and served to reinforce and reconfirm the family narrative. Unlike most of his peers in the residential program, Jack's capacity for self-management and impulse control are relatively high, which are reflected in reasonably high GAF and GARF scores.

Based on the clinical formulation, the following short-term and longer-term treatment goals can be specified. Given that Jack's outbursts are relationally specific (i.e., to his mother and stepfather) and have not generalized, a conservative treatment strategy would be to focus on short-term goal of reducing provocation and parental overreaction. This would involve a few sessions with parents only in which they are coached to reduce and eliminate "triggering" Jack's outburst. A therapist would work with them to find ways of engaging Jack in a less provocative and more nurturing but firm manner. Presumably, without such triggers, their relationship would be more like those that Jack experiences in school and the residential program. If this proves effective, no further individual or family treatment would be needed. If it is not sufficiently effective, a longer-term goal would be to address the unfair schema in focused individual sessions and the heroic struggle family story in family sessions. Coming from the narrative therapy tradition, restorying involves reflecting on the influence of particular events and relationships in a family's life and focusing on previously unexamined or unemphasized aspects of those experiences. The resulting story includes pieces of meaning and understanding that are new or different and that allow for a positive shift in the original family narrative. In this case, restorying should involve less emphasis on the achievement, obedience and loyalty, and more on relaxing and recognizing each other's uniqueness.

Table 5.1 summarizes these interventions and their potential sequencing. Note that the numbering represents the order in which interventions are sequenced; that is, parental coaching is first and second, whereas schema work and restorying are third, and so on.

Jack's prognosis remains quite good even without individual therapy, given that the parents are able to better modulate their communication and discipline style. If Jack's mother is unable to modulate her triggering behavior, then family therapy or even individual sessions with her would be necessary. A reasonable therapeutic marker of success would be for Jack to "graduate" from the residential program and return home.

Table 5.1 Pattern Analysis of the Case of Jack

Pattern Factors	Formulation/Treatment Targets	Interventions/ Sequence
Precipitant	Parental provocation	1. Parental coaching
Predisposition	Jack's "unfairness" schema and the family's "heroic, constant struggle" narrative	3. Schema work (Jack); restorying (family, particularly mother)
Presentation/ personal response(s)	Jack's angry outburst and disrespectful attitude	4. Anger management— if necessary
Presentation/family/ relational response(s)	Parental overreaction— increasing demands on Jack	2. Parental coaching

Case Commentary   This is a relatively straightforward and easy-to-treat case when viewed from the perspective of case conceptualization based on pattern analysis. But, as was previously pointed out, progress in the case has been essentially deadlocked because of using "standard" anger management treatment for Jack and a conventional focus on the impact of divorce on the "identified patient" in family therapy. Because anger and threats of physical were so circumscribed, and Jack was essentially a model student in school and in the residential program, the prognosis for this case is quite good. It will remain quite good provided the clinical formulation and treatment formulation continue to inform the treatment process, particularly the sequencing of treatment targets with designated interventions. Presumably, Jack can quickly return to a family with a more functional family narrative.

Case 2

H. W. is a 25-year-old married female, currently estranged from her husband of 6 years and who was referred for individual and couples therapy. She reported feeling depressed, hopeless, and helpless; having a lack of concentration; feeling tired; and being unable to sleep for several months. She also had a history of violent and vengeful behavior and was referred for individual and couple therapy as part of an after-care plan following a brief hospitalization. Prior to her hospitalization, the police were called to intervene during a domestic violence encounter. H. W. reported that her husband, who had been arrested on an earlier occasion for domestic violence, had hit her in the head with a shell during an argument. During the investigation, the client rescinded her story, indicating she had hit herself to get her husband into trouble. As a result, she was voluntarily admitted to a hospital for a three-week stay after disclosing a suicidal ideation with a nonlethal plan.

A review of her family revealed she was an only child, and that her mother died three years ago of cancer, while her father is alive and in good health, residing with his new girlfriend. She notes that she had a poor relationship with both parents from early childhood. Her mother was a nurse, and her father is a retired factory worker. Family values included hard work, obedience, and keeping family matters private. She remains uncertain about her parent's feelings for her, perhaps hoping that, even though they apparently did not demonstrate it, they really did love and care about her. Her mother was emotionally available to her, if only by being very concerned about her daughter's physical health. H. W.'s mother would never let her go outside to play with other children and refused to allow her to go outside or to school when she had a cold, had wet hair, or when the weather was threatening. She recalls her father was "never there for me" as he was off on business trips or spent time with his social friends when in town. Nevertheless, he did punish her with a strap for any perceived infraction, even when she was not guilty. At those times, her mother would retreat to a back bedroom and turn up the radio so that the neighbors wouldn't hear her daughter crying and screaming.

She reports having no friends while growing up and that other children made fun of her because of her health habits and the way she dressed. The first time she reported having any friends was during high school, during which time she had several boyfriends. This came about because she ran away from home at age 16 and lived with her paternal grandmother who "let me do whatever I wanted," apparently setting no boundaries or rules for her to follow. This experience was both liberating and confusing for her.

Her first job after high school was working for an escort service. She indicated she soon married her escort driver out of convenience only—it meant she could stop working as an escort—and that they did not love each other. Nevertheless, she reported being dependent on him for all her needs. When she tried to make some friends, he would not allow her to associate with them. He is 20 years older than H. W., and she reports that it is a volatile relationship. Once he was arrested and spent 2 months in jail for domestic violence.

They have a 5-year-old daughter, whom she really wanted to have "because there would be someone there for me, and I wouldn't lonely anymore." The child seemed to serve as a means of holding their relationship together, however tenuously. Their pattern was (a) for the couple to fight, (b) for her to retaliate at her husband, and then (c) for her to leave with her daughter. After a time, the husband would miss the child and then urge H. W. to return home. She would return, they would fight, and the cycle would start again.

In addition, features of pursuer–distancer relational dynamics appear to be operative and imposed on this cyclic pattern: She makes demands on him (pursuer), and he initially withdraws from her demands for attention and caring (distancer). She provokes him, and he recoils with exclusive demands, vengeful behavior, or in desperation retreats from the relationship. But because of their dependency on each other, they find themselves together.

Recently, the relationship had deteriorated and she admitted she had done some "crazy things" when she was mad. To spite him, she took her husband's beloved dogs, let them loose, and later told him they had been hit by a car. Another time she hit herself in order to get her husband arrested again for domestic violence, but the plan backfired and she was arrested instead.

She is unaware whether any extended family members had been diagnosed or treated for alcohol or substance abuse, but she recalls hearing that her maternal aunt had undergone electroshock treatment for depression. H. W.'s past mental health treatment has included a single hospitalization for depression and suicidality, as well as subsequent outpatient medication management. Unfortunately, H. W. soon stopped the medication. She herself has not been involved in individual, couples, or family therapy, but she is eager to begin. However, her husband, who has never been in any form of therapy, refuses to be involved.

Diagnostic Formulation   A five-axis DSM-IV-TR diagnosis can be specified with an Axis I of Major Depressive Disorder (296.23), Dysthymic Disorder (300.4), and Partner Relational Problem (V61.10), Axis II: Borderline and Antisocial Personality Features, Axis III: None, Axis IV: Partner Relational Problems and Economic Concerns, Axis V: GAP 40 now, 63 in past 12 months, and GARF: 55. A couples narrative with a story line of clinging while controlling and hurting the other is noted, along with the pursuer–distancer relational pattern.

Clinical Formulation   A pattern analysis suggests that, when her husband either ignores or provokes her, H. W. responds predictably by engaging in either attention-seeking or vengeful behavior, depending on the circumstance. This pattern of dependency–counterdependency arose in early life experiences when she came to view herself as someone who was deficient but strong and an outsider in world that is unfair and unpredictable. Despite her tendency to cling to and depend on others, she came to resolutely resist efforts to neglect, dominate, or hurt herself, and so she struggled to hold the attention and support of others while being demanding and oppositional.

In addition, it appears there may be some familial loading (behavioral and genetic history) for her depressive symptoms. Her attachment to her parents appeared to be anxious and insecure, and she would cling to anyone available and willing. Furthermore, strong parental injunctions encouraged keeping family matters private. The relationships she formed as a teenager were intense, and when she was not properly acknowledged, felt neglected, or was rejected, she felt desperate and would respond in a volatile and unpredictable manner. Her relationship with her husband was both physically and psychologically abusive as he isolated her from others and withheld psychological and physical support, such as leaving her at home for long periods of time, making her financially dependent on him, and so on.

Treatment Formulation The overall goal of therapy is to establish a better functioning relational pattern that meets the needs of both partners. In H. W.'s case, therapy should also support a reasonably healthy course of development of her young child. Accordingly, the following short-term and longer-term treatment targets can be specified. The first target is to reduce or eliminate the prominent depressive symptoms. H. W. agrees that such symptoms are wreaking havoc on her life and agrees to medication management, at least until the symptoms have remitted.

The second target is to address the triggering or precipitating factors. Accordingly, the therapists will attempt to enlist the support of H. W.'s husband to become involved as a "concerned family member" and meet in person or by phone with the therapist to come up with strategies—partner coaching—other than ignoring or provoking H. W. Not framing his involvement as a partner in couples therapy but as a concerned family member, it is quite likely that the husband will agree to this "safer" involvement in treatment.

At the same time, the third treatment target is diluting the pursuer–distancer pattern via partner coaching. Assuming that the husband finds the therapist understanding, safe, and helpful, the hope is that he will be receptive for the fourth target, which is to address the couple's narrative in a couples therapy format. If he refuses or starts but then drops out of couples work, the therapist can still address the couple's dynamics with H. W. alone. The heart of treatment for H. W. will involve intensive individual psychotherapy directed at her self-view, worldview, and dependency–counterdependency strategy, which is treatment target six.

She has agreed with the recommendation for individual therapy and believes that couples therapy is essential, although she is disappointed with her husband's refusal to be involved. It is anticipated that she may have considerable difficulty discussing personal matters with outsiders because of the privacy value held by her parents. Furthermore, her reversing pattern of intense relational dependency–counterdependency may pose challenges for the therapeutic relationship.

Table 5.2 presents a summary of the treatment targets, interventions, and the interventions' sequencing. Note that the numbering represents the order in which the interventions are sequenced; medication is first, followed by partner coaching, and so on.

Table 5.2 Pattern Analysis of the Case of H. W.

Pattern Factors	Formulation/Treatment Targets	Interventions/ Sequence
Precipitating factor(s):	Ignored *or* provoked by her husband	2. Partner coaching
Predisposing factor(s):	H. W.'s self-protective strategy of dependency–counterdependency; couples narrative: cling while controlling and hurting the other	6. Intensive individual psychotherapy 5. Couples therapy, with or without husband in sessions
Presentation/ personal response(s)	Attention-seeking *or* revengeful behavior; depressive symptoms	3. Partner coaching 1. Medication management re: depressive symptoms
Presentation/ family/relational response(s)	Pursuer–distancer dynamic: husband recoils from her demands, she provokes him, and he responds with vengefully or retreats; eliminate violent behavior	4. Couples session(s)

Case Commentary This case is considerably more complicated than the case of Jack. Here relatively intensive individual therapy will be, in all likelihood, a necessary adjunct to couples work. The major challenge for the therapist will be to first reduce the triggering of H. W.'s pattern, which requires that the therapist engage the husband in the process. If this cannot be achieved at the outset of therapy, it will be considerably more difficult to modify the couple's narrative—especially if only H. W. is directly involved. Furthermore, not diffusing this trigger and the subsequent relational response will cause the individual therapy directed at solving H. W.'s pattern of dependency–counterdependency to be that much more difficult. Suffice it to say, the prognosis for this case will be rather guarded and perhaps even poor if the decision is made to immediately begin treatment or directly work on the specified individual therapy and couples therapy treatment targets four and five without attending to targets one through three first.

SUMMARY

The purpose of this chapter has been to illustrate how case conceptualizations are developed and written. Specific guidelines have been offered for developing both clinical and treatment formulations. The two case examples, reasonably common presentations in family therapy practice today, detail how pattern analysis can be a useful tool for both establishing a treatment plan—including a tailored goal and a set of treatment targets—and a rationale for sequencing tailored treatment interventions. For didactic purposes, the matter of client versus therapist case conceptualizations was not addressed in either case in order to limit discussion to the essentials of developing and articulating case conceptualization. Nevertheless, eliciting the client's explanatory model or case conceptualization is highly recommended.

References

Fauman, M. (2002). *Study guide to DSM-IV-TR*. Washington, DC: American Psychiatric Press.

Nathan, P., & Gorman, J. (Eds.). (2002). *Guide to treatments that work*. New York: Oxford.

Sperry, L. (2001). Biopsychosocial therapy with individuals and couples: Integrative theory and interventions. In L. Sperry (Ed.), *Integrative and biopsychosocial therapy: Maximizing treatment outcomes with individual and couples* (pp. 67–99). Alexandria, VA: American Counseling Association.

Sperry, L., Blackwell, B., Gudeman, J., & Faulkner, K. (1992). *Psychiatric case formulations*. Washington, DC: American Psychiatric Press.

Sperry, L., Carlson, J., & Kjos, D. (2003). *Becoming an effective therapist*. Boston: Allyn & Bacon.

White, M., & Epston, D.(1990). *Narrative means to therapeutic ends*. New York: Norton.

Yingling, L., Miller, W., McDonald, M., & Galwaler, S. (1998). *GARF assessment sourcebook: Using the DSM-IV global assessment of relational functioning*. New York; Brunner Routledge.

6

TAILORING TREATMENT
The Impact of Culture

A therapist who wants to tailor treatment to meet the unique needs of specific families must be aware of all the variables that add to the complexity of family life. Given the steadily increasing diversity of the families we serve, culture is clearly among the most important of these variables. In fact, "the failure to see cultural and contextual issues actually denies and oppresses those whom we seek to help" (Ivey & Ivey, 2001, p. 221).

How can we meet the challenge of developing approaches that are alert to the cultural context? Lee (2001) pointed out that working from an "ethnically responsive paradigm" involves incorporating a number of approaches that have not always been part of the therapist's repertoire. For example, the effective therapist is aware of kinship influences and in fact can "find ways in which to make use of the kinship system in the counseling process" (p. 586). The ethnically responsive helper also appreciates and works with the central role played by language, by sex-role socialization practices, by religious–spiritual influences, and by the help-seeking attitudes and behaviors accepted among members of a particular group.

True *cultural responsiveness* may be an even broader construct than ethnic responsiveness. Consider the following definition of culture: "[Culture is] all of the learned behaviors, beliefs, norms, and values that are held by a group of people and passed on from older members to newer members, at least in part to preserve the group" (Hays, 1996, p. 333). If we accept this broad conceptualization, we begin to see that ethnicity is one of the central factors in culture, but not the only one. A number of building blocks can go into the construction of a particular family's cultural heritage. Along with race and ethnicity, a family's culture can be affected by age, language, social class, income, geographical location, education, religion, gender, sexual orientation, and myriad other factors. Family members may also hold values and worldviews that differ from those of the therapist. In fact, cultural differences may even occur among family members themselves. The key to a multicultural perspective is to embrace the reality of cultural diversity, recognizing the impact of culture on family life and working with all clients in accordance with their own cultural meanings.

The multicultural perspective has special repercussions for family therapy because culture so deeply affects even the most basic meaning that family life holds for each individual. Our effectiveness depends on our ability to understand how families are influenced by the values that underlie their notions of family life, by their experience of oppression, and by the conflicts inherent in acculturation.

THE VALUES UNDERLYING FAMILY LIFE

As they proceed on the journey toward multiculturalism, many family therapists find that they must stop and reexamine their own assumptions about what the concept of family really means. Suppositions that they believe to be universal sometimes turn out, on closer examination, to be culture-bound.

Individuation and Family Unity

The most basic definitions of family life vary from culture to culture. Consider, for example, the search for balance between the values of individuation and family unity. What family therapists perceive as unity within a family, or what counselors might view as an individual's tendency toward codependence, may in fact be a reflection of a cultural difference that should be honored.

Inclan and Hernandez (1992) addressed this issue in an analysis of the concept of codependence as it affects family therapy with Hispanic clients. They point out that, although separation, individuation, and clear boundaries are often considered positive goals of therapy, these concepts are not universally accepted across cultures. Therapeutic interventions designed to increase individual autonomy may be "unwittingly defining recovery and normality as the client's and family's ability to incorporate values, beliefs, and behavior that are more congruent with the ways of the Anglo culture than with their own" (p. 247).

If a therapist is unaware of the value placed by Hispanic families on family loyalty, on the preservation of traditions, on interdependence among family members, and on the subordination of individual needs to the needs of the family, the therapy may inadvertently undercut firmly held cultural values. Worse yet, the therapist may interpret culturally appropriate behaviors as pathological.

Inclan and Hernandez warned against therapeutic approaches that emphasize detachment and independence:

> This treatment approach is anchored in the cultural narrative of a Western-Anglo society that highly values individualism, action, mastery, and equality . . . Anchoring treatment goals and methods to such a social narrative is contrary to Hispanic family values and counterproductive to effective treatment. (1992, p. 251)

This concern is certainly not limited to Hispanic families. In fact, Sue and Sue (1990) suggested that, in comparison with the dominant culture in the United States, "almost all minority groups place greater value on families, historical lineage (reverence of ancestors), interdependence among family members, and submergence of self for the good the family" (p. 123). The fact that the dominant culture emphasizes individualism means that people whose cultures have a stronger relational dimension may be subjected to undue pressures to conform. "When the Euro-American worldview in psychology is used to determine normality and abnormality, then the cultural values of racial/ethnic minority groups may appear 'pathological'" (Sue et al., 1998, p. 22).

Women, as a cultural group, are also subjected to pressures to conform to changing views on what constitutes healthy behavior. The emphasis on relationships that was once considered appropriate for a woman now leaves her open to the criticism that she is enmeshed or codependent. As Walters (1993) pointed out, a woman is now expected to recover from her focus on nurturing others and to concentrate instead on meeting her own needs. Sometimes this new norm places a woman in an untenable position:

> It creates yet another of those ever-present, guilt-producing double binds for women: in your role as the *good* mother, you are expected to be a caretaker, responsible for the behavior of your children, protective, approving, available and self-sacrificing in

behalf of your family. But these very same behaviors will get you into trouble . . . . (Walters, 1993, p. 64)

Unfortunately, some of this trouble can actually stem from family therapy if therapists fail to recognize the impact of gender-role socialization processes that have their roots in the larger society.

The Extended Family

In addition to exploring cultural differences regarding individuation, Sue and Sue also contrasted the European-American emphasis on the nuclear family with the concept of the extended family. They stated that "middle-class White Americans consider the family unit to be nuclear (husband/wife and children related by blood), while most minorities define the family unit as an extended one" (p. 120). Ho (1987) pointed out that the conceptual framework of the nuclear family is often misused in services to Native Americans, whose family structures are more likely to be characterized by extended networks that include several households and active kinship systems. Boyd–Franklin (1989, p. 15) stated that "many black families have become extended families in which relatives of a variety of blood ties have been absorbed into a coherent network of mutual emotional and economic support." The Hispanic families described by Inclan and Hernandez (1992) are defined not just in terms of the nuclear unit but in terms of an extended kinship system that may include *compadres*, *comadres*, and *hijos de crianza* and that is expected to provide support in times of crisis.

Culturally based definitions of family have important implications for the therapeutic process. Clearly, therapists need to ask family members how they define the family before addressing any issues at all related to boundaries.

CULTURALLY BASED VIEWS OF FAMILY LIFE: THE IMPACT ON FAMILY THERAPY

Families define themselves within cultural contexts. These contexts have to be taken into account when therapists assess family systems and select interventions. Otherwise, family processes that are in fact normal within a particular culture may inadvertently be pathologized.

Ina (1994) provided an example that demonstrates the difficulties that can arise when a therapist is unaware of a family's cultural norms. She described a young Japanese-American college student who was referred to her by a Buddhist minister. The young man was in a state of deep depression following the intervention of his previous therapist. He had sought counseling initially because his father, a farmer in rural California, had announced he would be leaving the land to his eldest son. The client, who was the second son, had tried to earn his father's love and felt rejected.

After constructing a genogram, the previous counselor had diagnosed the family as dysfunctional, saying that the family was characterized by men who were authoritarian, remote, and emotionally unavailable, and women who were passive and personality-disordered. Boundaries between the parental and sibling subsystems were seen as diffuse. Communication patterns were assessed as triangulated because of the likelihood that one family member would approach another member indirectly by conveying a message through a third party.

Thus, family dynamics that in fact reflected the values of traditional Japanese-American families in this rural area were pathologized by a counselor who was uninformed about the culture. The young man was counseled to state his concerns directly in a public confrontation with his father. When this confrontation took place, the humiliated parent responded with an unremitting silence, refusing to speak to his son. The client, after being excluded from his family, fell into near-suicidal despondency.

Ina, working from a culturally sensitive perspective, helped the client understand the cultural beliefs underlying his father's behavior. The family's indirect communication pattern, far from being pathologized, was recognized as a culturally adaptive tool and was used to defuse this conflict. The client's eldest sister acted as an intermediary, taking a conciliatory message back to the father. Through this mechanism, the son was integrated back into the family, and a disaster rooted in cultural illiteracy was averted.

Falicov (1994) presented another example of the kind of problem that can occur when therapists are unaware of cultural norms. She described a situation in which a young child of Puerto Rican descent was hospitalized with a life-threatening illness. An elderly great-aunt, who was godmother to the child, spent innumerable hours at his bedside, praying, overseeing his treatment, and pampering him. The health care providers, exasperated with the aunt's constant "interference" and mystified by the fact that she was present more frequently than the child's parents, asked for a psychiatric consultation. The psychiatrist, who was unschooled in Latino culture, interpreted the aunt's behavior as a reaction formation based on her resentment at being forced to spend her spare time at the hospital in place of the child's mother. The hospital staff continued to discourage the aunt's participation.

What messages can we receive from these two examples? The counselor described by Ina was unaware of the risk involved in encouraging a client to exert a brand of individualism that was not accepted in his traditional family. The health care providers described by Falicov did not understand that their patient's definition of a "family" was much broader than their own. According to Falicov, the family's cultural values of strong kinship bonds, shared parenting, and three-generation involvement were misinterpreted by people whose own cultural values emphasized leisure, autonomy, and freedom from parenting in old age. Falicov stated that this event, which took place some years ago, would be less likely to occur today.

Although we may hope that such exaggerated ethnocentrism is a relic of the past, many therapists still fail to recognize the degree to which assumptions about the nature of family life differ among families and across cultures. Family therapists who are aware of cultural factors use their knowledge, not to make generalized assumptions about various ethnic groups, but to guide their exploration of each family's worldview.

THE EXPERIENCE OF OPPRESSION

Just as family therapists need to be sensitive to the cultural differences in family life, they also need to be aware of differences related to the experience of oppression. *Oppression* can be defined as "that state or condition within an ordered society . . . where one segment of the society is differentially and involuntarily limited access to all the available opportunities, resources, and benefits of that particular society" (Wilson, 1987, p. 19). Groups are targeted for oppression on the basis of such characteristics as ethnic and racial status, gender, and religious preference. The process of oppression is insidious because targeted people must face a lethal combination of overt bigotry, covert discrimination, and a socialization process that encourages internalization of negative self-views.

How could this process fail to affect the dynamics of family interactions? Consider, for example, the impact of racism on the family life of African-Americans:

The experience of being black in this country is almost a daily process of pulling out the arrows that racism hurls at us. The added burden that African-American families and couples must carry is to create an emotional atmosphere in which the arrows can be pulled out ... Unfortunately, many of the African-American families that we treat in family or couples therapy have redirected these daily arrows at each other. We cannot begin to address the anger and pain in these families unless we are willing to look at the racism that exists for them in society and in our field. (Boyd–Franklin, 1993, p. 55)

To be effective as family therapists, then, we need to be active in encouraging intense exploration of the impact of racism.

Addressing Racism Directly

Boyd–Franklin points out that African-American clients sometimes avoid talking about their experiences of racism even when these issues are foremost in their minds. "They know that many therapists will try to talk them out of what they are feeling because they do not understand the need for African-American individuals and families to vent their rage about situations in which there is an undercurrent of racism" (Boyd–Franklin, 1993, p. 56). When therapists are reluctant to address racism head-on, they impede the therapeutic process. As A. J. Franklin says,

> Once the pervasive impact of racism is acknowledged as a force in a black family's experience, the family can move on to confront other issues. But if the impact of racism is ignored, it's unlikely that therapy will go anywhere. (Franklin, 1993, p. 36)

"Healthy"

Racism and other oppressions are also relevant to family therapy because of their influence on the family's willingness to participate. People who have had to deal with a lifetime of racism and discrimination have many reasons to be suspicious of therapists and therapy (Boyd–Franklin, 1989; Willis, 1988). They may perceive extensive history-taking as an invasion of privacy, designed to place destructive labels on them. Negative experiences with the welfare system and other social and governmental agencies may have made distrust an appropriate response. Clients have no way to be certain that the agency providing family counseling is different and that confidentiality will be maintained. Family members may have been socialized from early childhood to distrust people who press for personal information. The referral for therapy may have come from the courts or from other systems that have agendas going beyond the well-being of the family.

Grier and Cobbs (1968) coined the term "healthy cultural paranoia" to describe the intense suspiciousness that may be the only route to survival in the context of racism. In the face of this reality, we should not be surprised by "minorities' help-seeking behaviors that include underutilization of family therapists who generally are monolinguistic, middle-class and ethnocentric in family problem diagnosis and treatment" (Ho, 1987, p. 14).

Oppression: The Impact on Family Therapy

Wilson stated that "empowerment is the antidote of oppression" (1987, p. 20). Therapy can lead toward empowerment when the therapist exhibits a belief in the client's potential ability to cope with problems; when problems are perceived as coming from a political, social, and economic context; when clients learn to understand and work with power dynamics; and when the therapist uses skill-building strategies to help clients gain control over their environments (McWhirter, 1991). Empowerment-oriented family therapy is built on the assumption that clients who recognize the role of oppression in their lives are most likely to move from the morass of self-blame to the solid ground of self-management.

Of course, exploring the experience of oppression is not an alternative to taking personal responsibility. Instead, it lays the groundwork that makes other therapeutic tasks possible. Consider, for example, an African-American family described by Franklin (1993). The family was seen in therapy primarily because of the adolescent son's behavior problems in school. The father was upset because the teacher and the school psychologist both seemed reluctant to speak to the father. He was also angered by his son's treatment in school, which he viewed as racist.

Some of the son's problems were, in fact, due to his own behavior, yet the racism experienced by both father and son was very real. As the therapist, Franklin knew he could not discount the family's accurate observation of institutionalized racism. He allowed time for family members, particularly the father, to express their sense that racism was a central problem in this situation. Once the issue of racism had been explored, the family was ready to move on and help the adolescent take more responsibility for his actions. As Franklin put it, "Therapy provided an opportunity to explore the crossroads where family dynamics and racism met" (1993, p. 36).

Anti-Oppression Advocacy

Sanders (2000) said that it is not enough simply to change the ways in which therapy services are offered. We need to look beyond the therapy office to the world beyond and take part in efforts to influence systems of oppression. Consider, for example, Sanders's list of ways to make systems work more effectively for African-American people (pp. 18–22):

- Cultural awareness if the first step
- Encourage self-advocacy
- Accountable training of professionals
- Use resources within communities such as churches and civic leaders to help spread the message
- Develop materials about mental health that are culturally appropriate
- Come out of your offices (which often represent institutions of oppression) and into African-American communities
- Challenge research and writings
- Raise awareness as you sit in on group and individual supervisions in your private and public practices
- Encourage educational professionals to provide accurate and inclusive instruction of American history to include the tremendous efforts of non-Whites and women
- Demystify the stigma associated with race talks by encouraging debate and dialogue
- Befriend African-American women's groups, sororities, and social clubs
- Support affirmative action and other antidiscrimination legislation
- Seek more funds to do empirical research of all socioeconomic levels within the African-American community to provide a more adequate picture of the heterogeneity
- Become an active participant in the numerous "watchdog" Web sites fighting for justice
- Encourage and advocate for the hiring and promotion of African-American educators, and support staff, and the admittance of African-Americans into master's and doctoral-level programs
- Challenge educational curriculum
- Challenge standards that continue to perpetuate ethnocentrism
- Fight institutions that discriminate against African-Americans

As Lee pointed out,

> The etiology of problems often is not in clients but rather in intolerant or restrictive environments. The only way in which clients will be able to solve problems or make decisions is to eradicate these systemic impediments. Ethnically responsive counselors often must assume the role of systemic change agents and help clients to challenge such impediments. (2001, p. 587)

CULTURAL VALUES AND CONFLICT

The concept of *worldview* is an important theme running through the current literature on multicultural counseling (Carter, 1991; Ho, 1987; Lewis, 1994; Sue & Sue, 1990). Cultural diversity creates differences in values that are so basic as to constitute alternate worldviews. For instance, Carter (1991), extending the work of Kluckhohn and Strodtbeck (1961), explained that cultures vary in terms of their orientations toward the following factors: *human nature, person and nature, time sense, activity,* and *social relations.*

In terms of human nature, cultures vary widely, with some teaching that people are born with evil inclinations that must be controlled, and others inculcating in their members a belief that people are basically good. The differences among cultures are even more apparent when we consider the relationship between person and nature. Some cultures believe in the subjugation of humans to nature and suggest that people cannot expect to control natural forces. Other cultures, in contrast, are built on the assumption that humankind can gain mastery over nature. An alternate worldview suggests that people can achieve partnership and harmony with nature.

Time sense is also central to cultural worldviews, with some cultures valuing the traditions of the past and others focusing on planning for the future. Closely associated with time sense is the orientation toward activity. Cultures that focus on *being* emphasize spontaneous self-expression, while those that focus on *doing* emphasize achievements that are measurable by external criteria. Finally, orientations toward social relations run the gamut from an acceptance of clearly established lines of authority to an emphasis on collective decision making, to an assumption that individuality and autonomy are more important than group goals.

On the basis of a review of numerous studies, Carter (1991) pointed out that "in general, these researchers have found significant differences between the dominant White middle-class value orientation and those of the cultural and ethnic groups with which they were compared" (p. 167). The value system of White middle-class Americans is characterized "by a belief in mastery over nature, future time, doing-oriented activity, and individual relationships" (p. 165). Studies of Latin cultures, Native American cultures, Asian cultures, African cultures, and Mediterranean cultures have pointed toward major value differences in all of these categories.

The fact that world views are so diverse has important implications for cross-cultural family counseling in that therapists have to see their own values in perspective. Again and again, they will face situations in which their own values and those of the families they are treating differ so greatly that the goals, assumptions, and processes of therapy will be affected:

> Middle-class therapists, no matter what their ethnic origins, have been socialized in terms of mainstream values. The therapist will be Future-oriented, expecting clients to be motivated and to keep appointments punctually. He or she will also expect families to be willing to work on therapeutic tasks (Doing), over reasonable periods of time (Future), with the prospect of change before them (Mastery-over-Nature) . . . And clients will be expected to separate themselves from enmeshment in the family structure and to develop increased autonomy (Individual). (Spiegel, 1982, p. 46)

Each therapist will have to respond with openness, adhering to his or her own value system but recognizing that it is one choice among many. "The therapist's beliefs, like those of the family, are only a 'comment on' the cultural context where they were learned, rather than the truth" (Schwartzman, 1983, p. 144).

Responding to these deep cultural differences is especially complex because the therapist can never assume that a client's value system necessarily coincides with his or her ethnic background. Adding to this complexity is the fact that many family systems are characterized by internal conflicts brought about by differences in acculturation among family members.

Conflicting Worldviews

Each individual and each family is affected by multiple cultural contexts. Within the United States, people may be influenced both by the traditional values of their families of origin and by the norms of the dominant culture. For instance, Garrett and Pichette (2000, p. 6) summarized the acculturation in Native Americans, which included the following levels:

- **Traditional** (holding traditional values and beliefs, following traditional practices, and speaking native language)
- **Marginal** (neither fully accepting traditional practices nor mainstream cultural values)
- **Bicultural** (accepting both dominant society and tribal society; knowing and accepting both mainstream and traditional values)
- **Assimilated** (accepting dominant society and embracing only mainstream cultural values)
- **Pantraditional** (assimilating but making a conscious choice to return to traditional cultural values and practices)

Within one family, all these levels of acculturation may exist at the same time, depending on differences in the life experiences of each member.

Similarly, in their discussion of Hispanics in the United States, Szapocznik, Scopetta, Ceballos, and Santisteban (1994) stated that much of the literature about this group is preoccupied with understanding the culture of origin while, in fact, no individual is purely a product of this idealized culture of origin:

> A Hispanic family in America, even in a very Hispanic region like Little Havana, is exposed to a complex melange of cultural influences which includes the culture of origin that exists in the living memories, values and behaviors of the older members of the family . . . This cultural melange also includes the hybrid culture in which the children are immersed both in school and with acculturating peers. (1994, p. 23)

This culturally pluralistic environment often leads to intensified generational conflict within families, with young people becoming acculturated into the mainstream while their parents try to maintain traditional values. Sometimes this culminates in a struggle wherein the adolescents strive for autonomy while the elders seek family connectedness.

Szapocznik and Kurtines (1993) described the conflicts they saw in clinical observations of Cuban refugees' families in the 1970s:

> The impact of a culturally diverse environment on these families resulted in the emergence of conflict-laden intergenerational acculturational differences in which parents and youths developed

different cultural alliances (Hispanic and American, respectively). These intergenerationally related cultural differences were added to the usual intergenerational conflicts that occur in families with adolescents to produce a much compounded and exacerbated intergenerational *and* intercultural conflict. As a consequence, parents became unable to properly manage youngsters who made strong claims for autonomy and who no longer accepted their parents' traditional Cuban ways. (1993, p. 403)

Szapocznik and Kurtines developed bicultural effectiveness training to work with these families. This strategy involved placing the cultural conflict itself in the role of identified patient and helping the family to develop a transcultural perspective. "Parents are encouraged to accept and understand the value of certain aspects of the American culture represented by their child, and the adolescents are encouraged to accept and understand the value of certain aspects of the Hispanic culture represented by their parents" (Szapocznik & Kurtines, 1993, p. 404).

CULTURAL CONFLICT WITHIN THE FAMILY: THE IMPACT ON THERAPY

Individual problems and family issues sometimes become clearer when they are reframed in terms of cultural conflict. Consider, for example, the case of Silvia, a 22-year-old woman, who had been living on her own since the age of 16. She left home at that time in the midst of an intense conflict with her father.

Silvia was an honors student in high school and wanted to continue her education, but her parents told her they would not be able to send her to college because they needed to save their money in case her older brother, Carlos, decided to go. In fact, Carlos had never shown any interest in higher education. Silvia felt that, no matter what she did, she could never win her father's approval.

Silvia's father, who had moved to Chicago from Mexico as a teenager, complained that Silvia was trying to turn her back on her family and her culture. Although he recognized that she was doing well in school, he criticized her lack of fluency in Spanish and her interest in "running around" with her friends in the evenings.

Once Silvia realized she would not be able to go to college, she gave up on school altogether, moving out and spending her time with a group of young people who had always succeeded in shocking her parents. After 18 months of living on her own, Silvia grew tired of awakening in too many strange places with no memory of what drugs she had ingested the night before and decided to return to the straight life. She finished her GED and got a clerical job. She soon established a strong relationship with Brent, an executive with her company. Brent asked her to marry him, but somehow Silvia was unable to make this commitment, although she was sure she loved him. She said she was so paralyzed in her own depression she could not make any decisions.

The main source of her depression had to do with her family. She had tried to reconnect with her family, but they said they could not forgive her for all that she had put them through when she left home. She thought her mother might have forgiven her but that her father would not allow it. Silvia had been able to forge some connections with her aunt, uncle, and cousins, but she said that being with them made her feel all the more lonely for her parents.

Another source of depression was that she had not disclosed to Brent any of the things that had happened to her in the 18 months after she left home. She feared he would leave her and that he would be right to do so. She did not believe that she deserved to have a happy relationship with someone like Brent.

Later Silvia ran into an old friend from her "wild days" and began to experiment with heroin. She was still involved with Brent, who could not understand the change to couples counseling with him. She felt she was on the edge of an abyss and that this therapy was her one last hope.

Although some therapists might seek the reasons for Silvia's drug use, depression, or her relationship problems with Brent, those with a multicultural perspective would recognize the salience of the cultural conflict within her family of origin. Silvia's attempts to be completely acculturated into the dominant Anglo culture ran the gamut from her unilingualism (English only) to her choice of a non-Hispanic mate. Even her drug use was a sign of her acculturation.

Despite her acculturation, however, Silvia could not come to terms with a lifestyle that others might call independent. Her separation from her family was a pain at the very core of her being. In essence, both she and her father were bicultural beings, each trying to maintain a hold on one of their cultures at the expense of the other. Her culturally aware therapist knew that Silvia and Brent could not move on in their lives until her need for connection with her family was addressed. Gradually, with the help of other members of the extended family, an accord was reached.

STRATEGIES FOR TAILORING FAMILY THERAPY

As the previous chapter indicated, "matching" and "tailoring" treatment are quite different. When it comes to multiculturalism, family therapists sometimes wish that they could use a simple matching strategy: learn about various ethnic groups and then match the treatment to the family's ethnicity. In fact, multiculturalism involves tailoring, not matching. The therapist must address the specific needs of the particular family while taking cultural factors into account. Thus, the therapist has to be knowledgeable enough to be sensitive to cultural norms and values without assuming that any generalization can apply to all members of a group. As Berg and Miller (1992) pointed out, the therapist has to be able to "balance consideration of the impact of culture on clients' world view with how clients personally experience ethnic and cultural influences" (p. 363).

Hardy (1989) helped to clarify the issue of balance by putting it in a historical perspective. First, family therapists have been trained according to the theoretical myth of sameness (TMOS), a belief system based on the assumption that all families are the same and that context could be safely ignored. A more contemporary view focuses on the difference between minority and nonminority families, but ignores differences within groups:

> Unless special topic areas give acute attention to the differences within any one group, be it women, gays or lesbians, or ethnic minorities, the inevitable consequence is a perpetuation of the epistemological error (TMOS) which these areas have been designed to rectify. Can there be a family therapy model that is effective for and applicable to *all* Hispanics? Is it possible for feminist family therapy to address the needs of all women given the vast number of gender-related permutations that may be a function of the interaction between race, ethnicity, religion, social class, etc.? Can we assume that a given technique or therapeutic principle that applies to *this* Hispanic family or *this* woman can be applied globally to all Hispanics or women? (Hardy, 1989, p. 21)

Cultural knowledge should serve as "a background from which the figure emerges" (Sue & Sue, 1990, p. 48). The process of tailoring begins, of course, with an appropriate assessment.

Culture-Aware Family Assessment

McGoldrick (1982) pointed out that "the language and customs of a culture will influence whether or not a symptom is labeled as a problem" (p. 7). Solomon (1992) also emphasized cultural differences in the expression of symptomatology and in the meanings of various behaviors. She gave an example of a Ghanian woman whose mother had recently died. The woman, who was living in America, was unable to return to Ghana for the funeral. The women reported seeing visions of her mother and hearing her mother's voice constantly in her head, telling her what to do. These symptoms led to a diagnosis of schizophrenia, triggered by traumatic life changes.

Solomon remarked that the diagnostic interview included no questions regarding the client's spiritual beliefs or the grieving process in her culture, although "normal grieving in some cultures includes elements that Western culture might view as psychotic (e.g., seeing the dead and communicating with them as they were in life or as transformed into birds, animals, or spirits)" (1992, p. 373). If the assessment had been sensitive to culture, the problem would have been seen in terms of depression or bereavement, rather than schizophrenia.

The point of taking culture into account is not to make stereotypical generalizations but to enhance the possibilities for understanding the particular family. Some of the following questions might need to be asked:

- If the therapist has difficulty understanding the family, might the therapist's own culturally biased assumptions and values be standing in the way?
- Are there aspects of the family's worldview that might help to explain individual behaviors or family dynamics?
- To what degree are the family members embedded in a traditional culture or acculturated into the dominant society?
- What differences in cultural identity exist among the family members themselves?
- How do the members define the boundaries of their family? Do they have an extended or multigenerational network that constitutes their family system?
- How do such cultural variables as gender, ethnicity, religion, and class interact to affect the family's values and concerns?
- How does this family view the balance between individual and family priorities?
- In what ways does oppression play a role in the life of this family?

If we consider again the case of Silvia, we can see how important such a culturally sensitive assessment process really is. The dynamics of Silvia's family make sense only when we carefully consider the alternate worldviews represented by Silvia and her parents, and when we recognize the depth of intrafamilial differences in cultural identity. The interaction of ethnicity and gender roles is also important in this case, with gender stereotyping playing an important role in limiting Silvia's perception of the options open to her.

Empowerment Strategies

Ho (1987) recognized that "racism and poverty dominate the lives of many ethnic minorities" (p. 14). Consider, for example, the impact of oppression on the African-American community. Because of the history of virulent racism and the prevalence of the "deficit view" of black families, Boyd–Franklin (1989) emphasized that empowerment should be seen as the most important goal of family therapy with African-Americans. Implicit in Boyd–Franklin's interpretation of the empowerment process are two basic needs: building a positive black identity and mobilizing the family's ability to interact effectively with outside systems.

People who have been subjected to oppression are often completely disempowered by this process. Instead of recognizing the social, political, and economic context of their difficulties, they may be mired in self-blame. In place of self-worth and self-efficacy, they could be caught in a cycle of victimization and helplessness. Far from having access to support systems, they may feel isolated and alone.

The practical implication of this is that therapy with families who are part of oppressed minority groups should be focused on empowerment. Specific empowerment strategies include reframing issues to recognize and focus on family strengths; directly addressing racism, sexism, and other oppressions; and building skills and support for navigating through hazardous environments. The therapist him- or herself has to redefine the meaning of systems theory, which "can be expanded to include society at large and problems such as prejudice, poverty, gender and ethnic minority issues" (Sue, 1994, p. 20).

Family issues can be reconceptualized if the following empowerment questions are addressed:

- How can the family's issues or problems be redefined in an empowering way? What strengths and competencies can be identified and encouraged?

  The value of these questions lies in the necessity of helping family members and the family as a whole recognize their potential for strength. Oppression is insidious because external discrimination is combined with socialization processes that bring about internalized oppression; victims learn to accept the negative views of themselves that have been inculcated by the mainstream society.

As we have seen in some of the examples presented earlier, the characteristics of families are often pathologized when they differ from those of the dominant culture. The therapist's ability to view families as having adaptive strengths, rather than as being inherently dysfunctional, makes the first step toward empowerment possible.

- How has this family been affected by oppression?

  Exploring this issue with family members can help to lay the groundwork for empowerment both by bringing about a release from self-blame and by readying the family to move toward considering the changes necessary for taking responsibility for their lives. A key issue here is that the therapist has to recognize the impact of broader systems in order to address the subject with the family.

- What therapeutic strategies can be used to overcome oppression-based barriers to healthy functioning?

  Beginning with a recognition of the role of oppression helps widen the range of possibilities considered by the therapist. Additionally, this question brings to the foreground the idea that the therapeutic strategies selected must be sensitive to the worldview of the client family. The therapist avoids the possibility that the therapy itself may play a role in the family's oppression.

- What positive environmental resources might be available to this family?

  The isolation of disempowerment can be addressed by helping the family identify potential sources of positive support in the broader environment. Moreover, this question points the therapist toward an acknowledgment of the important role of the informal helping network available in many minority communities.

If we return once more to Silvia's family, we can see the utility of addressing the empowerment questions. First, the strengths of Silvia and her family would be recognized. As an individual, Silvia has many strengths, including courage, intelligence, and a willingness to connect with others. Although some therapists might focus on the problems in her family life, an empowerment-oriented counselor would focus instead on the deep caring that has made complete separation impossible. A clear-headed exploration of the role of oppression in this case might also open new doors. Silvia has faced oppression as a woman; one aspect of therapy should focus on what she and her family view as the meaning of being male or female in traditional and contemporary cultures.

Internalized oppression might also play a role in this situation. Is Silvia's urgent desire to be completely acculturated based on an assumption that the dominant culture is superior? Could her feeling that she does not deserve "someone like Brent" relate to her awareness of their class differences? As Silvia develops a more integrated cultural identity, will she relate differently to Brent and to her parents? Clearly, these questions take the therapy down a road that would have been by-passed if a less contextual approach had been taken.

SUMMARY

A family's culture is affected by race, ethnicity, age, language, social class, income, geographical location, education, religion, gender, sexual orientation, and many other variables. Meeting the needs of a specific family requires that the tailoring process take these cultural factors into account.

When family therapists embark on the difficult work of becoming culturally aware, they often learn that their notion of what characterizes a healthy family is not universal. Cultural heritage affects such values as the desired balance between individuation and family unity. Families in various cultures also differ in terms of their definitions of the family unit and its boundaries.

The experience of oppression must also be recognized as a condition with a major impact on family life. Racism and other oppressions may need to be addressed directly before family members are ready to deal with other issues.

Family therapists are also learning that differences in worldviews have to be explored, whether they are between the family and therapist or among family members themselves. In fact, conflicting cultural values may sometimes be found to be at the heart of the turmoil, which seems incomprehensible to people who overlook the salience of culture.

Each of these issues has implications for therapeutic strategies, pointing to the need for a culturally aware family assessment and for case conceptualizations aimed toward empowerment.

References

Berg, I. K., & Miller, S. (1992). Working with Asian-American clients: One person at a time. *Families in Society: The Journal of Contemporary Human Services, 73,* 356–363.

Boyd–Franklin, N. (1989). *Black families in therapy: A multisystems approach.* New York: Guilford.

Boyd–Franklin, N. (1993, July/August). Pulling out the arrows. *Family Networker*, 54–56.

Carter, R. T. (1991). Cultural values: A review of empirical research and implications for counseling. *Journal of Counseling & Development, 70*, 164–173.

Falicov, C. (1994). *Cultural change on a global scale: Crossing cultural borders*. Paper presented at the 1994 Annual Convention, American Association of Marriage and Family Therapy, Chicago, IL.

Franklin, A. J. (1993, July/August). The invisibility syndrome. *Family Networker*, 33–39.

Garrett, M. T., & Pichette, E. F. (2000). Red as an apple: Native American acculturation and counseling with or without reservations. *Journal of Counseling & Development, 78*, 3–13.

Grier, W., & Cobbs, P. (1968). *Black rage*. New York: Basic Books.

Hardy, K. V. (1989). The theoretical myth of sameness: A critical issue in family therapy training and treatment. *Journal of Psychology and the Family, 6*(1–2), 17–33.

Hays, P. A. (1996). Addressing the complexities of culture and gender in counseling. *Journal of Counseling & Development, 74*, 332–338.

Ho, M. K. (1987). *Family therapy with ethnic minorities*. Newbury Park, CA: Sage.

Ina, S. (1994, April 24–27). *Culturally-sensitive family therapy*. Paper presented at the American Counseling Association Forum on Racism and Sexism: Promoting Dignity and Development Through Diversity, National Conference of the American Counseling Association, Minneapolis, MN.

Inclan, J., & Hernandez, M. (1992). Cross-cultural perspectives and codependence: The case of poor Hispanics. *American Journal of Orthopsychiatry, 62*(2), 245–255.

Ivey, A. E., & Ivey, M. B. (2001). Developmental counseling and therapy and multicultural counseling and therapy: Metatheory, contextual consciousness, and action. In D. C. Locke, J. E. Myers, & E. L. Herr (Eds.), *The handbook of counseling* (pp. 219–236). Thousand Oaks, CA: Sage.

Kluckhohn, F. R., & Strodtbeck, F. L. (1961). *Variations in value orientations*. Evanston, IL: Row, Patterson & Co.

Lee, C. C. (2001). Defining and responding to racial and ethnic diversity. In Locke, D.C., Myers, J., & Herr, E. (Eds.), *The handbook of counseling* (pp. 581–588). Thousand Oaks, CA: Sage.

Lewis, J. A. (1994). Issues of gender and culture in substance abuse treatment. In J. A. Lewis (Ed.), *Addictions: Concepts and strategies for treatment* (pp. 37–43). Gaithersburg, MD: Aspen.

McGoldrick, M. (1982). Ethnicity and family therapy: An overview. In M. McGoldrick, J. K. Peace, & J. Giordano (Eds.), *Ethnicity and family therapy* (pp. 3–30). New York: Guilford.

McWhirter, E. H. (1991). Empowerment in counseling. *Journal of Counseling and Development, 69*, 222–227.

Sanders, J. L. (2000). Advocacy on behalf of African-American clients. In J. Lewis & L. J. Bradley (Eds.), *Advocacy in counseling: Counselors, clients, & community* (pp. 15–24). Greensboro, NC: ERIC/CASS.

Schwartzman, J. (1983). Family ethnography: A tool for clinicians. In C. J. Falicov (Ed.), *Cultural perspective in family therapy* (pp. 137–149). Gaithersburg, MD: Aspen.

Solomon, A. (1992). Clinical diagnosis among diverse populations: A multicultural perspective. *Families in Society, 72*, 371–377.

Spiegel, J. (1982). An ecological model of ethnic families. In M. McGoldrick, J. K. Peace, & J. Giordano (Eds.), *Ethnicity and family therapy* (pp. 31–51). New York: Guilford.

Sue, D. (1994, spring). Incorporating cultural diversity in family therapy. *The Family Psychologist, 10*(2), 19–21.

Sue, D. W., Carter, R. T., Casas, J. M., Fouad, N. A., Ivey, A. E., Jensen, M., et al. (1998). *Multicultural counseling competencies: Individual and organizational development*. Thousand Oaks, CA: Sage.

Sue, D. W., & Sue, D. (1990). *Counseling the culturally different: Theory and practice*. New York: John Wiley & Sons.

Szapocznik, J., & Kurtines, W. M. (1993). Family psychology and cultural diversity: Opportunities for theory, research, and applications. *American Psychologist, 48*, 400–407.

Szapocznik, J., Scopetta, M. A., Ceballos, A., & Santisteban, D. (1994, spring). Understanding, supporting and empowering families: From microanalysis to macrointervention. *Family Psychologist, 10*(2), 23–27.

Walters, M. (1993, March/April). The codependent Cinderella and Iron John. *The Family Networker*, 60–65.

Willis, J. T. (1988). An effective counseling model for treating the black family. *Family Therapy, 15*(2), 185–194.

Wilson, M. (1987, spring). Classnotes on the psychology of oppression and social change. *The Family Psychologist, 20*(2), 18–19.

7

TAILORING TREATMENT

Families Under Stress

In situations of extreme stress, families need to call on all the resources that are available to them. Certainly, healthy families have the best chance of dealing successfully with new stressors. Even these families, however, may find that their usual ways of operating must change in response to serious pressures.

A family with a history of effective communication, mutual supportiveness, flexibility, and shared values has the tools for dealing effectively with stress. When family members are under severe stress, they need these adaptive characteristics more than ever. During these times, families need to communicate directly so they can find fresh solutions to pressing problems. They need to pull together without losing sight of individual needs and goals. They must also adapt to new stressors by being flexible enough to make systemic changes. With all these strengths in place, families sometimes manage to overcome seemingly insurmountable burdens.

Often, however, families under stress seem to lose the balance that they need most. Instead of communicating openly, they may depend on avoidance as their primary coping strategy. Instead of seeking intimacy, they may choose the extremes of distance and isolation or overprotection. Instead of making changes in their patterns of interaction, they may seek refuge in a rigid adherence to behavior that no longer works for them.

Any family—even one that has been characterized as healthy in the past—can be thrown into chaos in the face of extreme stress. What happens, then, to families that have been subject to numerous stressors over a long period of time? Madsen (1999) pointed out that when working with such multistressed families therapists sometimes find their clinical relationships dogged by losses of connection, competence, vision, hope, and balance. According to Madsen, these losses do not just represent family characteristics. They represent barriers that stand in the way of the therapeutic process. Not only the family but the therapist as well may disconnect in response to frustration and hopelessness. Both therapist and family may feel incompetent, resigned, and hopeless. When this kind of situation arises, the therapist may find it difficult to balance an understanding of the seriousness of the family's stressors with a sense of optimism about the family's strengths and resources. But that balance is exactly what the therapist and family, working in collaboration, must find. Madsen suggested that we can work with families from a strength-based perspective if we think in terms of constraints, rather than problems. "Anchored in a theory of constraints, therapy can become a collaborative effort in which the therapist works with the family to help them identify and address the constraints in their lives" (1999, p. 54).

When working with families under stress, therapists have to focus on ways to help family members mobilize whatever resources they have at their command. Sometimes the therapist will find that the family's unhealthy transactions preceded or exacerbated the current stressor. Often, he or she will find that the family's coping mechanisms and interaction patterns were simply overwhelmed by pressing demands. Tailoring treatment involves both recognizing the resources that might help the family function effectively and taking into account the realities inherent in the particular type of stressor involved. Consider, just as examples, the special needs of families dealing with each of the following specific stressors: addiction, illness or disability, and family violence or abuse.

FAMILIES AND ADDICTION

There is no doubt that tailoring treatment to the needs of an addiction-affected family requires at least some degree of focus on the nature and extent of the drug use. Clearly, the participants in therapy hope that at least one outcome of the process will be a change in the addictive behavior that has brought them there. Despite this concern with the individual's drug or alcohol use, however, the therapist's systemic focus must remain at the forefront. When an individual abuses alcohol or other drugs, his or her entire family is placed under severe ongoing stress. A parental addiction may leave children without stable supervision. Young people's substance abuse may leave parents feeling guilty, powerless, and fearful for their children's future. Couples may adapt to one member's addiction by creating imbalances in power and responsibility. Over time, families often get caught in rigid patterns of interaction that are adaptive to the presence of the drug but do benefit general family well-being. Attempts to keep the problem a secret may lead the family to develop impermeable boundaries that prevent members from seeking the help and support they need.

When a family member is addicted to alcohol or other drugs, this factor tends to become central to the family's functioning. The family adapts and organizes itself around the presence of the addiction. This adaptation supports and maintains the substance use.

Families develop consistent ways to adapt to the presence of alcohol or other drugs within their lives. Over time, of course, these patterns of interaction become deeply entrenched. Family members see few alternatives and continue carrying out behaviors that allow the substance use of the identified patient to continue. For instance, other family members often relieve the addict from carrying out normal responsibilities, picking up the slack by being steadfastly reliable themselves. Although this pattern may allow the family unit to survive intact, it also allows—even encourages—the substance use to continue unabated.

As is always the case with systems, a circular pattern emerges. Just as the working of the family system makes drug and alcohol use possible, the continuation of the family member's substance use allows the family to maintain its steady state. For instance, Steinglass, Bennett, Wolin, and Reiss (1987) studied a number of couples in which one member abused alcohol. They found that, in most cases, alcohol-related behavior served a systemic purpose by helping the family to cope, at least temporarily, with problems in daily living. Whether the problems being faced were internal or external, the families believed that they could cope with them only when alcohol was present. When problems arose and tensions mounted, intoxication would emerge as a response that allowed the system to become restabilized.

An addictions specialist and a family therapist often perceive this situation very differently. Substance-abuse-treatment providers try to recognize the impact of systemic thinking but tend to view the addiction as the root cause of the family's problems. Conversely, family therapists try to recognize the impact of the physiology of the addictive process but may view the alcoholic or addict simply as the identified symptom-bearer in the family, rather than as the primary focus of attention. A rapprochement between these two viewpoints depends on the ability of all therapists to focus on both the individual's health and on the functioning of the entire family. An important aspect of this effort is to take into account the family's situation at the time of the intervention. The appropriateness of a therapeutic strategy depends on the stage in the development and resolution of the addiction-related problem (Lewis, Dana, & Blevins, 2001). The goals and methods used depend on whether the drug use is currently active, whether the behavior is in the process of alteration, or whether a behavior change has been established.

Stages of Change

Five stages of change have been identified as common to a number of behavioral concerns, including substance abuse (Stages of change, n.d.). These stages of change are precontemplation, contemplation, preparation, action, and maintenance. *Precontemplation* is the stage at which no intention is made to change the behavior in the foreseeable future. *Contemplation* is when people are aware a problem exists and are seriously thinking about overcoming it, but have not yet made a commitment to take action. *Preparation* is a stage that combines intention and behavioral criteria. Individuals in this stage are intending to take action in the next month. *Action* is the stage in which individuals modify their behavior, experiences, or environment in order to overcome their problems. Action involves the most overt behavioral changes and requires a considerable commitment of time and energy. *Maintenance* is the stage in which people work to prevent a relapse and consolidate the gains attained during action. For addictive behaviors, this stage extends from 6 months to an indeterminate period past the initial action.

The stages of change are relevant not just to individuals but also to families. With family systems, of course, the process from readiness to change to maintenance is even more complex. Suppose, for example, family members differ in their levels of readiness. One may be solidly entrenched in precontemplation while another is primed for action. Family members who seek change will need assistance in recognizing and addressing the family's patterns of interaction. Otherwise, the system will simply reassert itself.

Clearly, systems interventions must fit the family's stage of readiness. One set of strategies is needed to help family members initiate changes in the systems that support alcohol and drug use. Still another set of strategies is needed to help families cope with the stress that accompanies the abrupt changes associated with individual recovery.

Making Initial Systemic Changes

We know that family members will not all be ready for change at the same time. Family therapy should be available to those who want to change their patterns of interaction even if the drug or alcohol abuser is not ready to take part. The key factor associated with success at this point is that family members explore the possibility of changing their customary roles. Family members may need help in making the choice between two difficult alternatives: (a) actively confronting the substance abuser in an effort to press him or her into treatment or (b) disengaging from an unhealthy focus on substance use as the central factor in family life.

Family members sometimes gather together to confront the individual substance abuser as a group. The focus of this kind of intervention is usually to convince the individual that his or her substance use is a problem and to press the individual into treatment. Ideally, the individual comes to accept the idea that his or her drinking or drug use is the source of the family's problems.

For families in pain, the appeal of this approach, with its promise of treatment as a potential "happy ending," is obvious. Unfortunately, however, it is in the very simplicity of the intervention that its shortcomings lie. The overriding purpose of the intervention is to make a convincing case that alcohol or another drug is the root cause of the problems affecting the individual and the family and to present treatment as an immediately available solution. Thus, the approach oversimplifies problem attribution, conceptualizing issues in linear, cause-and-effect terms (Lewis, 1991, p. 43).

Such an intervention should be approached with caution. First, the emphasis on the single cause of the family's pain overlooks the systemic nature of most problems. Second, the intervention assumes that the individual will face consequences if he or she refuses treatment. In fact, the interveners need to be prepared for the possible failure of the intervention to meet their goals. What might be the consequences for them and for the family as a whole if the identified patient refuses treatment? Third, the results of even a very successful intervention will be short lived if the family fails to make changes.

A valid option to the confrontation is to help those family members who are ready to change begin the process on their own. These people can be encouraged to improve their own lives, working toward goals that focus on their own growth rather than on the family behavior as a whole. If family members can interrupt rigid patterns of interaction and move away from accepting responsibility for each other's behavior, they may decrease the degree to which the system makes continued drug use likely. Even if this outcome is not achieved, the family members who have been involved in the process can benefit. They may enjoy their first opportunity to focus on meeting other family needs, rather than having their behaviors dominated by reactions to one family member's drinking or drug use.

Adjusting to Early Recovery

Families with a long history of transactional patterns based around a family member's addiction frequently face crises when the individual's substance use subsides. Behaviors that have been reasonably adaptive to the presence of the addiction are no longer appropriate when the identified patient moves out of his or her role. Families with newly abstinent members now need coping skills outside of their usual repertoires. The sudden need for change often comes as a shock, especially because substance use has previously replaced problem-solving and conflict resolution skills. In addition, families are often disappointed to find that the problems they have always attributed to substance use alone continue to exist.

Usher, Jay, and Glass (1982) called this situation the crisis of abstinence. They said that, although some families resolve the crisis successfully and make meaningful systemic changes, many respond to the crisis by splitting up or by reintroducing alcohol into the system. The way that alcohol and other drugs are "reintroduced" is through family members' return to prior patterns of interaction that can establish the familiar equilibrium.

How can family therapy address a family's needs during this crucial juncture? Bepko and Krestan (1985) said that the most important things to do at this point are to keep the system calm, defuse conflicts, address individual issues, and encourage members to focus on their individual needs. They suggested that the therapist work with the family to make minor structural changes that can give them time to adjust. Families can go through a process of negotiation, working out compromises so that individual needs are addressed. Later, after a period of stabilization, a family may be ready to make the more basic systemic changes that serve to rebalance the system.

A great deal of evidence indicates that couples counseling is especially effective in early recovery (O'Farrell, 1992). For instance, Wetchler, Nelson, McCollum, Trepper, and Lewis (1994) developed a program of systemic couples therapy for drug-abusing women. Their model calls for an assessment process that includes defining the problem, identifying interpersonal sequences surrounding the substance abuse, and examining multigenerational patterns. Components of the behavior change process include helping the couple learn to negotiate and altering dysfunctional couple sequences. Wetchler and his colleagues learned that the sequence of behaviors culminating in an individual's drug use can be interrupted most effectively when couples learn to notice them in their earliest stages.

Applying Couples Therapy

The context of understanding that addiction-related problems are viewed within should devote attention to the balance between family members in terms of power and responsibility. Among families affected by addiction, the years of drug or alcohol use have often affected this balance because of an impairment in the user's ability to carry out his or her responsibilities. Balance also enters the picture again as we consider the symmetry between separateness and connectedness. Among families affected by addiction, issues regarding boundaries are common, at least in part because of attempts to keep the alcohol or drug problem a secret from the outside world. The therapist must also attend to the larger systems within which the family operates. Addictive behaviors take place within a social context that may exacerbate the risk for problem development. With this understanding as a backdrop for action, the therapist can help the couple negotiate new behavioral patterns. Consider the potential impact of couples counseling in the cases that follow.

THE CASE OF RUTH AND JACK

Ruth and Jack, a young African-American couple, had lived together for over 6 years before Jack was arrested for selling a small amount of cocaine. Even in their own neighborhood, Jack had never been considered a major supplier. In fact, he had become involved initially only because he and Ruth had been unable to secure other employment despite their education and skills. His arrest, and subsequent imprisonment, came about because he was caught up in a large undercover operation. Still, Jack's involvement in the sale of cocaine had been the couple's main source of income. Although they were both users, they were able to live comfortably.

When Jack went to prison, Ruth had to find a way to support herself. (During her years with Jack, she had left it up to him to take care of their financial well-being and to decide what kind of lifestyle they would have.) She was not sure how to take care of the family business on her own because Jack's main suppliers were gone. She was prepared to go out on the street but was now more frightened of that life than she had been 6 years ago. Before she succeeded in gathering her courage, a neighbor suggested that she take a job temporarily cleaning rooms in a newly opened hotel. Ruth did get the job and, during the time Jack was away, stayed with the job and was promoted to housekeeper. Her current managerial job is quite demanding.

Now Jack has returned home. During his time away, Jack had become connected with a group of men who helped him get in touch with his religious and spiritual nature that had been buried during his years of drug use. Now, on probation and adamant about abstaining from drugs, Jack is hoping to find a career. In the meantime, they are both living on Ruth's salary.

When he first came home, both Ruth and Jack felt optimistic about their new life. It seemed miraculous that both of them were turning their lives around at the same time. Both of them were intent on living the straight life, yet some problems have arisen. Jack expected that their new lives would be a healthier, drug-free duplication of what their existence had been before. He expected to still be the main decision maker in the relationship and that Ruth would devote her attention to him. He felt she should be happy to spend all of her time with him after having gone through a painful separation. Ruth finds Jack's attitude unrealistic and thinks it is impossible to live up to his expectations. Her job is demanding and time-consuming, but Jack wants her to spend more time with him, to entertain his friends, and to take better care of the apartment. Also, she has become accustomed to making decisions on her own. Time after time, conflicts arise about money, about the apartment, about Jack's unemployment, and about the nature of the relationship. Twice, Ruth has left after one of these arguments and gone out to get high with one of her friends. When she returned, Jack was furious with her for using. The conflict became even more severe.

Conceptualizing the Situation of Ruth and Jack

A therapist working with this couple would recognize that the reestablishment of customary interactions would create a relapse risk for both

Ruth and Jack. Their former pattern left a major role to be played by cocaine; falling into this old pattern is as easy as it is dangerous.

One aspect of the couple's established pattern involves the balance of power in their relationship. Although their life may seem nontraditional to some people, Ruth and Jack have lived according to a conservative view of gender roles. Before the crisis of his imprisonment, Jack was both the primary breadwinner and powerholder in the relationship. Ruth's newfound economic power and the drain her job places on her time make it difficult for her to return to her prior role. Jack's ideal, that the relationship could be a drug-free equivalent of what it was before, is easy to understand. Yet this notion reflects a ubiquitous problem among recovering families. Family members often assume that the removal of the substance is all they need. In fact, an unchanged system clearly increases the likelihood that the drug will be reintroduced. The family context must be changed in order for the new behaviors (abstinance) to continue.

The balance between separation and connectedness is also relevant in this case. During Jack's absence, Ruth began to recognize herself as a separate entity. Again, Jack's reluctance to recognize these new boundaries is understandable but needs to be addressed in therapy. The fragile balance that Ruth and Jack seek is affected not just by their own attitudes and behaviors but by their cultural milieu. The racism that has limited their career opportunities and the gender stereotypes that have limited their social roles both play a part that the therapist needs to address.

Within the context of these systemic factors, the therapist can help Ruth and Jack make concrete changes in their interactions. Once they learn to recognize the signs of impending conflict, they can negotiate alternatives that prevent the disastrous endings of their previous friction.

THE CASE OF STEVE AND TIM

Steve and Tim were first introduced by a mutual friend at a bar that serves as the focal point of social life in the gay community. After seeing each other for over a year, they moved in together. They have lived for almost 2 years in an apartment close to where they first met. From the beginning, they have had an active social life, meeting their group of close friends at the bar or socializing over drinks at home.

Four months ago, Steve lost the job he had held as a paralegal in a large law firm. The late nights of drinking and socializing had taken their toll, and he found himself arriving at work either hung over or very late. (This has been less of a problem for Tim, who is a psychotherapist and has more flexible hours.) He was fired when one of the attorneys complained about smelling alcohol on his breath.

Steve has been seeing an addictions counselor and has been working hard at maintaining abstinence. He has been attending AA meetings and enjoys them. He hopes to find a new job and get his life back to what it was before.

Surprisingly, however, he and Tim have begun to have arguments for the first time in their relationship. Tim says that Steve has become fanatic about AA. He complains that Steve won't talk about anything else and that their social life has become nonexistent. He does not want Steve to drink and suggests that Steve have a soft drink when at the bar or when entertaining friends. Steve wants his life with Tim to get back to normal, but he is afraid to be around alcohol. Tim says he will simply go to the bar on his own, but that idea makes Steve feel jealous and abandoned.

Conceptualizing the Situation of Steve and Tim

Tim, like Jack, would like his relationship to be an alcohol-free duplication of the past. In fact, this ideal would be very difficult to achieve. At least in the earliest stages of recovery, Tim would find it problematic to spend a great deal of time surrounded by drinkers. Yet it is not realistic for Tim to expect the people around him—even Steve—to make drastic changes in their lifestyles. Oppression plays a role here, too. For many members of the gay community, bars have provided the most comfortable opportunity for socializing. Within this context, the therapist would help Steve and Tim negotiate short-term compromises that could allow each some separateness while maintaining the customary closeness and trust in the relationship.

FAMILIES' RESPONSES TO ILLNESS AND DISABILITY

Few problems are more stressful to a family than the illness of one of its members. The family's customary coping style may be inadequate, resulting in a situation in which resources are stretched to the breaking point.

Serious illness not only takes over the patient's life, it also greedily expands to consume the energy and resources of the patient's family. Far from being tightly confined inside the individual's skin, serious illness invades the entire network of connections around the sick individual. For some families, this crisis offers opportunities for emotional as well as physical healing. For others, the illness ravages everything in its path (McDaniel, Hepworth, & Doherty, 1993, pp. 20–21).

As is the case with addiction-related problems, the process of tailoring treatment for families affected by illness must balance the individual's health and the family's general level of functioning. Sometimes the treatment that seems most appropriate for the individual's needs, such as home dialysis, may be stressful and demanding for the family. In other instances, strategies that seem to be appropriate for the family may leave the needs of the medical patient unattended. The characteristics of the specific illness or disability also have a major impact on the nature of family stress and on the kinds of coping strategies that will be needed. Families find that different adaptations are needed, depending on the illness itself, the way it is treated, the extent of disability involved, and the way the family is structured.

Nature of the Illness or Disability

Rolland (1994) designed a topology of illnesses that emphasizes the varying effects of health-related problems in terms of their onset, course, likely outcome, degree of incapacitation, and degree of predictability. Each of these factors affects the kind and degree of challenge the family must meet. Moreover, families vary in terms of the degree to which their structures and styles tend to be successful in coping with particular types of illness.

Onset   Whether the onset of an illness is acute or gradual affects the kind of readjustment a family must make. A condition with an acute onset, such as a stroke, requires that the family mobilize quickly, using crisis management skills and making rapid adjustments. A gradual health problem, such as Alzheimer's, may require the same degree of problem solving and restructuring, but allow these changes to take place over a longer period of time.

Some families are better equipped than others to cope with rapid changes. Families able to tolerate highly charged, affective states, to exchange clearly defined roles flexibly, to solve problems efficiently, and to utilize outside resources effectively have an advantage in managing acute-onset illnesses. Other families' styles of coping may be more suited to a gradual change (Rolland, 1994, p. 23).

One cannot assume it is possible to distinguish between functional and dysfunctional family styles for coping with an illness. The same family that shows a high degree of success in responding to crises may be overwhelmed when called on to deal with illnesses characterized by a long-term, steady deterioration.

Course   Illnesses may also be characterized as progressive, constant, or relapsing/episodic. A progressive illness may require a family to reorganize itself again and again over time as the disability reaches new stages. The family with flexibility at its core is most likely to be successful in managing these changes, but even then the need to restructure can be so overwhelming that therapy aimed at deeper changes may still be needed. Illnesses that Rolland categorizes as constant become stable after the initial event. The family might need help to make a major adaptation but can assume that the new structure will suffice for a long period of time. Illnesses that are subject to relapses or episodes of disability bring their own special challenges because families have to reorganize for periods of health and relapse. Because these episodes are unpredictable, families cannot always prepare for change and must be on guard to deal with unexpected crises. Therapeutic needs will change over time as the family is buffeted by change.

Outcome   Rolland (1994) saw a continuum among illnesses that do not affect one's life span to illnesses that shorten life span to illnesses that are fatal. Family therapy needs differ according to the expected outcome of the illness. When the illness is expected to be fatal, families often need help dealing with anticipatory loss as well as with its associated conflict between the desire for intimacy with the ill person and a need to let go. Illnesses that shorten life span or that are characterized by an uncertainty about the possibility of sudden death have very complex effects on family life. Rolland said that, in families grappling with these kinds of illnesses, issues of mortality are "less prominent but more insidious in day to day living." Uncertainty makes varying interpretations and expectations of the situation possible. Family members may opt for overprotectiveness, for distancing, or for unpredictable swings between opposite behavioral poles.

Incapacitation   Of course, some illnesses and disabilities bring with them impairments that have a major impact on family life. Families are differentially affected according to the nature of the incapacitation (e.g., impairments in mental functioning, sensation, movement, or energy) and the extent of the disability.

Degree of Uncertainty/Predictability   Rolland's topology places a degree of certainty in the role of a metacharacteristic that affects all of the other categories. Illnesses vary in the predictability of their course, out-come, degree of incapacitation, and rate of progression. Uncertainty brings heightened stress.

Families coping with highly unpredictable diseases, such as multiple sclerosis, often state that these ambiguities are the hardest aspects to ac-cept. The more uncertain the course and outcome, the more a family must make decisions with flexible contingencies built into their plan-ning (Rolland, 1994, p. 33). Just as families are affected by the uncon-trollable course of the family member's illness, they are also affected by the sociocultural context within which the illness is viewed.

Sociocultural Context of Disability

Kirshbaum (1994) made the important point that families' responses to disabling conditions are colored by the tendency of the broader social trends to pathologize disabilities. Certainly, society as a whole is op-pressive toward disabled individuals. Of particular concern is the fact that the medical care system itself is not immune to oppressive atti-tudes. Health care providers may inadvertently place such a strong focus on individual and family deficits that they miss the importance of em-powerment. Moreover, the family is especially vulnerable to these neg-ative messages just at the times when they most need to be proactive in their adaptations to solve the problem or cope with the illness.

The cumulative effect of such pervasive and repetitive negative social messages is that we construct a personal framework of meaning regard-ing disability. This frame can, in turn, have a profound effect on indi-vidual family members' self-esteem, sense of defeat, and depletion. It can narrow our families' sense of what can be done together and of who the members can be together (Kirshbaum, 1994, p. 9).

When families respond to a disability or illness in ways that seem dys-functional, they may in fact be responding not just to their own inter-nal structures but also to an external stigmatization. Distancing within the family is sometimes a result of the dehumanizing stance of the cul-ture at large. Overprotectiveness may be a response to an onslaught of conflicting advice gleaned from health and social systems. Kirshbaum suggested that the process of therapy should focus on reframing the meanings inherent in the disability. Also, connections with the commu-nity of disabled persons enhance the process of depathologizing health-related problems.

The adult disability culture is inherently a reframe or a complex of reframes . . . People in disability traditions can experience profound shifts in meaning from contacts with individuals with long-term disability experience and disability community involvement . . . Being involved in the adult disability community is likely to expose one to a cultural perspective that values disability (Kirshbaum, 1994, p. 10). Similarly, recent years have seen the parents of disabled children take strong political action associated with their own success in overcoming deficit-focused beliefs.

Family Treatment Goals and Strategies

When therapists build their own practices on a recognition of the impact of the oppression, they are better able to help families develop the kind of positive reframe suggested by Kirshbaum. McDaniel, Hepworth, and Doherty (1993) stated that, even when the illness in question is fatal, a major goal of therapy must be to increase the family's "sense of agency." This means increasing their involvement and personal choices in managing the illness.

There cannot be many experiences, short of war, incarceration, or mass disaster, that so deplete feelings of personal competence and self-determination as being both very sick and caught in the tentacles of the modern medical health care system. A medical family therapist can help families maintain or reacquire the habit of making personal choices about medical decisions and take back aspects of members' lives that they have sacrificed to the illness (McDaniel et al., 1993, p. 28).

Helping families work together toward this kind of empowerment requires an emphasis on open communication. In fact, McDaniel and her colleagues suggest that an equally important goal of family therapy involves enhancing the communion found in emotional bonds. Family members may be stuck together in a tight clump of single-minded preoccupation with the illness and its costs, while at the same time feeling deeply isolated from one another. Their love and concern for one another can become fused with guilt, anguish, resentment, and depression that completely distort the quality of family life. The previously mentioned communion is meant to be a restoration, where possible, of human connections within the family and between the family and the community. These connections are based on qualities of affection, humor, friendliness, common interests, and mutual respect that may have given way in the collective isolation imposed by the illness (McDaniel et al., 1993, p. 62).

Rolland also emphasized the role of the family therapist in opening up communication within the family. He suggested that, in the couple relationship, members be encouraged to "revise their closeness to include rather than avoid issues of incapacitation and threatened loss"

(Rolland, 1994, p. 237). Among the subjects he suggests for discussion are the demands of the illness over time, the couple's beliefs about the factors that caused the disorder and might affect its course, ways to live with loss, priorities for the relationship, patient and caregiver roles, and ways to maintain balance and mutuality in the relationship. For families with children, he suggests open, age-appropriate communication about all the health issues being faced.

The levels of personal disclosure that may have been functional before a disorder appeared often become inadequate. Discussions about living with the threat of a loss may represent new territory (Rolland, 1994, p. 238). Underlying all these discussions is the need to "find a place for the illness within the family while at the same time ensuring that the illness is kept in its place" (Steinglass & Horan, 1988, p. 139). Somewhere between the extremes of denying or overemphasizing the illness lies a functional balance.

THE CASE OF THE PETERSON FAMILY

By the time Jim and Julie Peterson had reached their late thirties, they had come to view their lives as stable and predictable. Their two children, Linda and Scott, were weathering early adolescence without anything more than the standard degree of conflict. Although Jim's professional work as an architect was very demanding, it was also lucrative. Julie was glad that she had been able to stay home with the children when they were younger. She was now working part-time as a designer.

The Petersons barely noticed the subtle symptoms of Jim's illness at first. It was only when the symptoms became impossible to ignore that he sought a medical diagnosis and realized he had multiple sclerosis. Even after the diagnosis, Jim and Julie had difficulty taking in the reality of the situation. Jim had long periods of time when he was free of symptoms and could almost forget he had M.S. At first, the Petersons thought they could postpone discussing the illness with the children.

In time, however, the family members became conscious of changes in their lives. Julie knew she had to think about some kind of career plan for herself but felt helpless about moving in a new direction. Linda's grades dropped and she began to spend long hours alone in her room. Scott's teachers reported he was acting out in school. The solid structure of their family life seemed to be crumbling, even though Jim was still functioning well.

The need for a major adaptation became pressing when Jim's health no longer allowed him to perform effectively at work. Now he cannot always predict whether he will be able to finish a project. Although his work is still excellent, he and the family have begun to realize their traditional roles are changing. Jim's work can no longer be the only source of support for the family. Julie will have to make her work more central to her life, even to the extent of securing a job with family health insurance that will cover preexisting conditions. The children will have to adapt by taking on more adult responsibilities than they are used to.

Conceptualizing the Case of the Petersons

The Peterson family has virtually had to reinvent themselves in response to the illness of one member. Although they held their solid stability and success in carrying out traditional roles as sources of pride, Jim and Julie must now learn to practice and value flexibility. Clearly, as each family member must accept new roles and responsibilities, the new structure that has been created may have to be dismantled and rebuilt again and again as Jim's physical abilities and the needs of the family change. Within the context of this constant renewal, the family will have to "put the illness in its place," making sure that the roles of parent and child remain intact despite their transformations.

The importance of open communication about health-related issues is clear in this case. The parents' assumption that silence could protect their children was quickly proven to be inaccurate. Open family discussions about the nature of this new stressor and the best ways of coping with it will be crucial to the Petersons' adjustment. These family members will have to use every possible resource and coping skill at their command.

VIOLENCE AND ABUSE

The need to tailor therapy in accordance with the stressor affecting the specific family becomes especially salient in cases of violence or abuse. When it comes to violence and abuse within a family, systems thinking is often called into question. The concept of circularity ignores power differences and fails to provide a mechanism for focusing on the individual responsibility of the perpetrator.

When applied to problems such as battery, rape, and incest, circular causality subtly removes responsibility for his behavior from the man while implying that the woman is coresponsible. "Similarly, systemic notions of neutrality emphasize that all parts of the system contribute *equally* to the production and maintenance of problems/dysfunction, and render totally invisible differences in power and influence between family members" (Avis, 1988, p. 17).

One way to address this issue is to view family systems through a lens that takes in the larger systems within which families operate. Although it is always important for family therapists to focus on sociocultural factors, it is even more vital to keep these factors in the forefront when dealing with violence and abuse.

The right of men to control their wives and girlfriends is widely assumed in our society despite the economic and social gains made by women within the last thirty years. Violence is rooted in disparities of power based on gender, race, class, sexual orientation, or interlocking combinations of these and other factors. Violence is an act which signifies domination and power over another person (Arnold & Sobieraj, 2000, pp. 113–114).

As these critiques of conventional therapy make clear, tailoring treatment for situations involving violence requires several special adaptations, including (a) acknowledging and addressing the role of the larger culture in encouraging violent and abusive behavior, (b) recognizing the need to keep the safety of the vulnerable woman or child as the most important goal of treatment, and (c) accepting a focus on individual responsibility, even at the expense of the pure notion of circularity. These adaptations are necessary both for situations of domestic violence and for intrafamilial sexual abuse.

Domestic Violence

Domestic violence is "a pattern of coercive behavior, which must include physical aggression or threat, commonly accompanied by other forms of controlling behaviors, that adults or adolescents use against their intimate partners" (Kemp, 1998, p. 226). Brooks (1992) offered a perspective on domestic violence that highlights the salience of culture. According to Brooks, "one of the most serious errors in the treatment of violent men is to ignore the cultural context in which this violence takes place" (p. 29). Therapists often assume that individual abusers have not been successfully socialized against violence and that they need to be taught to comply to society's normative behavior. In fact, men are socialized toward violence as a solution for problems. Brooks therefore suggests that violence is the product of factors such as the message that violence is manly and the pressure to maintain an inegalitarian role of leadership in the family.

In addition to the urgent need for a broad cultural perspective, family therapists dealing with violence and abuse must also make special adaptations in therapeutic goals. Ensuring the safety of the victim and changing the behavior of the perpetrator must provide the central focus of the therapeutic process. For example, Brooks (1990) presented a model for treating spousal abuse in which the male perpetrator and the vulnerable woman are first treated separately. The therapist works to enhance the woman's empowerment and to support the man's positive efforts toward change. Conjoint therapy is begun only when three conditions have been met. "The woman's empowerment should be secure; the husband should be committed to her continued empowerment and to an egalitarian marital relationship; both parties independently, without coercion, choose to pursue the therapy" (Brooks, 1990, p. 61).

Carden (1994), in her overview of the literature related to the sources of domestic violence, recognized the differences among various perspectives. The sociopolitical response to the question "Why does he do it?" has been that the man does it because cultural norms support his belief that (a) violence is an acceptable and effective method of resolving interpersonal conflict, (b) he is entitled to dominate and expected to control his wife, (c) it will get him what he wants, and (d) he can get away with it (p. 552).

Psychological perspectives, on the other hand, emphasize the impact of the perpetrator's developmental experience as well as the possible role of dysfunctional transactions. Differences in perspective lead in turn to differences in treatment. According to Carden, the sociopolitical perspective implies the use of social control strategies that hold the batterer accountable for his violence, while psychological perspectives use either cognitive–behavioral interventions such as anger management training or conjoint therapies emphasizing such skills as conflict resolution.

Carden recommended an integrative perspective that takes into account the combined influences of cultural, intrapsychic, and interpersonal variables. She cites, for example, the work of Dutton (1985), who suggested that the violent behavior of an individual will be affected by variables within four layers of experience: (a) individual experience; (b) the microsystem of the family; (c) the exosystemic layer, made up of such systems as work, religious affiliation, social setting, and neighborhood; and (d) the macrosystem of society's rules and norms. The approach she describes uses an array of treatment options dedicated to three general goals: "(a) the safety and well-being of victims; (b) the empowerment of men to live emotionally enriched, cognitively aware, violence-free lives; and (c) the prevention of the intergenerational transmission of violence." Her treatment program includes psychoeducational strategies addressing issues within each of Dutton's ecological layers, group work confronting gender-role issues, and finally conjoint therapy in a separate or group milieu.

Child Sexual Abuse

Barrett, Trepper, and Fish (1990) used an equally well integrated approach for the treatment of intrafamilial child sexual abuse. They accepted as valid the feminist critique of the application of family systems therapies for treating sexual abuse. Although Barrett and her colleagues recognized the peril of overlooking sociopolitical factors, ignoring power differentials, and allowing vulnerable family members to shoulder part of the blame for the perpetrator's behavior, they suggested that family therapy can provide the context for addressing these concerns. "Protection of the incest victim, while at the same time empowering her to defend herself, is best done through a gender-sensitive, family systems approach" (1990, p. 164).

For Barrett, Trepper, and Fish, the child is the primary concern and the cessation of abuse is the first goal of treatment. With this caveat always in mind, they use systemic approaches to try to equalize power in the family. Their goal for the offender is not only to end his denial but also to help him become engaged in a nurturing role as a parent and in an appropriate sexual relationship with a partner of an appropriate age.

The Multiple Systems Model (Trepper & Barrett, 1986) recognizes that abuse results from a combination of external, family, and internal systems. This does not supplant the fact that the ultimate responsibility for the abuse rests with the offender, who after all is the older of the two and is responsible for the well-being of his children. This perspective merely recognizes that responsibility is not the cause, and that to fully understand the cause of incest, so that we may effectively intervene, we must accept that complex interactions among various systems make a family more or less vulnerable to the development of incest (Barrett & Trepper, 1991, p. 130). Differentiating between responsibility and cause, Barrett and Trepper said that attributing blame is not enough; other contributing factors must be addressed if long-term change is to take place.

Although they were aware of this modality's complexities, Barrett and Trepper used conjoint treatment, along with individual therapy and dealing with larger social systems, as one of their methods. They suggested that this approach is practical for several reasons. First, the victim often does have contact with the offender, and this contact may keep her in a powerless position if she does not have the opportunity to confront the perpetrator in a safe environment. Second, families often do intend to remain together and need conjoint meetings to discuss their future plans. Finally, discovery of the abuse throws the entire family into a crisis that should be addressed in therapy.

Treating Adult Survivors of Early Abuse

Of course, the early effects of abuse follow the individual throughout his or her life span. Many women survivors are plagued with such on-going symptoms as depression, anxiety, guilt, self-blame, and problems with relationships and sexuality (Ratican, 1992). Often, women have a history of repeated experiences of revictimization in childhood, adolescence, and adulthood. Addiction-related problems are very common (Barrett & Trepper, 1991). Family therapists may be especially helpful to such individuals because of their ability to view the problems from a systemic perspective. Even when the client is being seen individually, the family perspective remains an underpinning of the therapy.

Whether or not the individual remembers the experience of abuse, she may be unaware of its connection to her current problems. The creation of a safe environment for bringing these issues to the surface makes it possible for the survivor to decide when she is ready to begin exploring them. Individual interventions may be combined with group procedures that actually give some clients the first experience they have ever had in making connections with other women.

THE CASE OF MARY

Mary appeared at a hospital emergency room complaining of severe abdominal pain. She was admitted to the hospital detoxification unit because she began showing signs of withdrawal from alcohol and because it was suspected that she was also addicted to barbiturates. She admitted she had been using tranquilizers and occasionally sleeping pills for some time. Mary was kept in the hospital until she was medically stabilized and then referred to a nonmedical substance abuse treatment facility.

Mary is a divorced, 28-year-old woman of Irish and German descent. She has three children, aged 6, 8, and 10. She says that she has some experience doing secretarial work but has been unemployed for several years. She has no income other than what she gets in public assistance but says that a legal aid attorney has been trying to get some of the child-support money owed to her by her former husband, Carl. She is not optimistic about obtaining this money, because her ex-husband has been a long-term heroin addict. She has not seen him for some time, but has no reason to expect that there has been any change in his condition since their marriage ended 5 years ago.

Mary has had very little contact with her family of origin since her marriage at the age of 18. Her parents disliked Carl but insisted that she marry him when she became pregnant at 17. Mary says her father is an alcoholic and that she and her mother have never been close. Mary says that several times in recent years she has thought about visiting her family. Each time she has become so anxious that she has gone on a binge and become too ill.

Now she feels uncertain about her future. She says she wants to change because she is a bad mother and wants to take better care of her children. She says if she didn't feel responsible for them she would have no reason to live. She wishes she could get her life together but says she is unable to find employment. She has not been able to work because of a lack of child care. Now that the children are in school, she could work but believes her career history is too spotty to allow her to be employable.

Mary says she has no social life, although she does drink with a group of women. She sees these acquaintances regularly but does not feel close to them and reports she does not trust them. She believes that she "gets along better" with men, but in fact she has had several bad experiences. Since her divorce, one man moved in with her but left because of impatience with her children. Another left when neighbors heard him beating her and called the police. Her drinking and drug use began during her marriage, when her husband wanted her to keep him company, but she says that her heaviest use began at the time of their breakup.

Conceptualizing the Case of Mary

The chance that there was abuse in Mary's background shows up in subtle ways. Her experience of repeated victimization, her attempts to find salvation in a relationship with a man, her escape into drugs and alcohol, her difficulty in forming trusting relationships, her extreme anxiety at the thought of visiting her family of origin, all these factors indicate the possibility of early abuse. The therapist's role is to walk a narrow line, giving Mary the opportunity to explore her history and believing her when she describes abuse, but avoiding placing even the slightest pressure on her to delve into areas that she is not ready to consider. Both Mary and her children certainly have an improved outlook for success if Mary's substance abuse is interrupted. The therapist must recognize, however, that slips are likely to occur even if Mary sincerely desires abstinence. Throughout her adult life, drug and alcohol use has formed her primary coping strategy for dealing with the anxiety and depression that might otherwise have overwhelmed her. Moving toward health will have to be a gradual process that recognizes the client's fragility. At the same time, Mary's recovery depends on her ability to move from the morass of self-blame to the high ground of empowerment.

SUMMARY

Families dealing with highly stressful situations need effective coping mechanisms in order to meet the pressing demands that might otherwise overwhelm them. In fact, however, families under severe stress sometimes lack the ability to adapt effectively or lose sight of the strategies that worked for them in the past. In these circumstances, tailoring treatment involves both assessing the family's general functionality and recognizing the impact of the specific stressor.

In this chapter, we have examined three examples of serious family stressors: addiction, illness, and violence or abuse. In the case of addiction, the therapist should devote attention to the individual's drug use with a focus on dynamics within the family. When working with addiction-related family issues, the therapist needs to fit his or her strategies to the solution of the problem. In order to make initial changes, family members will need help in disengaging from their focus on substance use as the central factor in the family's life. In the stage of early recovery, family members will have to be prepared for the fact that they are entering a point of crisis when their usual ways of interacting are no longer effective. It may be because of the urgent need for systemic change at this point that couple counseling is among the most effective treatment available for substance abuse.

Families affected by illness or disability may also be faced with the need to make major systemic changes. Tailoring treatment involves taking into account not only the way the family functions but also the nature of the specific illness or disability. The demands on the family differ drastically in accord with the onset, course, outcome, degree of incapacitation, and degree of uncertainty that characterize the illness. Among the general goals for working with health-related issues are increasing the family's "sense of agency," enhancing the family's ability to communicate openly, and finding an appropriate balance between denying and overemphasizing the illness.

Tailoring treatment for families dealing with violence or abuse also brings unique concerns to the surface. In response to feminist critiques of systemic approaches for dealing with abuse, family therapists have learned to take into account the culpability of a culture that condones violence and domination. When violence or abuse is an issue, therapy must be adapted to acknowledge the role of cultural factors, to recognize that the safety of the victim is the most important goal, and to keep the responsibility for the violence focused on the perpetrator.

References

Arnold, M. S., & Sobieraj, K. (2000). Domestic violence: The case for social advocacy. In J. Lewis & L. J. Bradley (Eds.), *Advocacy in counseling: Counselors, clients, & community* (pp. 113–124). Greensboro, NC: ERIC/CASS.

Avis, J. M. (1988). Deepening awareness: A private study guide to feminism and family therapy. In L. Braverman (Ed.), *A guide to feminist family therapy*. New York: Harrington Park Press.

Barrett, M. J., & Trepper, T. S. (1991). Treating women drug abusers who were victims of childhood sexual abuse. In C. Bepko (Ed.), *Feminism and addiction* (pp. 127–145). New York: Haworth Press.

Barrett, M. J., Trepper, T. S., & Fish, L. S. (1990). Feminist-informed family therapy for the treatment of intrafamily child sexual abuse. *Journal of Family Psychology, 4*, 151–166.

Bepko, C., & Krestan, J. A. (1985). *The responsibility trap: A blueprint for treating the alcoholic family*. New York: The Free Press.

Brooks, G. R. (1992). Gender-sensitive family therapy in a violent culture. *Topics in Family Psychology and Counseling, 1*(4), 24–36.

Brooks, G. W. (1990). Traditional men in marital and family therapy. In M. Bograd (Ed.), *Feminist approaches for men in family therapy* (pp. 51–74). New York: Harrington Park Press.

Carden, A. (1994). Wife abuse and the wife abuser: Review and recommendations. *The Counseling Psychologist, 22*, 539–582.

Dutton, D. G. (1985). An ecologically nested theory of male violence toward intimates. *International Journal of Women's Studies, 8*(4), 404–413.

Kemp, A. (1998). *Abuse in the family: An introduction*. Pacific Grove, CA: Brooks/Cole.

Kirshbaum, M. (1994). Family context and disability culture reframing: Through the looking class. *The Family Psychologist, 10*(4), 8–12.

Lewis, J. A. (1991). Change and the alcohol-affected family: Limitations of the "intervention." *The Family Psychologist, 7*(2), 43–44.

Lewis, J. A., Dana, R. Q., & Blevins, G. A. (2001). *Substance abuse counseling: An individualized approach* (3rd ed.). Monterey, CA: Brooks/Cole.

Madsen, W. C. (1999). *Collaborative therapy with multi-stressed families: From old problems to new futures*. New York: Guilford.

McDaniel, S. H., Hepworth, J., & Doherty, W. J. (1993, Jan./Feb.). A new prescription for family health care. *Family Networker 17*(2), 18–29, 62–63.

O'Farrell, T. J. (1992). Families and alcohol problems: An overview of treatment research. *Journal of Family Psychology, 5*, 339–359.

Ratican, K. L. (1992). Sexual abuse survivors: Identifying symptoms and special treatment considerations. *Journal of Counseling & Development, 71*, 33–38.

Rolland, J. S. (1994). *Families, illness, and stability: An integrative treatment model*. New York: Basic Books.

Stages of change (n.d.). Retrieved July 2002, from http://www.uri.edu/research/cprc/TTM/StagesOfChange.htm.

Steinglass, P., Bennett, L. A., Wolin, S. J., & Reiss, D. (1987). *The alcoholic family*. New York: Basic Books.

Steinglass, P., & Horan, M. E. (1988). Families and chronic medical illness. *Journal of Psychotherapy and the Family, 3*(3), 127–142.

Trepper, T. S., & Barrett, M. J. (1986). *Treating incest: A multiple systems perspective*. New York: Haworth.

Usher, M. L., Jay, J., & Glass, D. R. (1982). Family therapy as a treatment modality for alcoholism. *Journal of Studies on Alcohol, 43*, 927–938.

Wetchler, J. L., Nelson, T. S., McCollum, E. E., Trepper, T. S., and Lewis, R. A. (1994). Couple-focused therapy for substance-abusing women. In J. A. Lewis (Ed.), *Addictions: Concepts and strategies for treatment*. Gaithersburg, MD: Aspen.

8

TAILORING TREATMENT
Work and Family Concerns

The portrait of the traditional American family is fading fast, yet the frame still hangs on the walls of American corporate and government offices, as well as those of psychotherapists. The portrait shows a white male with two children and a wife who doesn't work outside the home. He puts in a 9-to-5, five-day workweek, and he leaves his work at the office or shop. He rarely allows family matters to impinge on his work life and vice versa.

Replacing the fading portrait is the picture of today's family. The majority of today's families do not consist of a married couple with a single breadwinner and two children. Rather, many types exist, including single parents, couples without children, and dual-earner couples. The workday may really be a night shift or a rotating shift. Some or all of the work might be done at home (telecommuting or flex work), or considerable traveling or long-distance commuting may be involved. The workweek may be compressed (flextime) into four 10-hour days or three 12-hour shifts a week. More likely than not, family matters impinge on work life, and work life clearly affects family life.

Unfortunately, most government officials, many corporate executives, and even large numbers of family therapists have clung to the faded family portrait of the past. Although therapists admit that a sizable portion of their case loads consists of single-parent families and dual-earner couples, their therapeutic sensitivity to work–family issues and practice patterns may not have appreciably changed. To date, relatively little coverage of work–family issues appears in marital and family therapy books and journals. Therapists can effectively help today's couples and families but only if they fully understand the entire range of issues faced by couples and families.

THE RELATIONSHIP OF WORK LIFE
AND FAMILY LIFE

The relationship between family and work changes across cultures and over time. The tension between the two primal themes of individualism and communitarianism is reflected in this evolving relationship. In many ways, the history of work and family reflects the issues of merging, splitting, and balance that families typically experience. Consider, for example, the historical background of the family types that have come to dominate American middle-class culture.

In the beginning of communal living, work was centered in the home. Families—husbands, wives, and children—hunted and grew food, built shelter, and raised their young. Even with the rise of the merchant and craftsman classes in the Middle Ages, work and family remained interdependent, with the craftsman/merchant working in the home or out of sheds or shops nearby. Male children apprenticed with their fathers, and mother and daughter often were involved in the work.

With the dawn of the Industrial Revolution in the mid-1800s, a distinct split occurred between family and work. In Europe and the United States, many men now worked away from home at a factory from dawn to dusk while their wives lost their roles in the workforce. For many people, home became independent from work, a supposed refuge from the travails of earning a living. At the same time this was happening, of course, slavery persisted and even grew in economic vigor. Among poor urban families, children entered the workforce in large numbers:

> So for every 19th-century middle-class family that was able to nurture its women and children comfortably inside the family circle, there was an Irish or German girl scrubbing floors, a Welsh boy mining coal, a black girl doing laundry, a black mother and child picking cotton, and a Jewish or Italian daughter making dresses, cigars, or artificial flowers in a sweatshop. (Coontz, 2000, p. 15)

With the arrival of World War II, women's labor was needed outside the home. Among those families that had been characterized by male bread-winning and female domesticity, change was rapid. Women went to work in droves. As the war ended, however, the work–family supports that had been present, including childcare, were quickly eliminated. Many middle-class women once more left the work force while their husbands became loyal members of a corporate milieu. An unspoken agreement mandated that the corporation's needs always had priority over personal and family needs. Furthermore, it was assumed that family problems were the worker's concern, not the corporation's.

For some families with children, the suburbs became a middle-class ghetto during the 1950s. It was during that brief time that what some people think of as the "traditional American family" reached its pinnacle. In fact, as Coontz points out, the family of that decade was neither traditional nor idyllic.

Though many people found satisfaction in family life during that period, we now know the experiences of many groups and individuals were denied. Problems such as alcoholism, physical abuse, and incest were swept under the rug. So was discrimination against ethnic groups, political dissidents, women, elders, gays, lesbians, religious minorities, and the handicapped. Rates of divorce and unwed motherhood were low, but that did not prevent 30% of American children from living in poverty, a higher figure than at present (Coontz, 2000, p. 17).

During the 1960s and 1970s, more people began questioning the values and functions of all social institutions, including the corporate workplace. Many workers concluded that their dependence on the corporation was akin to "selling their souls to the company store" in exchange for security. Not surprisingly, the recognition of this reality brought with it a new degree of conflict between management and labor in the 1970s and early 1980s.

In the mid-1980s, a wave of corporate takeovers and downsizing essentially broke whatever "psychological contract" had been perceived. If worker loyalty had previously been rewarded by corporate security, that situation no longer existed. The loss of corporate security brought with it the demise of the "organization man" (Bennett, 1990). The corporate world seemed cold and calculating as mergers, acquisitions, and downsizing escalated. Both workers and executives with decades of seniority were fired or forced into early retirement. Not surprisingly, the incidences of stress-related medical disorders, alcohol and substance abuse problems, and other effects of occupational stress increased dramatically. The seemingly secure organizational and family-like cultures of the manufacturing and service corporations disappeared almost overnight. The purges seemed to be convincing proof that if corporations were workers' second families, they were hostile and dysfunctional families.

Baby boomers now constitute the largest segment of the workplace. Their values of personal development and balance among family, self, and job reflect the need for a flexibility in work schedules, family leaves, and dependent care along with adequate remuneration, benefits, and an enriched work environment. Although a few corporations have tried to rise to this challenge, family concerns generally remain unmet. Women are employed in great numbers, but are forced to balance work and family life without support from the workplace or the community. The gap between rich and poor has radically increased and, at this point in time, unemployment and underemployment are increasing as well. Families have become more aware of what they need, but their desires remain largely unmet.

COMMON WORK–FAMILY CONFLICTS AND THEIR CONSEQUENCES

With few exceptions, most U.S. corporations function as if the significant changes of the late 20th and early 21st centuries had never occurred. Despite the increasing number of women in the workplace, many government, school, and corporate leaders seem to harbor a delusional belief that mothers are indeed not in the workplace but rather at home where they can attend to the needs of their spouses, children, and elderly relatives. As a result of this institutional blindness, families are expected to adapt, adjust, and singly manage the stresses and strains of ever increasing social, economic, political, and cultural changes. It is becoming increasingly apparent that government's hands-off-the-family policy and the corporate world's reluctance to establish realistic family policies are shortsighted and counterproductive.

As work–family conflicts increase and the balancing of work and family responsibilities becomes more complex, the need for better support systems increases. The alternative is to continue with the inequitable and dysfunctional systems currently in place. A major challenge of the new millennium is to reshape work–family relations, increase productivity, and create new opportunities for intimacy. This challenge will require an increased awareness of and honesty about the complexity of the issues and their ownership beyond the family. No longer can government shrink from responsibility with moral claims about the sanctity of family privacy. Other social institutions that have been resistant to change must begin the process of reconfiguration and accommodation. Schools and corporations will have to change their hours and their leave policies, providing the social services they previously resisted.

A majority of current work–family conflicts arise because major social institutions, such as the school system and government, have organized their resources and structure around obsolete concepts of family and society. These institutions seem complacently blind to the plight of the contemporary family. The lack of external social support for families often generates stress and conflict within family systems. It remains difficult for families to maintain both togetherness and economic stability. Although two-parent families are now two-paycheck households, real family earnings have dropped. The two-adult family now works an average of 80 hours a week outside the home compared with 40 hours a generation ago (Googins, 1991).

These pressures have brought with them increases in the type and frequency of work–family conflicts. A variety of such conflicts exist. They include role strain, role overload, and role conflicts, as well as problems involving child care, elder care, and issues of balance among career, family, and personal needs.

Work–family conflicts exist when role pressures from work and family demands are mutually incompatible, as when participation in one role precludes participation in another. Three general classes of work–family conflict have been articulated: time-based conflicts, strain-based conflicts, and behavior-based conflicts (Greenhaus, 1987; Greenhaus & Beutell, 1985). *Time-based conflict* refers to how time devoted to one role detracts from another, as when late-night meetings conflict with a child's school conference. *Strain-based conflict* refers to the intrusion of strain symptoms such as fatigue and irritability from one role to the other. *Behavior-based conflict* refers to the incompatibility of behavior in one role with behavior expected in another, as when a worker is expected to be detached and objective on the job but warm, nurturing, and emotional in the family.

Greenhaus, Parasuraman, Granrose, Rabinowitz, and Beutell (1989) studied strain-based and time-based conflicts. They found that men and women experienced similar levels of strain-based conflict, but in different ways. Work scheduling was associated with strain-based conflict for men but not for women. Women experienced high levels of work–family conflict because of their work, and they did not experience as much stress when their partners exhibited high work salience, but the pattern was reversed for men. Men's work–family conflicts were unrelated to their job involvement, whereas women's job involvement was clearly related to work–family conflicts.

Several types of role strain are particularly noticeable in dual-career relationships. These problems include career versus personal and family demands, competition between spouses, division of labor, child care arrangements, time allocation, job-related geographic mobility, social networks, and identity maintenance versus identity diffusion.

Shaevitz and Shaevitz (1980) listed a number of questions that must be addressed regarding role strain. How will household tasks be assigned? Who will do what and according to what standards? Who controls the money? Separate or joint accounts? What are the rights of each in spending money? How should partners deal with job relocation? Is one spouse's commuting a realistic solution? What if one spouse is more successful in his or her career than the other? How can partners recognize and deal with overload and burnout? Who will be responsible for child care? Who will be available in emergencies? Are child care facilities available in emergencies? Are child care facilities available at all? What special things must the partners do to enhance their relationship?

Work–family conflicts have been present throughout history, but the challenges in this new millennium are especially severe. One serious issue involves the increasing isolation of family members. Overworked parents may have little time to invest in their children, in their spouses, or in themselves. When friendships arise in the workplace rather than in the community, spouses may not share the same social contacts.

Another pressing issue has to do with conflicts over priorities. If the time spent at work compromises family life, the employer's values and expectations may pervade the person's thinking and decision making. At some level the worker thinks, "If I only could find better child care, I could pay more attention to the real priority, which is my work." Should adults have to choose between work and family or feel guilty and apologetic about rescheduling a meeting or arriving late because a child or elder is sick? For many individuals, the workplace has come to replace the home as the haven of safety, the center of life's meaning, and the source of self-worth. Previously, work provided the financial means to keep the home secure.

Finally, economic stress is a primary factor in marital discord. Economically stressed couples struggle with a wide variety of issues. These stressors may precipitate marital conflict or exacerbate existing marital problems. During times of financial stress, a couple's communication may be considerably affected. The couples may engage in fewer rewarding exchanges, and negative communication may increase. Spouses may covertly or overtly attempt to control the other. Consequently, ample opportunity exists for disappointment and disillusion as one spouse blames the other for their financial difficulties. Both spouses may become psychologically absorbed with the family's financial concerns. They may lack the energy needed to devote time to marital issues, because they work longer hours, attempting to deal with overdue bills.

The result is a diminished amount of both time and energy to devote to family matters.

Recently, researchers have begun focusing on the family dynamics affected by economic hardship. Conger, Elder, Lorenz, and Conger (1990) described a process model of marital dysfunction involving economic hardship. They noted that economic hardship leads initially to a subjective sense of "economic strain." This strain engenders cognitive, affective, and behavioral changes, which then leads to an increase in spousal hostility. As hostility continues to increase, warmth decreases, marital quality decreases, and the relationship becomes unstable. A second study (Lorenz, Conger, Simon, Whitbeck, & Elder, 1991) confirmed this model and concluded that efforts to increase warmth and decrease hostility improved the relationship stability even amid financial stressors.

Although financial stress clearly affects the lives of working couples, it tends to be even more severe in single-parent families. Gladding (1998) pointed out that single-parent families are six times as likely to be poor when compared with nuclear families. This disparity in income is due to the fact that women, who still tend to receive lower wages than their male counterparts, head many single-parent families. The high cost of day care adds even further to the financial strain.

That the portrait of the American family is changing is indisputable. That clinicians and counselors working with couples and families will be sensitive and effective regarding this changing reality is another matter. A central theme of this book is that treatment efficacy can be greatly enhanced by tailoring treatment to the unique needs, circumstances, and expectations of couples and families. Tailoring treatment requires a comprehensive, integrative assessment of the unique needs, circumstances, and expectations of the client system.

TAILORING TREATMENT

The family therapist wanting to tailor treatment must attend both to family types and to differences within family types. In the following sections, we will present as examples ways to tailor treatment for two family types: dual-career couples and single-parent families.

Overcoming Therapist Bias

Providing effective family therapy around issues of work and family is impossible if the therapist holds negative or unrealistic attitudes about the relational pattern of the family. Clinicians need to make sure their own biases do not intrude into the treatment process. They must examine whether their own value system is incompatible with the assumptions underlying the work–family lifestyle of their clients. Therapists who are ambivalent or opposed to women pursuing careers, to men engaging in family chores, or to changes in traditional gender roles may find it difficult to understand and effectively counsel individuals or couples whose families reflect these values. The dual-career spouse who detects a therapist's bias about role stereotypes, for instance, is likely to withdraw, feel threatened, or be pessimistic about being understood (Goldenberg & Goldenberg, 1984).

Particularly crucial to an effective therapeutic interventions is the recognition that the experiences of men in dual-career or single-parent systems are different from those of women. Because the gender-role socializations of men and women differ dramatically, the areas they experience as problematic and the factors contributing to the problem areas can be markedly different. For example, the traditional structuring of professional careers has presented an obstacle for men's full involvement in family life, whereas the traditional division of labor in the home has presented obstacles to women who want to become more involved in professional careers. These differences surface in the day-to-day conflicts of dual-career couples and in the pressures faced by single parents. Thus, while men may struggle with esteem issues such as a perceived loss of power, a loss of prestige, and involvement with "women's work" within the family, women may struggle with esteem issues regarding role conflict, redefinition, the roles of wife and mother, and expectations of a spouse's involvement in family work (Gilbert & Rachlin, 1987).

Common Issues

From her comparative review of marital therapy literature, Stoltz–Loike (1992) noted six underlying themes related to effective dual-career couple functioning: (a) couples must establish boundaries between themselves and others; (b) spouses must be able to express supportiveness, both emotional and physical, to each other; (c) effective couple relations depend on mastering and using basic communication skills; (d) effective couple relations depend on mastering and using conflict-resolution skills; (e) dysfunctional couple patterns can be framed as problems in need of solutions; and (f) effective couple relations involve the process of change that couples tend to fear and resist. The obvious implication is that therapist-guided change can greatly enhance the functioning of dual-career couples.

The therapeutic issues identified by Gladding (1998) as being important for work with single-parent families show some commonality with the ideas expressed by Stoltz–Loike. Gladding suggested that approaches to working with single-parent families should include helping family members communicate clearly and frequently with one another. Clearly, an emphasis on developing communication skills cuts across both family forms. Gladding went on to suggest, however, two additional areas of emphasis: (a) linking family members and the family as a whole to sources of social support and (b) assisting families in getting their financial matters resolved. This accent on the social–economic–political environment may well be a key factor in both family types.

An ecological perspective reminds counselors that person–environment interactions can be changed in numerous ways for any given client. This can be achieved, for example, by changing the environment through the counselor's or client's initiative, thereby making systems more helpful or affirming; helping clients identify and practice skills to cope with the environment more effectively; or addressing the client's cognitive processes that shape his or her transactions with the environment (Cook, Heppner, & O'Brien, 2002, p. 297).

Cook et al. suggested, for instance, that "many women who work outside the home continue to be primarily responsible for the care of the home and children" (p. 299). They say that a key to helping women manage multiple roles is to change societal norms and values regarding flexible work hours. This concept may be as important to couples as it is to people in single-parent families.

Psychoeducational Strategies

Therapeutic interventions can take two forms: prevention or treatment. The preventive form involves educating individuals regarding potential problems and challenges they might face. The purpose of this type of intervention is consciousness raising and skill acquisition. Individuals are provided the opportunity to learn about day-to-day realities of their career; to examine their personal values, attitudes, and life goals, particularly in terms of the concept of equity; and to assess their receptivity to making the attitude and behavior changes needed to accommodate the dual-career or single-parent lifestyle. Such psychoeducational strategies remain important for working with families already experiencing work-related difficulties.

Generally speaking, family therapists should be able to provide dual-career couples with accurate information, link them with appropriate social supports, and intervene with strategies and techniques appropriate to the dual-career couple's unique needs. A generic five-step intervention protocol has been described by Jordan, Cobb, and McCully

(1989) that is representative of the psychoeducational approach. The steps include (a) the clarification of goals and values; (b) communication training, (c) negotiation and contracting skills training, (d) time-management techniques, and (e) stress-management techniques.

First, the couple's role expectations are assessed with regard to career, marriage, parenting, and personal life. The therapist assists the couple in identifying the discrepancies between expectations and reality so that mutually satisfying goals can be established.

Second, because successful communication patterns at the workplace may not generalize to parental and marital relationships, deficits in communication skills are assessed. Particular attention is given to communication issues of power and control. The couple is assisted in practicing such skills as active listening, clarification, "I" statements, feedback, request-making, self-expression, and positive aspects of nonverbal communication.

Third, when the couple can communicate their needs directly and positively, they have the prerequisite for negotiating areas of conflict through formal and informal contracts. Contracting can help spouses overcome resentments caused by unmet needs or an inequitable division of household duties. The issue of equity is, of course, a cornerstone of treatment for dual-career couples.

Fourth, time management involves setting priorities and scheduling tasks. The couple is assisted in establishing their career, family, and personal priorities so that realistic decisions about scheduling can be made.

The final step of the protocol is stress management. Even though realistic goals; priorities; and effective time management, communication, and conflict-resolution skills can greatly reduce stressors for the dual-career couple, additional stress reduction skills are needed. The couple is counseled on rules for low-stress living that include deep relaxation, breath control, exercise, sensible eating, hobbies, guarding personal freedom, and so on.

These five areas represent the traditional relational skills that most psychoeducational and behavioral marital therapists deem essential for effective and satisfying marital functioning. In addressing work–family concerns, the therapist might want to add *negotiation* to the skill set. Cook et al. (2002) stated that women with extensive parenting responsibilities often find they need negotiation skills in order to ask for what they need in the workplace. These same negotiation skills are important not just for heads of single-parent households but also for members of dual-career families, as "many women may also benefit from assistance in negotiating the sharing of responsibilities with their partners" (2002, p. 299).

Interpersonal-Systems Strategies

Goldenberg and Goldenberg (1984) believed that effective therapy with dual-career couples can best be achieved within an interpersonal systems perspective. They noted that the relationship between dual-career spouses is too complex and interdependent for individual psychotherapeutic interventions to succeed. Goldenberg (1986) maintained that successful treatment needs to involve the spouses conjointly and be highly focused. Frequently, the conjoint sessions are the first time one spouse has had to attend to the other spouse's agenda. They may see that their relationship system needs reorganizing. Sometimes a first session will create dramatic changes from this new vision of the relationship.

From his relationship-systems perspective, Goldenberg (1986) emphasized the importance of social and professional networks. He contended that dual-career couples function better if they are not in social isolation. Thus, it is important for them to develop a network of friends and professional colleagues with whom they can share experiences. Feedback provided from being with other couples is useful because it highlights how couples can work out their differences. Similarly, a professional support network of individuals or a group of colleagues is most helpful for discussing and venting workplace problems and frustrations. Without a professional support network, the temptation is to dump the day's accumulated stresses and complaints on one's spouse.

Goldenberg also believed that the clinician must continuously maintain a systems perspective and view issues, stress, and problems in light of a flexible view of marriage. The therapist must understand that each developmental lifestyle is important and also must not identify with the person whose life stage is closest to the therapist's own. For example, if the husband has had an ongoing career, the therapist needs to be reminded that the wife also deserves a turn to have a career, even if it comes later in life. The wife has just been periodically interrupted and has made achievements in a less orderly or orthodox manner.

Like most other writers on treating dual-career couples, Goldenberg believed that the essential goal of therapy is to achieve or restore a sense of relationship equity and assist the couple in nourishing their relationship. Because therapeutic impasses are common in conjoint therapy of dual-career couples, Goldenberg used the following two therapeutic exercises. In the first, the couple is encouraged to reverse positions emotionally and honestly attempt to offer arguments as though they were the other partner. In the second, the couple is asked to imagine themselves as 15 to 20 years older and construct an autobiography noting what has happened to their relationship, their careers, and their children. This exercise helps couples foresee the balance of family and career. The therapist's role is to focus each spouse on the other's agenda. As a result, each spouse can become more sensitive to the fact that more is happening in their relationship than his or her own individual unhappiness.

Interpersonal-systems strategies take a different approach in the case of single-parent families. Gladding (1998) pointed out that single-parent families are often more democratic than other family types, with parents and children relating to one another through collaboration. "When decisions have to be made, the needs of all parties, parents and children, are usually taken into consideration" (p. 294). Although this equity in decision-making represents a strength among families, it also has limitations.

Within single-parent families, the democratic nature may blur needed boundary distinctions between a parent and child. If boundaries are not clear, chaotic and confusing interactions may result and children may get out of control (Gladding, 1998, p. 295). Across family forms, systemic issues differ while the need to attend to systems remains the same.

Psychodynamic Strategies

Although psychoeducational and systemic strategies aim to teach relational and coping skills or adaptive solutions, these approaches tend to be of limited use in helping dual-career couples work through a resistance to change or the obstacles that prevent relational and therapeutic progress. Therapeutically confronting these resistances and impasses may require exploring issues from early in each spouse's development. Confronting and resolving the unfinished developmental business of one or both spouses is often part of the process of working with couples. Glickhauf–Hughes, Hughes, & Wells (1986) considered the developmental issues that underlie six common conflict areas for dual-career couples. Three of these will be briefly considered here: power conflicts, competition, and commitment.

Glickhauf–Hughes et al. contended that power conflicts often reflect each spouse's childhood experience that others cannot be counted on to meet their needs. As adults, they are likely to develop a "look out for number one" attitude. In addition, when parents are insensitive to their children's needs and frustration level, these children will likely become adults who have difficulty tolerating the frustration of unmet needs. Thus, compromises with a spouse may be both difficult and painful because they are associated with loss rather than mutual gain. Equity is often proposed as the corrective solution for resolving power conflicts or struggles, but this solution requires several things.

First, each spouse must keep one's needs in mind; second, each must develop the ability to tolerate the frustration of not getting one's needs met immediately; and third, each spouse must view the other's requests as legitimate and not as attempts at control or domination. In terms of Erikson's stages of psychosocial development, the resolution of power conflicts by equity is difficult if either or both spouses have insufficiently mastered the developmental tasks of trust and autonomy.

Another common conflict of dual-career couples is competition. The opposite of competition is cooperation or collaboration. Collaboration requires the capacity to separate one's own feelings from the spouse's feelings and behavior, the ability to sustain and augment self-esteem via encouragement, and an acceptance of competitive feelings, both within oneself and in one's spouse. The developmental obstacle that can impede a couple from resolving conflicts about competition results from an insufficient mastery of autonomy and initiative by one or both spouses.

A third common conflict involves commitment. Because many dual-career spouses value success, achievement, and independence, and because individuals in dual-career relationships are usually intelligent, verbal, and successful individuals used to solving problems with cognitive analysis, they frequently resort to the defenses of intellectualization, rationalization, and isolation of affect when faced with conflict. So it is not surprising that both spouses view strong feelings as obstacles to problem solving. Often such couples are undeveloped when it comes to identifying and sharing feelings. Rice (1979) noted three common problem areas that dual-career couples contend with in marital therapy: issues about children, time management, and relationships with others. These three problem areas often involve manifestations of underlying power struggles between the spouses.

In therapy with single-parent families, human development is approached in a different way. Gladding (1998) pointed out that children in single-parent families often go through developmental stages at a more rapid pace than children in two-parent families. In the context of the democratic style, children take responsibilities quite early and have an aura of maturity in relating to adults. The parentification of the child may be an issue that needs to be addressed over time.

Integrative Strategies

Stoltz–Loike (1992) described what she calls an integrated approach to counseling dual-career couples. She believes that dual-career couples do not represent a variant of traditional couples in which the career responsibilities of the woman are simply attached to her family role and the man's family commitment is formed by his career role. She advocates that an integrated approach is essential to effectively address the unique demands of dual-career couples who present for consultation.

This integrated approach is based on several assumptions:

- A family has a variety of responsibilities that must be performed and comfortably divided depending on the skills, talents, and preferences of the family members.
- Attitudes toward responsibilities need to be communicated, and conflicts need to be discussed and resolved.
- Since dual-career couples typically have few role models for balancing career and family roles, therapists must provide such information. This may include dual-career couples and groups that can facilitate functional modeling in being an effective dual-career couple.
- Because conflicts and ways of resolving them change throughout the couple's life span, communication, negotiation, and problem solving need to be viewed as ongoing processes.
- Because of individual differences, gender concerns, and personal needs, effective solutions to a couple's family and career conflicts will vary, and the therapist must be cognizant of tailored interventions.
- A spouse must balance his or her own family and work responsibilities with those of the other spouse.
- Solutions to dual-career issues must be made within the larger context of each spouse's life within a specific corporate and community setting. Thus, the therapist must comprehensively assess the couple's life space and circumstances.

The goal of the integrated approach is to achieve balance and negotiate family and career equity. The focus is on helping couples recognize how family and career concerns and role conflicts evolve and how both rewards and challenges differ over time. Strategies are drawn from life-span development counseling, marital and family therapy, career counseling, and gender counseling to deal with the unique problems.

Because dual-career couples have overlapping roles and responsibilities, reducing the overlap and balancing the responsibilities in order to achieve equity is only possible when a couple has mastered communication, negotiation, conflict resolution, and life-span success. Stoltz–Loike believes that the therapist's primary responsibility is to help spouses develop these skills and reinforce their acquisition. She notes that successful dual-career couples are characterized by a mutual respect for achievement at home and performance in the workplace, as well as a deep commitment to personal and spousal accomplishments. Furthermore, the sense of equity associated with both spouses' achievements enriches their relationship while enhancing career productivity.

Stoltz–Loike's book (1992) *Dual Career Couples* offered a wide range of assessment devices for many areas. These included family–career status and priorities, the perceived balance between family and career, couple communication, gender sensitivity, conflict-resolution style, the definitions of career and family success, couple goals, and career stepladders. The second section of Stolz–Loike's book illustrates a variety of strategies for skill training and therapeutic interventions regarding communication and negotiation, conflict resolution, gender sensitivity, and life-span success. Stoltz–Loike notes that developing success goals as a couple depends on the commitment of each spouse to his or her own achievement, as well as that of his or her partner. Life-span success is achieved when both can benefit according to their own standards, rather than when one spouse's self-defined success overshadows or obviates the other's ability to achieve. Basically, life-span success is reached by pursuing a series of short-term goals that represent distinct achievements and lead to long-term objectives. Each of these goals can be achieved in various ways, even amid the timeouts or workloads that occur for any number of reasons.

The integrated approach has been used in a variety of settings: in the clinical setting with one or both spouses in a dual-career relationship; in groups of dual-career couples in a clinical setting; in groups of dual-career couples in a corporate setting; or in a seminar or series in a corporate setting. The comprehensiveness of this approach allows psychoeducational approaches to be used concurrently with structural, strategic, cognitive, and dynamic intervention methods.

Group Strategies

Group treatments, which involve either homogeneous or heterogeneous formats, have become increasingly available and useful in working with couples. Traditional group therapy is heterogeneous, including individuals or couples with a wide variety of presentations and concerns, and it tends to be ongoing and long term. Homogeneous groups, in contrast, provide a structural social network for individuals or couples with a common presentation or concern. These groups tend to be shorter and time-limited, and can have either a dynamic–interpersonal or psychoeducational focus. Furthermore, these groups vary in their use of different therapeutic group factors, yet they rely heavily on cohesiveness and universality, as well as imparting information. Groups specifically for dual-career couples are, of course, homogeneous groups and tend to have a psychoeducational format.

The following description by Prochaska and Prochaska (1982) illustrates a typical group format. A six-session format with 90-minute sessions is advertised. Prospective couples are told they can share their experiences and learn a variety of new coping skills to help each other with the typical conflicts arising in balancing a career, marriage, and family. Usually, the group comprises five to six couples at differing stages, which is important for providing role modeling and anticipatory experiences for couples who have not faced certain dilemmas. Because of the therapy's psychoeducational focus, a variety of methods, including group discussion, minilectures, handouts, role playing, and exercises, are used.

The first session focuses on eliciting the issues and concerns of each couple and their learning needs. The goal is to create a relaxed atmosphere that will foster therapeutic group factors of cohesiveness and universality. The second session introduces the concept of equity in dual-career relationships, and equity is distinguished from equality. Problem-solving skills oriented toward equitable alternatives to the demands facing dual-career couples are described and discussed.

The third session centers on children, the effect dual-career relationships have on them and vice versa. Usually one or more of the couples are in various stages of deciding whether or when to have children, and they are trying to anticipate the ways in which their lives will change. Usually in this session skills are taught for implementing weekly family meetings in which equitable rules and decisions are arrived at by a process of consensus. This forum provides an opportunity for families to change and grow as the needs of the family group and individuals change.

The fourth session focuses on time issues. Time-management concepts and skills are presented, including "time borrowing" whereby someone outside the family is hired to perform time-consuming tasks. Empathy training exercises in dyads and triads also occur in this session. The fifth session focuses on styles and methods of conflict resolution. Role playing with prompt cards is also used to address typical dual-career conflict issues.

The sixth and last session emphasizes role flexibility. A group dinner is planned the session before so that each member can contribute in a unique and novel way. Typically, one or more of the men who usually never cook prepare the meal, while the woman or women who usually take total responsibility for the meal relax. The dinner discussion centers on being out of the usual roles, the advantages of increasing their flexibility, and termination issues. It is not unusual for groups to decide to continue to meet monthly as a support group to further discuss issues of mutual concern.

That these seminars and workshops are beneficial is beyond question. That they may not be reaching those most at risk is another matter. King and Winnett (1986) reported data suggesting that clerical and other hourly workers have as great a need or greater than professional workers for stress management and conflict resolution training. Typically, however, it is the professional worker who is targeted for such programs. These researchers further noted that men in dual-earner marriages appear to be less interested in attending such training programs than men in dual-career marriages.

Many excellent resources are available for training seminars and workshops. Stoltz–Loike (1992) provided a number of simple inventories that are useful in group formats involving individuals or couples. Michaels and McCarty's book (1992) is one of a number of recent trade publications that can be suggested or assigned as reading for participants.

Consulting on Work–Family Issues

Marital and family therapists/consultants also can have a significant effect on work–family functioning through consulting on policy and programming matters, including hiring practices, parental leave, flexible work scheduling, and child care. Vanderkolk and Young (1991) focused most of their efforts regarding policy and programming changes on work–family matters that corporations have already successfully implemented. They also provided a number of worksheets, surveys, and strategies to aid in overcoming management's resistance to such changes. They pointed out that these changes not only result in increased worker satisfaction and productivity but are also cost-effective and necessary for a corporation to maintain its competitive edge in a changing world economy.

An extended section of the Stoltz–Loike (1992) book is entitled "Corporate Response to Dual-Career Couples" in which she describes the needed policy changes that corporations must make to become more family friendly. She describes policies and programming for child care and elder care, flexible scheduling, leave policies, recruitment and retention, relocation, and the type of corporate culture that is consistent with such family-friendly policies. A professional therapist and consultant,

Stoltz–Loike believes that clinicians have a unique opportunity to consult on the development and implementation of various family-friendly programs. She states that both internal relational dynamics and external sources of corporate stress must be addressed for the concerns of dual-career couples to be effectively resolved.

Sekaran (1986) also argued that both internal and external sources of work–family stress must be addressed. Sperry (1993) contended that clinically trained individuals with knowledge and experience in family systems theory are much better suited to consult with organizations on work–family issues than nonclinically trained management consultants. Cole (1992) also indicated that business and management consultants are trained to approach organizational issues from a linear and rational perspective, whereas family therapists are trained to think systemically and circularly. Cole further noted that an increasing number of marital and family therapists are being called on to serve as consultants on work and family interactions.

A SAMPLE PROTOCOL: MATCHING/TAILORING TREATMENT WITH DUAL-CAREER COUPLES

The protocol proposed here is simple, perhaps deceptively simple. It involves four steps: (a) a comprehensive assessment, (b) matching to a therapeutic strategy and treatment format, (c) tailoring the chosen strategy, and (d) implementation, review, and revision of the matching/tailoring efforts.

Assessment

The assessment format includes the situation, severity, system, skill, style, and suitability for treatment, as well as the dimensions of support network and synchronism/asynchronism. As described by Sekaran and Hall (1989), *synchronism is* a condition under which an individual's or a couple's experience is "on" schedule with some "timetable" of development, while *asynchronism* refers to being "off" schedule. The family, the couple, and the work organization define these timetables.

For instance, couples who marry and have children late are usually considered out of sync with social norms, also called family *asynchronism.* If one spouse's career started later than the other, or if the progress of one was slower than the other, this would illustrate couple *asynchronism.* But when an individual is not promoted to a managerial level by the age of 40, that individual is considered behind schedule and subsequently may never receive such a promotion. This is called *organizational asynchronism.*

Among dual-career couples, the more types of asynchronism, the more stress the couple is likely to experience (Sekaran & Hall, 1989). Assessing the dual-career couple's career timing, family timing, and synchronism/asynchronism is thus useful in formulating a matched/tailored treatment plan.

Matching a Therapeutic Strategy and Treatment Format to the Couple

Clinical experience with dual-career couples suggests that matching a couple with a therapeutic strategy should be based on the dimensions of situation/severity, system, support network, and skills. As noted in chapter 4, the situation/severity can be operationalized by the level of marital discord (Guerin, Fay, Burden, & Kuetto, 1987), the level of functioning (Weltner, 1985), or the level of distress (Worthington, 1989).

Using the level of marital conflict is particularly helpful. The first level of marital conflict involves couples who demonstrate a preclinical or minimal degree of marital conflict. Such conflict has lasted for less than 6 months, and most often the couples are newlyweds. Level two consists of couples who are experiencing significant marital conflict lasting longer than 6 months. Although their communication patterns remain open and adequate, criticism and projection have increased. Level-three couples present with severe marital conflict. Often this conflict has lasted longer than 6 months, and projection is intense. The levels of anxiety and emotional arousal are high, as are the intensity and polarization of surrounding triangles. Communication is closed with marked conflict, the level of criticism is high, and blaming is common. Finally, couples at level four are characterized by communication that is closed, poor or nonexistent information exchange, high levels of criticism and blaming, and an absence of self-disclosure activity. In the vast majority of level-four cases, attempts to keep the marriage from dissolution appeared doomed.

For instance, if the dual-career couple is recently married with a level-one conflict, a psychoeducational intervention strategy would likely be necessary, particularly if the couple also displays skill deficits in one or more areas such as communication, negotiation, conflict resolution, time and stress management, or goal clarification. A consultative intervention might also be a good match. In contrast, with a couple presenting with a level-two or level-three conflict, an interpersonal or psychodynamic intervention might be a better match than a psychoeducational one. However, psychoeducational input might be selectively used at some point in the course of treatment.

A second consideration at the matching stage of the protocol is treatment format. Whether an individual, conjoint couple, or couples group therapy format is indicated depends on a number of factors, including the nature of the presenting problem situation and systemic factors. The situation/severity and systems dimensions can provide useful information with regard to matching. Generally speaking, the individual format is indicated if a single spouse is experiencing difficulty adjusting to or coping with stress within his or her career and relationship. In contrast, the conjoint format tends to be more appropriate if the issue affects the dynamic within the relationship, particularly when issues of equality, power, boundaries, and intimacy are prominent. The couples group format is helpful if the stressors are largely external to the couple, that is, from the workplace, or the couple's concerns reflect level-one marital conflict (Guerin et al., 1987).

Usually, decisions about matching treatment are made before, during, or after the first session. However, tailoring decisions tend to be made at various points throughout the course of treatment. This is because tailoring involves a fine-tuning or fitting of the matched treatment strategy to the couple's unique needs, expectations, and treatment readiness.

Tailoring the Chosen Therapeutic Strategy

Once a therapeutic strategy and treatment format match has been made, the therapist can focus on tailoring treatment to the couple's unique needs and expectations. Clinical experience suggests that tailoring be based on the dimensions of style, synchronism, and suitability for treatment.

The style dimension reflects the intrapsychic dynamic of each spouse. As Rice (1979) observed, narcissistic features are often prominent in both spouses in dual-career marriages. Obsessive-compulsive features may be noted in the achievement focus, along with the workaholic patterns of one or both spouses. Irrespective of the therapeutic strategy used, an effective therapist will reconfigure the treatment keeping these individual dynamics in mind. In other words, the therapist's questions, clarifications, confrontations, reframes, interpretations, or any combination will be tailored to "fit" that couple or spouse. Lazarus's BASIC ID model (1981) is likewise valuable in tailoring interventions to dual-career couples, particularly because of its emphasis on specifying specific interventions with specific treatment methods.

The therapist must also consider the dimension of synchronism/ asynchronism in tailoring a strategy. A therapist's sensitivity to family, couple, workplace asynchronism, or any combination can aid in both reducing stress and empowering one or both spouses.

Finally, the dimension of suitability for treatment is valuable in decisions regarding tailoring. Spousal expectations for treatment and their treatment readiness are the major considerations. If one or both spouse's treatment expectations are unrealistic or conflicting, the therapist must address them in the initial sessions. Not to do so is to risk premature termination, which is not uncommon with dual-career couples. Similarly, the couple's level of readiness (Myers, 1992) is an important consideration in tailoring a particular treatment strategy. To maximize the treatment efficacy, the therapist needs to adapt how much direction and support he or she provides the couple. For the couple with low task readiness, the therapist who responds in a highly supportive or delegating style will be out of sync, while being quite in sync with a couple high in task readiness.

Implementation, Review, and Revision of Matching/Tailoring

In this last step of this protocol, the therapist continues the therapeutic intervention(s) while monitoring response and outcomes. Usually, the therapeutic strategy remains the same, whereas the treatment goals may need to be modified and the tailoring of the chosen therapeutic strategies continues. However, it may be necessary to change the strategy or even the treatment format. For instance, although treatment may begin in a conjoint format, it may be useful or necessary to switch or to add individual sessions for one or both spouses.

CASE EXAMPLE OF MATCHING/TAILORING WITH A DUAL-CAREER COUPLE

The following case illustrates the matching/tailoring process with a dual-career couple experiencing moderately severe marital discord. Given the chronicity of the couple's discord, a successful outcome following 21 sessions is likely, due to the tailored nature of the treatment. By the careful blending and sequencing of interpersonal, psychoeducational, and dynamic strategies with a conjoint treatment format, the couple was aided in redirecting and reclarifying their relationship.

Dale and Claire Justen have been married 6 years and have a 3-year-old son. They presented for therapy after a particularly vitriolic disagreement in which Dale pushed Claire into a wall. Although this was the first such incident, both were shaken sufficiently to seek professional help.

Dale, 43, is chief financial officer for a national fast-food chain. Claire is 40 and a junior partner in a high-visibility corporate law firm. She had worked full-time for 6 years in her firm before her son was born. She then took a 3-month maternity leave and returned to her job on a 20-hour-a-week basis. She hoped to be made a full partner 6 months ago but was told she would not even be considered until she returned to full-time status. This greatly distressed her because she felt strongly about spending "enough" time with her son, at least until he began first grade. She felt some guilt about working at all during her son's "most formative years," as her mother continued to remind her.

Both Claire and Dale come from traditional families in which their mothers were full-time homemakers and their fathers were the sole breadwinners. Claire and Dale were also the first generation of their respective families to attend college. Both began careers immediately and were quite successful. They met about 2 years before their marriage and discussed their desire to balance a family while continuing their careers. Things never quite worked out that way after the baby was born. Claire ended up assuming nearly total responsibility for child care. When the child was 2 1/2 , Claire and Dale decided they would change from half-time to full-time day care so that Claire could return to her career full time. But Dale never seemed to be free to drop off or pick up the child from daycare, and he was always too tired to help with household chores or spend time alone with Claire. For 3 weeks she attempted to juggle her work and home responsibilities before dropping back to 20 hours a week, much to the consternation of the senior partners and Dale, but to the delight of her mother. Dale insisted that they needed a full-time income from her to meet their increasing expenses since they had recently purchased a ski lodge condo.

These events served to fuel an already chronic, incendiary relationship marked by periods of sharp verbal exchange followed by the same "cold shoulder" treatment or "stonewalling" (Gottman, 1994) they had noted in their parents' relationships. Although they have never seriously considered separation or divorce—"our religion doesn't permit it"— they noted a decline in sexual relations since the baby was born. Last year Dale complained he had "lost all interest, because I'm too tired and stressed out."

Dale's corporation was recently involved in a hostile takeover, and he has spent considerable time and effort making the merger work. It has been considerably stressful for him because of the increasing travel demands and the fact that he has much less time to play golf and ski with his buddies.

When Dale was transferred after they were married, Claire had to leave behind the support network of friends she had been a part of since college. Except for one unmarried woman in the firm, Claire has not had or taken the time to develop other friendships.

After two sessions of comprehensive assessments had been completed, issues of power inequality, gender stereotyping, and inhibited sexual desire were prominent. The results of FACES-III (Olson, Portner, & Labee, 1985) confirmed the therapist's impression of low marital cohesion and adaptability with unclear boundaries. The negative effect of Claire's mother was obvious to the couple. The Millon Clinical Multiaxial Inventory-II (MCMI-II) showed elevations on the narcissistic and obsessive-compulsive scales for Dale and histrionic elevations for Claire. Although both were quite successful in their careers, skills of communication, negotiation, encouragement, conflict resolution, and empathy were not evident in their relationship, although the time management skills seemed adequate. Although Dale's support network was adequate, Claire's was not. Also, Claire experienced considerable couple and career asynchronism, which she experienced as a moderate stressor.

Because of the chronicity of their presenting concerns, the couple met criteria for level-three marital discord (Guerin et al., 1987). Blaming and projection were common and reflected both their hostility and increasing hopelessness (Gottman, 1994). Their different personality styles, lack of relational skills, and issues regarding power, boundary, and intimacy led to their ongoing conflict and inability to resolve their differences. Given their relatively strong motivation to make changes and a commitment to stay together, their prognosis appeared favorable. The relevant goals were mutually negotiated to increase the likelihood that the couple would assume ownership and be more motivated and adherent to the treatment process. The treatment goals were as follows:

- Reduce the present level of conflict and distress
- Establish clearer boundaries regarding careers and families of origin
- Establish a more equitable relationship and increased gender sensitivity
- Develop more effective relationship skills regarding communication, conflict resolution, negotiation, empathy, encouragement, and time management
- Increase the understanding of individual and couple dynamics

- Assist Claire in better understanding and resolving her career and family asynchronism

These six goals were stated in the developmental order in which they would be addressed therapeutically; that is, symptom relief and boundary restructuring would be a prerequisite for working on equity and gender sensitivity along with skill building, which would be followed by insight and awareness. (L' Abate [1986] advocates such a sequential process of marital and family interventions.) Based on the assessment dimensions of situation/severity, systems, skills, and support networks, three therapeutic strategies were matched. The interpersonal-systems strategy would be employed to achieve the first three goals. A psychoeducational strategy was planned for the fourth goal, while a psychodynamic strategy was envisioned for the fifth and sixth goals. Tailoring treatment was based on the dimensions of style, synchronism, and suitability for treatment. Because the couple had high levels of task readiness, a commitment to the marriage, and motivation for treatment, it was assumed that the therapist would easily form a therapeutic alliance. Anticipating that the alliance would be collaborative and that the therapist would probably encounter minimal resistance to symptom reduction, boundary issues, and skill training, an active, albeit supportive, therapist style would be well tolerated.

Tailoring with regard to the psychoeducational strategy was manifested by considerable in-session modeling of effective communication, conflict resolution, and negotiation skills, given the couple's incendiary style, family history, and limited success in this area. It would have been inappropriate to simply prescribe workbook exercises to learn these skills, which would have been possible with some other couples. For this reason, the use of a co-therapist was necessary in this case. Both therapists could model and enact potentially conflictual situations for the couple to observe, discuss, and then role play. Similarly, because both spouses reflected cultural gender stereotyping in which histrionic behavior in females has been considered feminine and obsessive-compulsive behavior in males tends to be rewarded professionally, more androgynous co-therapist interaction could greatly enhance the efforts to increase gender sensitivity.

Because of Dale's empathic deficits, reflective of his narcissistic personality style, the therapist used mirroring as well as empathy training. However, the therapist's use of encouragement through reframing and stroking was necessary for both spouses, given their narcissistic and histrionic styles.

As anticipated, the treatment process eventually became a collaborative endeavor, but not until they were able to reduce their hurtful, incendiary communication and establish reasonable boundaries involving their job and family demands. Surprisingly, they responded quickly to skill-building tasks and other psychoeducational interventions. By the eighth session, they met the first four treatment goals and stabilized their relational system.

The next 12 sessions primarily focused on individual and family-of-origin dynamics that Claire and Dale brought to their marriage. During this time, relapse prevention strategies were introduced. The last session reviewed their progress and current level of functioning. Both agreed they were less stressed and much happier about their relationship and career. Dale recognized the need for additional work on issues of entitlement and blame. Subsequently, he continued for six additional individual sessions with the therapist.

THERAPEUTIC INTERVENTION WITH THE SINGLE, WORKING PARENT

Therapeutic work with the working, single parent who has child custody can be considerably challenging. In addition to the unique system stressors of the single-parent family, the therapist must account for the job component and its unique stresses and challenges. This section briefly describes some treatment strategies and resources.

Initially, the therapist must remain mindful of the psychological presence of the absent parent, as this individual probably exerts considerable influence on the therapist–family dynamics. The therapist must assess the manner in which single parenthood occurred, including the ages of children and the stage of the marriage in which the death, divorce, or desertion occurred.

Second, the therapist must assess the family structure, including boundaries and coalitions, particularly observing for the presence of a parentified child. An assessment also includes the type of work, stressors, child care plan, and the type and quality of the support network the working parent has both on and off the job. Particularly, attention should be focused on the relationship the working parent has with job supervisors and on work–family policies at the place of employment, such as schedule flexibility, child care, leave, absenteeism, and personal time.

Third, the therapist begins to assist the family in thinking of themselves in systems terms, as this can facilitate a later intervention aimed at changes in both family structure and work relations. Generally, the therapist begins with strengthening the executive function of the parent and restructuring the system so that the child or children assume some responsibility for supportive tasks. Because support systems are critical to the single-parent family, the therapist encourages the parent to develop and/or strengthen support on the job, in the community, and from relatives if possible.

Fourth, often single parents will need to develop parenting skills to remediate specific family concerns. The single parent may also need to develop a number of additional self-management and self-care skills to better cope with day-to-day realities.

Fifth, the "fit" between the single parent and her or his job may need attention. A poor fit may be the source of considerable stress because of role ambiguity, role conflict, role overload, or spillover into the family. The therapist's knowledge of career-counseling methods and strategies can be quite useful in such situations. Although Burden (1986) ruled that single, female parent employees functioned at high levels, she believed they do so at great expense to their physical and psychological well-being. Thus, the therapist must assist the working parent in inventorying her work–family stressors along with her personal and corporate coping resources. They must also decide on whether more self-management or self-care skills must be acquired or if a job change might be necessary.

Although few resources focus on working with single parents, what is available is excellent. Michaels and McCarty (1992), for instance, focused specifically on the working, single parent. They suggested eight critical areas that should be considered: (a) evaluating and reevaluating one's job and career, (b) building effective support networks, (c) dealing with depression, (d) acquiring needed life-management skills (that is, delegating, planning, priorities, and so on), (e) developing self-care skills, (f) finding and keeping appropriate child care, (g) getting sufficient sleep, and (h) financial planning.

SUMMARY

This chapter has reviewed a wide variety of treatment strategies germane to work–family problems and concerns, particularly those of the dual-career couple and the working, single-parent family. The detailed case example illustrated a method of matching and tailoring treatment based on a comprehensive, integrative assessment. The reader should note that the published literature on counseling and consulting with families and couples on work–family issues is steadily increasing, but it is relatively small in comparison with general marital and family therapy literature. As those who teach, supervise, research, and practice family therapy continue to respond to the changing portrait of the American family, particularly regarding the work–family connection, our therapeutic expertise should correspondingly increase.

References

Bennett, A. (1990). *The death of the organization man.* New York: William Morrow.

Burden, D. (1986). Single parents and the work setting: The impact of multiple job and homelife responsibilities. *Family Relations, 35,* 37–43.

Cole, P. (1992). Family systems business: A merger at last. *Family Therapy News, 23*(2), 29.

Conger, R., Elder, G., Lorenz, F., Conger, K., Simans, R. L., Whitbeck, L. B., et al. (1990). Linking economic hardships to marital quality and stability. *Journal of Marriage and the Family, 52,* 643–656.

Cook, E. P., Heppner, M. J., & O'Brien, K. M. (2002). Career development of women of color and white women: Assumptions, conceptualization, and interventions from an ecological perspective. *Career Development Quarterly, 50,* 291–305.

Coontz, S. (2000). The changing family: History and politics. In M. Hutter (Ed.), *The family experience: A reader in cultural diversity* (pp. 13–19). Boston: Allyn & Bacon.

Gilbert, L., & Rachlin, V. (1987). Mental health and psychological functioning of dual-career families. *The Counseling Psychologist, 15*(1), 7–49.

Gladding, S. T. (1998). *Family therapy: History, theory, and practice.* (2nd ed.). Upper Saddle River, NJ: Merrill.

Glickhauf–Hughes, C., Hughes, G., & Wells, M. (1986). A developmental approach to treating dual-career couples. *American Journal of Family Therapy, 14*(3), 254–263.

Goldenberg, H. (1986). Treating contemporary couples in dual-career relationships. *Family Therapy Today, 1,* 1–7.

Goldenberg, I., & Goldenberg, H. (1984). Treating the dual-career couple. *American Journal of Family Therapy, 12,* 29–37.

Googins, B. (1991). *Work/family conflicts: Private lives—public responses.* New York: Arburn House.

Gottman, J. (1994). *Why marriages succeed or fail.* New York: Simon & Shuster.

Greenhaus, J. (1987). *Career management.* Chicago: Dryden Press.

Greenhaus, J., & Beutell, N. (1985). Sources of conflict between work and family roles. *Academy of Management Review, 10,* 76–88.

Greenhaus, J., Parasuraman, S., Granrose, C., Rabinowitz, S., & Beutell, N. J. (1989). Sources of work family conflict among two-career couples. *Journal of Vocational Behavior, 34,* 133–153.

Guerin, P., Fay, L., Burden, S., & Kuetto, J. (1987). *The evaluation and treatment of marital conflict: A four-stage approach.* New York: Basic Books.

Jordan, C., Cobb, N., & McCully, R. (1989). Clinical issues of the dual-career couple. *Social Work, 34*(1), 29–32.

King, A., & Winnett, R. (1986). Tailoring stress-reduction strategies to populations at risk: Comparison between women from dual-career and dual-worker families. *Family and Community Health, 9*(3), 42–50.

L'Abate, L. (1986). *Systematic family therapy.* New York: Brunner/Mazel.

Lazarus, A. (1981). *The practice of multimodal therapy.* New York: McGraw-Hill.

Lorenz, F., Conger, R., Simon, R., Whitbeck, L., & Elder, G. (1991). Economics pressure and marital quality. *Journal of Marriage and the Family, 53,* 375–388.

Michaels, B., & McCarty, E. (1992). *Solving the work/family puzzle*. Homewood, IL: Business One Irwin.

Myers, P. (1992). Using adaptive counseling and therapy to tailor treatment to couples and families. *Topics in Family Psychology and Counseling, 1*(3), 56–70.

Olson, D., Portner, J., & Labee, Y. (1985). *FACES-III*. St. Paul, MN: University of Minnesota, Family Social Sciences.

Prochaska, J., & Prochaska, J. (1982). Dual-career families are a new challenge for spouses and agencies. *Social Casework, 63,* 118–120.

Rice, D. (1979). *Dual-career marriage: Conflict and treatment*. New York: Free Press.

Sekaran, U. (1986). *Dual-career families*. San Francisco: Jossey–Bass.

Sekaran, U., & Hall, D. (1989). A synchronism in dual-career and family linkages. In M. Arthur, D. Hall, & B. Lawrence (Eds.), *Handbook of Career Theory* (pp. 159–180). Cambridge: Cambridge University Press.

Shaevitz, M., & Shaevitz, H. (1980). *Making it together as a two-career couple*. Boston: Houghton-Mifflin.

Sperry, L. (1993). *Psychiatric consultation in the workplace*. Washington, DC: American Psychiatric Press.

Stoltz–Loike, M. (1992). *Dual-career couples: New perspectives in counseling*. Alexandria, VA: American Association for Counseling and Development.

Vanderkolk, B., & Young, A. (1991). *The work and family revolution*. New York: Facts on File.

Weltner, J. (1985). Matchmaking: Choosing the appropriate therapy for families at various levels of pathology. In M. Mirkin & S. Koman (Eds.), *Handbook of adolescents and family therapy* (pp. 237–246). New York: Gardner.

Worthington, E. (1989). Matching family treatment to family stressors. In C. Figley (Ed.), *Treating stress in families* (pp. 44–63). New York: Brunner/Mazel.

9

TREATMENT ADHERENCE
AND RELAPSE PREVENTION
Ensuring Therapeutic Results

Therapists are traditionally trained to identify, diagnose, and remediate the full spectrum of psychopathology (Sperry & Carlson, 1996). Although therapists are initially successful in helping couples and families improve their status, follow-up research shows that these gains seldom maintain themselves (Gottman, 1994b; Jacobson, 1989; Jacobson, Schmaling, & Holtzworth–Munroe, 1987; Snyder, 1999). The degree to which a couple or family follows through with (or adheres to) the planned treatment change process is very low. Failure to adhere is a major obstacle to a successful change, although therapists often deny or are very surprised that it is so common.

Therapists have extensive training in frontloading the helping process by putting all their resources into identification, diagnosis, and remediation, and very little into treatment adherence and relapse prevention (RP). Thus, it is necessary for therapists to have a clear conception not only of how to help distressed couples and families learn to function more effectively but also of how to maintain those gains once they are reached. It is becoming increasingly obvious that termination should not imply an end to treatment as much as it should a change in treatment intensity.

A great challenge for therapists is to gain the ability to predict therapeutic success and maintenance. Some treatments are likely to have long-term effectiveness, whereas others are probably temporary at best. What can therapists do to change the therapeutic conditions in order to increase long-term treatment success and prevent a return or relapse to previous levels of dysfunction? How long do effects last after a successful intervention? What percentage of couples/families relapse after a successful intervention? What distinguishes those who maintain treatment gains from those who relapse? What causes or creates a relapse? Can a relapse be prevented or minimized? This chapter will answer these and other questions in describing how treatment adherence and RP principles can be used with couples and families. It is hoped that the professional community will begin to understand the importance of these concepts as both research and clinical issues.

TREATMENT ADHERENCE

No one set of adherence-enhancement procedures will be successful across populations. More than 20 years ago, Epstein and Masek (1978) catalogued more than 30 different techniques designed to increase medical patient adherence. Some examples of the techniques that we have found helpful are as follows:

- Provide specific appointment times.
- Use reminders (mail or telephone).
- Elicit and discuss reasons for previously missed appointments.
- Involve family/couple in planning and implementing the treatment program.
- Tailor treatment plan.
- Simplify treatment directives.
- Use psychoeducation and check for comprehension.
- Anticipate side effects.
- Process any negative feedback.
- Teach self-management skills.
- Use a graduated regimen implementation.
- Involve significant others.
- Use role-playing and paradoxical techniques when appropriate.
- Use a combination of approaches rather than single strategies.

We have found that it is essential to diagnose and assess each instance of nonadherence, be flexible, and tailor procedures to the specific circumstances and characteristics of the family/couple. For example, a couple came back after 1 week, indicating that the assigned homework of conducting a daily 10-minute dialogue was completed on only 1 day. The couple was asked to discuss why the assignment had not been completed, and after each person gave his or her explanation a more detailed assignment was developed. A specific time was established, and a modified plan to meet every other day was agreed to. The couple was willing to conduct the activity, but they needed assistance in changing present behavioral patterns.

TREATMENT ADHERENCE GUIDELINES

As we have previously discussed, the therapist needs to begin the treatment process with a comprehensive assessment. He or she not only needs to diagnose the family/couple's clinical condition but also to diagnose or assess the chances and reasons for nonadherence. The therapist must assess the family's adherence history, relationship beliefs, expectations, and possible obstacles to adherence. Once this has taken place, the following guidelines (adapted from Meichenbaum & Turk, 1987) will be useful.

Anticipate Nonadherence

Therapists must think about adherence at the beginning of treatment, often when information is provided by the referral source. The therapist must carefully weigh all data provided, especially those about treatment, the duration of the problem, the locus of responsibility, and the extent of the problem. Many clients are confused and misinformed about the process of marriage and family therapy (that is, who does what). It is usually helpful to begin therapy by asking the following questions:

- Why have they come to treatment?
- What have they heard or been told about treatment?
- What do they expect to happen during treatment?
- What will be different after treatment?

The therapist also needs to assess factors that may facilitate or impede treatment, such as rapport, the readiness to learn or change, and the willingness to accept responsibility.

Specifically, therapists need to assess factors such as

- The family's expectation for treatment (If treatment is successful, how will you know? What will be different?)

- The beliefs and misconceptions about the cause, severity, and symptoms of the problem (Would you each give your explanation of the problem and describe how your believe it can be changed?)
- The goals of treatment (What do you want to accomplish in therapy?)
- The family's commitment to treatment, or how badly they want to change (On a scale of 1 to 10, with 1 being low and 10 high, how important is it to you that change occurs?)
- The present level of skills
- The sense of helplessness and hopelessness versus resourcefulness and self-efficacy (How optimistic are you that the situation can be changed? Give a ranking on the 1 to 10 scale; have you ever brought about change in other aspects of your or your family's live?)
- Educational or physical limitations
- The life circumstances that may affect adherence, that is, limited time and limited financial resources (What are some things that might get in the way of successful change?)

The preceding information is usually gathered directly using questions similar to the examples or indirectly in the initial interview. The information is used in tailoring the approach to deal with possible adherence problems. The therapist who anticipates nonadherence can usually make the corrections necessary to maximize treatment adherence.

Consider Treatment from the Family's Perspective

The therapist should not assume that his or her perceptions of events are the same as the family's. Families come into treatment with certain attitudes, beliefs, expectations, and resources. The therapist should essentially *join* the family (Minuchin, 1974). In this process, the therapist adjusts to the communication style and perceptions of the family.

Certain aspects of personality style conviction guide a family or couple's behaviors and habits. These beliefs form an explanatory model that aids the family in making sense of problems and events: how they respond, how they describe events, and how they cope with situations. This model also gives an insight into the family's expectations for treatment, the outcome, and the level of participation. The therapist must understand the family's explanatory model in order to develop a lasting intervention.

Additionally, the therapist must realize that families have other commitments, demands, and life circumstances that may make the problem easier to maintain or support than its solutions. Families live and have their problems supported within a social network. It *cannot* be assumed that just because someone has a problem and brings it to a therapist that they will adhere to the change.

Facilitate a Collaborative Relationship Based on Negotiation

A wise therapist knows how to avoid resistance by involving the family in the decisional process regarding their treatment: "An acceptable treatment plan that is carried out appropriately is much better than an ideal one that is ignored." The therapist must be willing to negotiate within reason.

The therapist must use the family's words, ideas, and explanatory model in developing a treatment plan. The plan should flow from the family, and the therapist should use statements such as "It sounds like you all want to . . . " or "It looks like you want this to happen in this way . . . " or "All of you seem to be in touch with the need to . . . ."

Be Family-Oriented (Understand the Family's Views/Explanatory Model)

What are the family's views, expectations, and knowledge concerning the problem? Do they believe they can successfully adhere to the treatment? Do they think the treatment will actually work? How important do they feel the treatment is? What barriers does the family envision will prevent or impede a successful treatment? What does the family believe can be done to make adherence easier?

It is important to listen not only to what the family says but also to what they fail to say. The failure of the family to answer certain questions usually indicates they are not collaborating and will not follow the treatment plan.

Tailor Treatment

As we have discussed throughout this book, no standard treatment exists for any couple or family. In considering a set of treatment recommendations, the therapist must consider, adjust, and modify treatment to fit each family.

As a general rule, treatment plans should be effective, simple, and convenient. They produce the fewest side effects and require the least interference with normal daily activities. Whenever possible, connect adherence behavior to normal daily routines such as meals, bedtime, time of awakening, and so on. Families will need assistance when integrating new demands into their daily routine. For example, a suggestion of talking for 10 minutes each night at bedtime is more likely to be adhered to than talking during the day.

Enlist Family Support

Generally, it is useful to make sure that family and other significant people understand the treatment plan and goals in order to be allies. Therapists need to keep making statements such as "Tell me again what you believe needs to be done and what exactly you are working on."

Provide a System of Continuity and Accessibility

Families need to know that the therapist views the treatment process as lifelong and is therefore accessible at various stages in the family or couple's life cycle. The therapist needs to be an ally who is accessible, nonjudgmental, respectful, and sincere in the willingness to cooperate with the family or couple. The open-ended therapy model (Lebow, 1995) sees the clients making use of treatment at various times in the cycle.

Don't Give up

Many therapists write off nonadherence to system resistance. This allows them to blame the family or couple and excuse themselves of any responsibility. However, skilled therapists must navigate the waters of resistance and develop tailored treatment plans. A well-designed plan will create cooperation and treatment adherence. It is this challenge that makes working with couples and families so rewarding.

WHAT IS RELAPSE PREVENTION (RP)?

RP is a self-control program designed to teach couples and families that are trying to change their behavior how to anticipate and cope with the problem of relapse. In a very real sense, relapse refers to a breakdown or failure in a system's attempt to change or modify behaviors and adhere to treatment. Traditionally based on the principles of social-learning theory (Bandura, 1977), RP is a psychoeducational program that combines behavioral skill-training procedures and cognitive intervention techniques with systems thinking.

The RP model was initially developed as a behavioral maintenance program for use in the treatment of addictive behaviors (Marlatt & Gordon, 1985). In the case of addiction, the typical goals of treatment are either to refrain totally from performing a target behavior (for example, to abstain from drug use) or to impose regulatory limits or controls over the occurrence of a behavior (for instance, to use diet as a means of controlling food intake).

The concept of RP has become a central focus of research and practice in health psychology and behavioral medicine. Because nonadherence, previously called noncompliance, with treatment is so high, ranging from 30% to 80% (Sperry, 1986), clinicians have sought ways to reverse this phenomenon. At the most general level, relapse is the return of a problem behavior following a problem-free period.

The recent *Webster's New Collegiate Dictionary* refers to relapse as both an outcome and a process. The *outcome* is reflected in the use of the term "relapse" to denote "a recurrence of symptoms of a disease after a period of improvement," and the *process* is captured in the phrase "the act or instance of backsliding, worsening, or subsiding." The process implies that something has occurred that may or may not lead to a full relapse.

Whether the process or outcome definition of relapse is chosen has obvious implications for the conceptualization, prevention, and treatment of a relapse. Viewing a relapse as a process and not an outcome implies that the therapist and family can intervene at choice points in the process (Ludgate, 1995). Marlatt and Gordon (1985) distinguished between "lapse" and "relapse," arguing that a lapse implies a temporary state of affairs that might, under some circumstances, lead to a relapse. How a family responds to an initial lapse will determine whether a full relapse will occur. It is generally conceded that the prediction and prevention of relapses is desirable because the continuation of behavioral problems may reduce a family's quality of life and place limitations on their successful pursuit of goals. The understanding of a relapse and the RP program can be used to ensure treatment adherence.

RP Research

Unfortunately, most research studies have been designed to measure the outcome of treatment rather than long-term maintenance or effectiveness. The identification of RP properties in treatment is usually post hoc rather than a part of the original research plans. However, some research can be useful in helping to understand the importance of RP. Research by Bogner and Zielenbach–Coenen (1984) demonstrated that lengthening the intervals between the final therapy sessions facilitates a couple's ability to benefit from marital therapy initially and in the long term.

Whisman (1991) investigated the effectiveness of booster sessions on RP. This research used two mandatory booster sessions at 3 and 6 months after therapy and three optional sessions during the same 6-month period. The results were not statistically significant. However, these findings seem to suggest that booster sessions deserve further attention and refinement; however, they do not unequivocally support booster sessions' efficacy. Whisman, however, outlined several ways the efficacy of booster sessions could have been improved, including using an experienced therapist, improving the booster session content, scheduling additional booster sessions during the first three post-therapy months, and extending the length of the maintenance component.

Truax and Jacobson (1992) felt that, although no treatment differences can be supported at this time by research, some treatment characteristics appear to emerge. These characteristics seem to support the use of matched and tailored treatment. The use of the traditional one-size-fits-all therapy does not seem to be supported by long-term maintenance assessments. The following are the treatment characteristics that emerged in their research.

Flexibility in Treatment Content   Despite many common themes among couples and families, each is unique. The treatment must therefore be carefully tailored. The content of therapy may focus on thoughts, behavior, feelings, the past, the present, the future, and so forth.

Flexibility in Treatment Format   Therapists need to structure the length and spacing of sessions according to the interaction and purpose of the therapy. For example, traditional 1-hour weekly sessions seldom work during the initial sessions of family therapy or when skill training is needed.

Identifying and Modifying Salient Behaviors (Overt, Emotional, Cognitive)   It is important to gather a complete picture of the couple's functioning. Often therapists and families stop treatment after the presenting problem disappears only to resume treatment after a short passage of time.

Focusing on Reasonably Changeable Behaviors   Many behavioral changes may temporarily improve couple or family satisfaction, but it is unlikely that they all can be maintained. It is important, however, to focus on the ones that can be. For example, if a couple is guided to an interaction that leads to an increased understanding and a spontaneous hug, this interaction is most likely to be repeated.

Effectively Generalizing from Therapy to the Client's World   This is perhaps the greatest challenge to RP. In addition to the tailoring ideas discussed in this book, the therapist must be able to design interventions that facilitate generalization from the therapeutic environment to the daily life of the couple or family. Several steps have been recommended by Truax and Jacobson (1992) to improve generalization:

- Maximizing the couple's natural reinforcement potential
- Assigning homework throughout therapy
- Lengthening intervals between final sessions
- Including booster sessions
- Predicting stressful life events (1992, p. 315)

WHY COUPLES OR FAMILIES RELAPSE

Essentially, couples and families relapse because they are supposed to. Seldom does behavior permanently change so that former behaviors never occur. However, a relapse has often been seen as synonymous with treatment failure, a return to a previous behavior after a period of gain or change, and it is often viewed as an end state. This all-or-nothing perception fails to take into account that a relapse is a common component of an effective change. Mistakes and lapses are "human" and common in the change process. By allowing room in the treatment process for mistakes (relapses) to occur, it is possible to avoid what has been called the *oscillation effect*, whereby a system is either in control or out of control. When a relapse is expected and planned for, the affective and cognitive reactions to a slip become significantly less intense, and the treatment program can be quickly reinstated. The length of the relapse period often depends on the personal expectations of the people involved. So rather than a relapse being a dead end, it becomes a fork in the road with one path moving toward the old patterns and the other to new ones.

Many people believe that quitting a pattern of behavior has to be all or nothing. Once a mistake has occurred, they believe it is for all time and that the intervention did not work. Many attribute the cause of a relapse to a personal or family weakness or failure, such as the lack of will power, a weakness of character, or a problematic family composition, rather than to the difficulty of the task and the predictability of slips occurring during the course of change. The belief that "total control is the only control" needs to be challenged. People need to be taught how to view change on a continuum that includes where they are and where they hope to be.

The therapist must be aware that the combination of high-risk situations with no coping responses and negative expectancies increases the likelihood that a relapse will occur. High-risk situations pose a threat to the system's sense of self-control and increase the risk of a potential relapse. The three most common high-risk categories associated with a high relapse rate (Marlatt & Gordon, 1985) are (a) a negative emotional state, (b) interpersonal conflict, and (c) social pressure. To this list we might add (d) highly charged anniversary dates. It is often helpful to work with couples and families to plan responses to these challenging situations. A simple discussion and the ability to be aware of high-risk situations are simple yet effective procedures.

If couples and families are taught a coping response in these high-risk situations, the likelihood of a relapse can be decreased. This results in developing a feeling of control or mastery similar to the concept of self-efficacy (Bandura, 1977). The couple or family thereby develops feelings of confidence and knowledge that they can handle life's problems. Bandura's research indicates that if someone is successful in coping in one situation, this increases the likelihood that he or she will be successful in another.

The family's belief or expectation that a relapse will occur seems to be a powerful predictor of relapse. Thus, successful RP needs to address the belief structure of the family. Negative expectancies must be replaced with positive ones that serve as compelling goals. It is important to offer a new story or metaphor for the family that will prevent relapses (O'Hanlon, 1994).

Relapse Prevention (RP)

RP is an intervention consisting of specific skills and cognitive strategies that prepare clients in advance to cope with inevitable slips or relapses in compliance with a change program (Marlatt & Gordon, 1985). Although the early work on RP was developed in alcohol and drug treatment programs in which relapses and returns to addictive substances were very high, RP principles have been applied to smoking cessation, pain control, weight management, sleep disorders, exercise adherence, and other health-promotion areas (Lewis, Sperry, Carlson, & Englar–Carlson, 2005.) With the possible exceptions of Jacobson and Holtzworth–Munroe (1986) and Truax and Jacobson (1992), RP has not been introduced into the family therapy literature.

Daley (1989) described five different RP models, of which Marlatt and Gordon's (1985) is the most well known and researched. This cognitive–behavioral model emphasizes the following points:

- Identification of individual high-risk situations
- Development of coping skills for high-risk situations
- Practice in coping with potential lapses
- Development of cognitive coping strategies for use immediately after relapse

Marlatt noted that the majority of relapses in adults occurs in response to stressful situations involving conflict or social pressure. He stressed that reframing the relapse as a mistake rather than a factual error or moral shortcoming is an important preventive measure that can help the individual get back on track and learn from the experience. RP helps the individual apply the brakes so that once a slip occurs it does not escalate into a full-blown relapse.

Wilson (1992) identified several different types of RP strategies that have been developed and evaluated to varying degrees with different types of problem behaviors. The techniques include:

- Booster sessions
- Treatment programs with RP strategies integrated into the initial treatment
- Procedures that require minimal therapist contact, such as periodic reminder letters (White & Epston, 1990), telephone calls, or the provision of therapy-related reading materials

Problem behaviors are explained as a series of acquired habit patterns governed by cognitive and experiential processes in which antecedent events, beliefs and expectations, learning history, and behavioral consequences play important roles. The maintenance stage of intervention must be considered as a period in which an opportunity exists for new learning to occur as the family or couple is faced with situations, events, moods, and beliefs that might increase the risk of returning to previously ineffective behavioral patterns.

According to Wilson (1992), a relapse may occur because of a failure at any time between initial treatment and maintenance, and an effective treatment may not necessarily lead to perceived control or enhanced self-efficacy. Clients may fail to recognize and respond appropriately to high-risk situations. They may fail to develop adequate coping responses and may still have negative outcome expectancies about the use of effective strategies in future situations. Clients may use ineffective responses, or they may have positive expectancies about the effects of old coping strategies that in reality have failed in the past.

A major component of the RP program is the identification of high-risk situations for self-monitoring, self-efficacy ratings, and a detailed analysis of past relapse episodes. These activities aim to increase the therapist's knowledge of factors that might lead to a relapse and to increase the family's awareness of how these factors operate.

Throughout family therapy, applying therapy to daily life is facilitated through weekly homework assignments and easing out of therapist reinforcement by increasingly drawing attention to natural reinforces within the family. By tailoring treatment, the therapist can use homework assignments that are unique to each family. To increase the likelihood that families will continue active problem solving, the therapist must find a format that incorporates the family's natural problem-solving style. For example, some families can be initially instructed to note problems for family meetings by jotting them down on a list that is kept in an accessible place in the home. Other families, however, may find it uncomfortable to wait, and they will want to solve problems on the spot. Thus, it is important for the therapist to identify procedures a family can easily use. Again, the success of therapy seems to be related to the careful analysis and tailoring of treatment.

Change in Treatment Focus

Traditional therapy strategies are much more effective at reducing negative behaviors than at increasing positive ones. Research continues to show that the differences between distressed and nondistressed families is that distressed ones engage in more negative behaviors, whereas nondistressed families exhibit more positive behaviors. Although these findings are not surprising, they do suggest a simple reduction of negative behaviors without an increase in positive ones is probably not sufficient to help distressed couples and families be genuinely happy.

Certain researchers (Baucom & Hoffman, 1986; Gottman, 1994a; Truax & Jacobson, 1992) believe that the identification and creation of positive intimate experiences can improve therapy's durability. Unfortunately, most therapy seems to be focused on the elimination of negative behaviors. This has the effect of making couples or families into better friends but not necessarily better spouses or family members.

The communication skills that are taught are generally aimed at problem solving. Thus, a number of destructive forms of communication that interfere with the process often tend to be emphasized. To have meaning, many positive communications must be spontaneous, emerging from the person's internal thoughts and feelings about the partner or the topic at hand (Baucom & Hoffman, 1986, p. 600). Therefore, by focusing on increasing positive behaviors, families and couples can learn to define progress based on realistic goals. It may also be wise to help clients use the problem-solving process to become more intimate with one another rather than using it to solve problems themselves (which are often not reasonably solvable).

Determining an operational definition of intimacy and positive communication is difficult. Generally, intimacy and positive communication refer to knowing and being known by another person. Skinner (1974) indicated that the extent to which someone is known is synonymous with the extent to which his or her behavior can be predicted. Therefore, a primary goal of intimate interventions is to help clients create a context in which they will be likely to get into contact with the reinforcing feelings of the mutual knowledge of one another. Therefore, the goals are to increase the expression of internal experiences and to encourage this expression. This involves clients learning how to express as well as accept emotions. Truax and Jacobson (1992) felt that specific interventions are needed to help couples increase their intimate behaviors:

- Providing directives about how to behave more intimately
- Making suggestions about how to express internal experiences that may have never been aired
- Reminding the couple of the positive feelings derived from their behavioral differences
- Emphasizing behavioral sequences that exemplify how the relationship benefits from their difference
- Pointing out that behavioral differences are a result of different learning histories rather than something each does to the other
- Educating the couple on how expressing and listening to one another's internal experiences will be mutually reinforcing
- Helping the couple understand that the interactions that promote intimacy may have more reinforcement potential than actually solving the problem (1992, pp. 298–299)

In addition, if marital and family success is based on huge individual compromises and changes, relapse is much more likely. A focus on marriage and family satisfaction to the exclusion of individual well-being may also obscure potentially important differences. It is perhaps most important to help families and couples learn to appreciate differences than to make large behavioral changes.

Whisman (1991) conducted research that seems to support the notion that a couple's or family's ability to maintain therapeutic gains may well be affected by the discrepancy between their satisfaction levels. Thus, one must focus attention on reasonable and maintainable behavioral changes. Unfortunately, therapists often bite off more than they can chew. When clients attempt to resolve conflicts that are not solvable, they may become more deeply entrenched in helplessness. It is often more helpful for the therapist to first focus on helping clients understand one another's internal experiences without rushing to a conclusion. Therapists also need to pay special attention to behaviors that are naturally reinforcing both in and out of sessions for families.

A typical response to a relapse is to increase the number of treatment interventions in order to create a more comprehensive, broad-based package. This response seems to be based on the belief that "more is better:" the more treatment components, the longer the results will last. However, evidence suggests that the more techniques and procedures are applied, the more difficult it becomes to maintain compliance. In addition, it seems that most intervention techniques are aimed at an *initial* behavior change and not at the *maintenance* of the changed behavior. One of the main differences between initial and maintenance procedures is that the therapist usually administers the initial techniques, whereas the maintenance procedures are mostly self-administered. An obvious exception to this distinction is the use of booster sessions, which will be described later.

Open-Ended Couple–Family Therapy

A useful perspective for therapists is to think in terms of treating couples and families over a lifetime. The likelihood of one set of meetings putting a permanent end to problems throughout a life span is not great. It's much more helpful to view problems as occurring at different points in the life span and seeing couple–family therapy as a resource that can be used to resolve these difficulties. The therapist therefore becomes a resource, similar to the family doctor. Regarding therapy in this way establishes a direct manner of dealing with the deterioration that seems to occur after successful marital and family therapy.

At the beginning of therapy, the therapist presents the notion of termination of treatment with an open-ended viewpoint. He or she discusses the benefits of having a planned termination, but he or she also discusses the value of ongoing involvement. Working toward termination occurs throughout the therapeutic meetings.

Lebow (1995) highlighted 10 tasks that are central to ending most family therapy:

- **Tracking progress in therapy to determine the appropriateness of ending.** This task involves a regular assessment of how the family/couple is progressing toward treatment goals.
- **Reviewing the course of treatment.** The therapist provides time for the family/couple to review the changes and events that occurred in the treatment process.
- **Emphasizing the gains made and the client's role in these gains.** Often clients do not fully understand the extent of change or their role in how change occurred. It is important to help the couple or family realize the sense of competence and confidence that can occur by understanding one's role in successful change.
- **Abstracting what has been learned from treatment and how it may be applied later.** The therapist helps the family and couple understand the behavioral, affective, and cognitive skills that have been developed and how they may be used as future problems occur.
- **Internalizing the therapist.** The family/couple needs to learn how to have the therapist remain with the family, not as an active member or participant in the family but as an internalized member. Family members are often encouraged to develop skills by imagining what the therapist would say or suggest at a particular moment.
- **Regarding the ending through the lens of other endings in life.** Therapists should develop an understanding of each client's unique history of endings. Some families have a difficult time with endings, whereas others find them comfortable
- **Saying goodbye with an opportunity to express gratitude and exchange feelings.**
- **Discussing the conditions for returning to treatment.** Booster sessions may be used to promote the durability of change. These sessions are scheduled at regular intervals to renew skills and insights.
- **Referring.** Sometimes ending work with one therapist opens the door to future work with another, such as moving on to a self-help group or educational class. In some cases, the ending of treatment with one therapist occurs when a referral is made to another professional who has different skills.
- **Defining post-treatment availability.**

STEPS TO RP

RP has many potential applications for marital and family therapy. One of the most obvious involves providing therapy for families in maintenance (that is, open-ended treatment), whereby the therapists will not only predict relapses but preventively intervene by preparing the family for them. Five steps can facilitate RP:

1.) Create a treatment alliance.
2.) Tailor treatment.
3.) Learn to manage stress.
4.) Increase and maintain positive-to-negative interaction ratio.
5.) Provide skill training.

Create a Treatment Alliance

An effective intervention involves engaging couples and families in the therapy process, helping them actively and collaboratively participate through complying with the homework assignments. Success seems to be based on the couple's or family's level of involvement in and adherence to therapy. Researchers consistently discover that the level of client involvement is related to the therapy's outcome (Holtzworth–Munroe, Jacobson, DeKlyen, & Whisman, 1989). Active collaboration in the tasks appropriate to the treatment process may be conceptualized as treatment alliance.

Tailor Treatment

It appears that a high level of involvement needs to be sustained in the family or marriage to produce an effective long-term therapeutic change. How can this level of involvement be maintained to produce a permanent change? As we have pointed out, the ability to engage a family or couple effectively in the therapeutic process depends largely on the therapist's ability to provide highly structured treatments tailored to the needs of particular clients. In addition, as we also mentioned, matching intervention strategies to a particular client is an often-neglected area of treatment. However, it is not surprising that the "one size fits all" therapies are not as durable as those than can directly address each couple's or family's specific concerns. The ability to match and tailor treatment according to how particular clients conceptualize their distress will greatly increase the maintenance of positive behavior.

Although many therapists advocate the ideas of matching and tailoring in theory, practice shows that therapists tend to treat all clients with basically the same methods and approaches. The therapists act as if their ideas and intervention strategies are good for everyone. However, Jacobson, Schmaling, and Holtzworth–Munroe (1987) reported that individual tailoring of treatment plans and the resultant idiographic flexibility can significantly reduce relapse.

Manage Stress

Another important consideration is the need to predict the external stressors on the family. These are often related to stages of marriage or family life and are predictable. Research indicates that booster sessions and training in stress management (Sperry & Carlson, 1994) can be very helpful in this area. However, one should remember that just using booster sessions alone does not appear to be enough to prevent relapse. The therapist should initiate RP programming in the early stages of therapy and maintain it throughout treatment, rather than wait for a re-lapse problem to occur.

Increase and Maintain the Positive-to-Negative Interaction Ratio

Gottman (1994a; 1994b) and Gottman, Driver, and Tabares (2003) con-cluded after extensive research that the ratio of positive-to-negative interactions needed to maintain a functioning marriage or family can be quantified. They found that satisfied couples, no matter how bad their marriages stacked up against the ideal, were those that maintained a 5-to-1 ratio of positive-to-negative moments. The good moments of mutual pleasure, passion, humor, support, kindness, and generosity outweigh the bad moments of complaint, criticism, anger, disgust, con-tempt, defensiveness, and coldness.

Skill Training

Perhaps the most important determinants of relapse are whether or not effective skill training has occurred and whether or not these strategies were tailored to the family in advance of stressful situations. To have strong, effective, and healthy marriages, for example, couples must also have effective marriage skills (Dinkmeyer & Carlson, 2003). The fol-lowing six skills are among the most important to be acquired. They form the basis for all relationships within the marriage:

- Making the relationship a priority
- Communicating regularly
- Practicing encouragement

- Having marriage meetings and choices
- Setting up negotiations, rules, and conflict resolution
- Having regular fun

Couples who learn and practice these skills are able to create and maintain successful relationships.

Carlson and Dinkmeyer (1991) also identified the following traits that contribute to emotional and psychological intimacy in satisfying family relationships:

- Understanding one's self and being willing to share feelings, thoughts, and beliefs in a sensitive manner
- Flexibility and responsibility
- Acceptance of self and partner
- Permanence of the relationship
- Trust
- Ability to negotiate
- Sharing positive feelings

Perhaps the greatest challenge in promoting RP involves designing skills and interventions that facilitate applying the therapy to the family's daily life. Unless each family member becomes self-sufficient and all members are able to reinforce one another, the therapy is likely to fail once the session has ended. As mentioned previously, researchers have established several steps to improve the transition from therapy to home life: (a) maximize the family's natural reinforcement potential, (b) assign homework through therapy, (c) lengthen intervals between final sessions, and (d) predict stressful life events (Truax & Jacobson, 1992).

RP CASE HISTORY

The Shank family presented for treatment after a Thanksgiving celebration resulted in a family feud. Present at the initial session were the parents, Mary and Al, and the children, Rich, 19, Bill, 17, Susan, 15, and Tammy, 11. Apparently, the dinner was ruined for all family members by the constant bickering of the girls and boys. Their battles are described as "frequent" and "cruel."

Session 1

At the initial session, questions were asked to determine the family dynamics. It appears that the family is divided along gender lines with little overlap. This pattern appears long-standing, as both parents report similar dynamics within their families of origin. All family members stated that they wanted the fighting and bickering stopped, but they were not optimistic about whether this could actually occur, because each person believed he or she was not the locus of the problem and was therefore powerless to resolve the problem.

Most family members reported half-hearted attempts in the past to bring about a change. The likelihood of an effective change appeared low and the likelihood of relapse great. The therapist was careful not to own the problem and made it clear that they needed to discover their own resources to change the situation and to learn to help one another. Further questioning made it clear that effective communication, problem solving, and encouragement skills were absent. The family seemed willing to change their responses and agreed to verbally congratulate each family member for a change response at least once before the nest session. This activity was practiced within the session, and a simple encouragement strategy was taught (Dinkmeyer & Carlson, 2003).

Comment   This session began the RP process by empowering the family, tailoring the treatment, offering skill training and practice, and providing a homework assignment. The salient behavior to change was to increase the number of positive exchanges through encouragement. This seemed to be behavior that was reasonably changeable.

Session 2

The entire family returned for the second session. They reported no change in the family dynamics, but they also reported not having done the homework assignment. The therapist asked the family members if they expected relationships to change while they themselves could remain the same. All laughed at this and recommitted to doing the homework in the upcoming week. The therapist asked each family member to encourage the others in the way he or she would have done the previous week. This created a positive exchange, especially when done across the gender line. Considerable joking and anxiety took place as this occurred. The family was asked what needed to occur to make sure the assignment was followed. A discussion took place, and the family agreed to put up a chart for each family member to mark each time she or he encouraged another family member.

Comment   This session involved not overreacting to the homework noncompliance and the family's development of their own monitoring system. Further skill practice also occurred.

Session 3

Only the parents came to this session. A discussion occurred on the gender dichotomy within their families of origin. The couple indicated that this seemed familiar to them, although they did not like it. Each person agreed to write to each of their opposite gender siblings a brief "thinking of you" note. Additionally, they agreed to do one couple activity each week and engage each opposite-gender child in at least 30 minutes of conversation or shared activity during the next week.

Session 4

This session occurred 2 weeks after session 3. The session began by having each family member report what they had done differently during the previous 2 weeks. All seemed willing to share exactly what they had done. Comments were also made as to the decreasing feelings of hostility. The therapist indicated that the family needed to think about what could be done to ensure that these changes were maintained and what should happen if they were not. The family wanted to continue the chart and agreed that any member could call for an unscheduled family therapy session if problems could not be resolved among themselves. The next session was set for 3 weeks.

Comment   The family took an increasing amount of responsibility for themselves. The therapist gradually increased the time between sessions and made the family members more dependent on one another.

Session 5

The family reported a period of " uneventful" activity. All family members had 90% or greater compliance on the chart. There were no presenting problems, and all family members wished to stop treatment; however, they agreed to return at 2-month intervals for the next 6 months.

Comment   The family took responsibility for a change. Each person was performing at a 90% compliance rate, and the family agreed to stop treatment. Booster sessions were scheduled.

Overall, this brief intervention was accomplished by creating a treatment alliance, tailoring treatment, managing stress, increasing the percentage of positive and negative exchanges, and providing skill training.

SUMMARY

Once skills are taught and learned, therapists can develop a follow-up program to monitor families in much the same fashion as automobile and other service contracts are prepared. Of course, we cannot be so bold as to say that families need to come in every 10,000 miles, but it is not unreasonable to think that couples and families can benefit significantly from quarter, semi-annual, or yearly checkups. At these sessions, therapists can make sure that each family is (a) taking time for regular communication, (b) practicing encouragement, (c) setting aside regular time to resolve conflicts, (d) having regularly planned leisure activities, and (e) developing clear plans and methods to ensure the implementation of future activities and time together. By monitoring these checkpoints, it is possible for the family and therapist alike to be able to pinpoint areas that may need further work, just as a mechanic is able to spot carburation, acceleration, or wheel-alignment problems. Research on booster sessions (Whisman, 1991) seems to show a number of advantages to conducting booster sessions, with a gradual decrease of treatment from regular weekly to less frequent visits. Although therapists are not trained to think in this fashion, it may prove to be the most effective solution to the high levels of relapse in marriage and family therapy (Sperry & Carlson, 1991).

Effective marriage and family life is not a privilege but a responsibility. Families, couples, and their therapists need to understand how to create and maintain effective relationships. Traditional methods of helping focus on the front end of change rather than on the maintenance of a successful intervention. We urge therapists who work with families to be aware of the important strategies to prevent a relapse and increase treatment adherence. Again, as a recap:

1.) Engage the family/couple and involve them in homework assignments throughout therapy.
2.) Match strategies to the family's unique needs.
3.) Use booster sessions and planned procedures to handle normal external stress.
4.) Train families in the essential skills.
5.) Gradually increase the time between visits, allowing the family to be gradually less dependent on therapy.

References

Bandura, A. (1977). *Social learning theory.* Englewood Cliffs, NJ: Prentice Hall.

Baucom, D. H., & Hoffman, J. A. (1986). The effectiveness of marital therapy: Current status and application to the clinical setting. In N. S. Jacobson & A. S. Gurman (Eds.), *Clinical handbook of marital therapy* (pp. 597–620).

Bogner, I., & Zielenback–Coenen, H. (1984). On maintaining change in behavioral marital therapy. In K. Hahlweg & N. S. Jacobson (Eds.), *Marital interaction: Analysis and modification* (pp. 27–35). New York: Guilford.

Carlson, J., & Dinkmeyer, D. (1991). *The basics of marriage.* Coral Springs, FL: CMTI Press.

Daley, D. C. (1989). *Relapse prevention: Treatment alternatives and counseling aids.* Blaze Ridge Summit, PA: TAB Books.

Dinkmeyer, D., & Carlson, J. (2003). *Training in marriage enrichment.* Bowling Green, KY: CMTI Press.

Epstein, L. H., & Masek, B. J. (1978). Behavioral control of medicine compliance. *Journal of Applied Behavioral Analysis, 11,* 1–9.

Gottman, J. (1994a). *What predicts divorce: The relationship between marital processes and marital outcomes.* Hillside, NJ: Lawrence Erlbaum Associates.

Gottman, J. (1994b). *Why marriages succeed or fail.* New York: Simon & Schuster.

Gottman, J. M., Driver, J., & Tabares, A. (2003). Building the sound marital house: An empirically derived couple therapy. In A. S. Gurmon & N. S. Jacobson (Eds.), *Clinical handbook of couples therapy* (pp. 373–379). New York: Guilford.

Holtzworth–Munroe, A., Jacobson, N. S., DeKlyen, M., & Whisman, M. A. (1989). Relationship between behavioral marital therapy outcome and process variables. *Journal of Consulting and Clinical Psychology, 57*(5), 658–662.

Jacobson, N. S. (1989). The maintenance of treatment gains following social learning based marital therapy. *Behavior Therapy, 20,* 325–336.

Jacobson, N. S., & Holtzworth–Munroe, A. (1986). Marital therapy: A social learning/cognitive perspective. In N. S. Jacobson & A. S. Gurman (Eds.), *Clinical handbook of marital therapy* (pp. 29–70). New York: Guilford.

Jacobson, N. S., Schmaling, K. B., & Holtzworth–Munroe, A. (1987). Component analysis of behavioral marital therapy: Two-year follow-up and prediction of relapse. *Journal of Marital and Family Therapy, 13,* 187–195.

Lebow, J. (1995). Open-ended therapy: Termination in marital and family therapy. In R. H. Miksell, D. Lusterman, & S. H. McDaniel (Eds.), *Integrating family therapy: Handbook of family psychology and systems theory* (pp. 73–86). Washington, DC: American Psychological Association.

Lewis, J. A., Sperry, L., Carlson, J., & Englar–Carlson, J. M. (2005). *Health promotion and health counseling.* Boston: Allyn & Bacon.

Ludgate, J. W. (1995). *Maximizing psychotherapeutic gains and preventing relapse in emotionally distressed clients.* Sarasota, FL: Professional Resource Press.

Marlatt, G. A., & Gordon, J. R. (1985). *Relapse prevention: Maintenance and strategies in the treatment of addictive behaviors.* New York: Guilford.

Meichenbaum, D., & Turk, D. C. (1987). *Facilitating treatment adherence: A practitioner's guide.* New York: Plenum Press

Minuchin, S. (1974). *Families and family therapy.* Cambridge, MA: Harvard University Press.

O'Hanlon, B. (1994). The third wave. *The Family Therapy Networker, 18*(6), 19–29.

Skinner, B. F. (1974). *About behaviorism.* New York: Vintage Books.

Snyder, D. K. (1999). Affective reconstruction in context of a pluralistic approach to couple therapy. *Clinical Psychology: Science & Practice, 6*(4), 348–365.

Southan, M. A., & Dunbar, J. M. (1986). Facilitating patient compliance with medical interventions. In K. Holroyd & T. Creer (Eds.), *Self management of chronic disease.* New York: Academic Press.

Sperry, L. (1986). Contemporary approaches to family therapy: A comparative and meta-analysis. *Individual Psychology, 42,* 591–601.

Sperry, L., & Carlson, J. (1991). *Marital therapy: Integrating theory and practice.* Denver, CO: Love Publishing.

Sperry, L., & Carlson, J. (1994). *The basics of stress management.* Coral Springs, FL: CMTI Press.

Sperry, L., & Carlson, J. (1996). *Psychopathology and psychotherapy: From diagnosis to treatment.* Philadelphia: Taylor & Francis.

Truax, P., & Jacobson, N. S. (1992). Marital distress. In P. H. Wilson (Ed.), *Principles and practice of relapse prevention* (pp. 290–321). New York: Guilford Press.

Whisman, M. A. (1991). *The use of booster maintenance sessions in behavioral marital therapy.* Unpublished doctoral dissertation. University of Washington, Seattle.

White, M., & Epston, D. (1990). *Narrative means to therapeutic ends.* New York: W.W. Norton.

Wilson, P. H. (Ed.). (1992). *Principles and practice of relapse prevention.* New York: Guilford.

INDEX

A

abuse
case study, 162–163
families under stress, 158–162
addiction, tailoring treatment, 144–149
Adler, Alfred
goals, 20
techniques, 21–22
theories, 19–22
treatment, 21
Adlerian formulation, 106
affective reconstruction, 73
aging, 10
anchoring, 28
anti-oppression advocacy, family life
and, 129–130
assessment
dual-career couples, 184–185
integrative behavioral couples
therapy, 65
integrative problem-centered therapy,
63–64
tailoring treatment, 87–95
attachment, family therapy and, 10

B

Bateson, G., 31–34
behavioral theories, 46–48
goals, 46
techniques, 47–48
treatment, 46

biological formulation, case
conceptualization and, 105
boundaries, family therapy theories, 19
Bowen, M., 22–25
goals, 23
techniques, 24
treatment, 23–24
brain and physiological research, family
therapy, 9

C

case conceptualization
clinical formulation, 100–101, 105–107
clinical illustrations, 110–119
clinical value, 101–102
diagnostic formulation, 100, 104–105
pattern analysis, 107–110
tailoring treatment, 100–107
therapists *vs.* clients, 102–104
treatment formulation, 01
case studies
dual-career couples, 187–191
families under stress, 149–152, 157–158
relapse prevention, 212
tailoring treatment, 99–119
violence and abuse, 162–163
ceremonies, 33
change
family therapy, 9
transtheoretical therapy, 58–59, 59–60
change stages
families under stress, 146–147

219

change stages *(continued)*
  transtheoretical therapy, 59
circular questioning, 33
client/extratherapeutic factors., 9
clinical formulation, case conceptualization,
          100–101, 105–107
clinical protocol, tailoring treatment, 87–96
clinical value, case conceptualization,
          101–102
clues, 37
coaching
coaching, family therapy, 10
coalitions, family therapy theories, 19
cognitive-behavioral formulation, 105
cognitive-behavioral theories, 46–48
communication theories, 25–29
complementarily and differences, family
          therapy theories, 20
conflict and cultural values, 130–133
constructivist/narrative theories, 34–36
  goals, 34
  techniques, 35–36
  treatment, 35
consulting, work and family concerns,
          183–184
counterparadox, 33
couples
  families under stress, 149
  relapse prevention, 203–209
cultural conflict within family, 133–134
cultural diversity of families, celebration
          of, 12
cultural values, conflict and, 130–133
culturally based views, family life, 124–126
culture-aware family assessment, 135–137
culture impact, tailoring treatment, 121–122

D

deconstruction, 35, 37
denominalization, 28
detriangling, 24
diagnostic formulation, case
          conceptualization, 100, 104–105
differential therapeutics, tailoring treatment,
          86–87
distress level, tailoring treatment, 86
divorce, 6–7
DNA, and family therapy, 9
Doherty, W. J., 5–6

dual-career couples
  assessment, 184–185
  case example, 187–191
  therapeutic strategy, 185–187
  work and family concerns, 184–191

E

emotionally focused couples therapy, 66–68
empathy, 49
empowerment strategies, family therapy,
          137–139
experiential theories, 29–31
extended family, family life, 124
externalizing, 35

F

families
  cultural conflict within, 133–134
  relapse prevention, 203–209
  tailoring treatment, 144–149
families under stress
  adult survivors of abuse, 162
  case study, 149–152, 157–158
  change stages, 146–147
  child sexual abuse, 161
  couples therapy, 149
  domestic violence, 159–160
  family treatment goals and strategies,
          156–157
  illness or disability, 153–155
  recovery, 148–149
  response to illness and disability, 152–157
  sociocultural context of disability,
          155–156
  systemic changes, 147–148
  tailoring treatment, 143–144
  violence and abuse, 158–162
family dynamics, family therapy
          theories, 19–20
family functioning level, tailoring
          treatment, 81–83
family life
  anti-oppression advocacy, 129–130
  culturally based views, 124–126
  extended family, 124
  fact chronology, 27
  individuation and family unity, 122–124

multicultural factors, 5
  oppression and, 126–130
  racism, 127
  realities, 2–5
  values, 122–124
family maps, 27
family-orientation treatment adherence, 199
family support treatment adherence, 200
family systems formulation, 106
family therapy, 1–15
  aging, 10
  attachment, 10
  brain and physiological research., 9
  change factors, 9
  changes in profession, 10
  client/extratherapeutic factors., 9
  coaching, 10
  cultural diversity of families, 12
  culture-aware family assessment, 135–137
  divorce, 6–7
  empowerment strategies, 137–139
  family life, 2–5
  gender role socialization, 12
  happiness/optimism, 10
  hierarchy, 3–5
  human genome project, 9
  interventions, 12
  model/technique factors, 9
  motivational interviewing, 10
  multicultural factors, 5
  practice, 11–13
  professional practice, 7–10
  psychoeducation, increasing importance of, 12–13
  relationship factors, 9
  responses to change, 5–6
  shamanism, 9
  smart marriages, 10
  special needs of families, 11–12
  spirituality, 9
  strategies for changing environment, 1–2
  strength building, 10
  tailoring strategies, 134–139
family's perspective treatment adherence, 198–199

G

gender role socialization, family therapy, 12
genograms, 24

goals
  Adler, 20
  behavioral theories, 46
  Bowen, 23
  constructivist/narrative theories, 34
  Milan theories, 32
  object relations theories, 49
  Satir, Virginia, 25–26
  solution-focused theories, 37
  strategic family therapy theory, 39
  structural family therapy theory, 43
  theories, family therapy, 17–50
  Whitaker, Carl, 29–30
group strategies, work and family concerns, 181–183

H

hierarchy, family therapy, 3–5
human genome project and family therapy, 9
hypothesizing, 33

I

illness or disability, families under stress, 153–155
implementation, tailoring treatment, 96
individual functioning level, tailoring treatment, 84–85
individuation and family unity, family life, 122–124
institutional families, 6
integration, integrative treatment, 54–58
integrative behavioral couples therapy, 64–66
  assessment, 65
  techniques, 66
  therapist's role, 65
integrative family therapy, 68–70
integrative formulation, 106
integrative problem-centered therapy, 61–64
  intervention and assessment, 63–64
  problem focus, 62–63
integrative strategies, work and family concerns, 179–181
integrative treatment, 53–77, 70–72
  integration, 54–58
  transtheoretical therapy, 58–61
  treatment efficacy, 53–54
intergenerational theories, 22–25

interpersonal-systems strategies, work and
        family concerns, 177–178
interventions
    family therapy, 12
    integrative problem-centered therapy,
        63–64
    transtheoretical therapy, 60–61
intimacy, family therapy theories, 19

J–L

joining, 43–44
letters, 35
listening, 49

M

metaphors, 27
Milan theories, 31–34
    goals, 32
    techniques, 32–34
    treatment process, 32
model/technique factors, family therapy, 9
models, tailoring treatment, 79
motivational interviewing, 10
multicultural factors
    family life, 5
    family therapy, 5
mutual trap, 65
myths, family therapy theories, 20

N

narrative theories, 34–36
negotiation, treatment adherence, 199
nonadherence, treatment adherence, 197–198

O

object relations theories, 48–50
    goals, 49
    techniques, 49–50
    treatment, 49
Olsen, David C., 68–70
open-ended couple-family therapy, relapse
        prevention, 208–209
oppression and family life, 126–130

P

pattern analysis
    case conceptualization, 107–110
    strategy, 99
patterns of communication, 20
perpetuants, 107
pluralistic theory, 72–75
polarization, 65
positive connotations, 33
power, family therapy theories, 19
practice, family therapy, 11–13
precipitant, 107
prescriptions, 33
problem maintenance system, 63
professional practice, 7–10
protocol, tailoring treatment, 79
psychodynamic formulation, 105
psychodynamic strategies, 178–179
psychoeducation
    family therapy, 12–13
    work and family concerns, 175–176

Q–R

questions, 36
racism, family life, 127
readiness level, tailoring treatment, 85–86
reauthoring, 35
reconstruction, 35
recovery, families under stress, 148–149
reflecting team, 35–36
reframing, 28, 41, 45
relapse prevention, 200–215
    case history, 212
    couples, 203–209
    families, 203–209
    manage stress, 211
    open-ended couple-family therapy,
        208–209
    research, 201–203
    skill training, 211–212
    tailor treatment, 210–211
    treatment alliance, 210
    treatment focus, 206–208
relational conflict level, tailoring treatment,
        83–84
research, relapse prevention, 201–203
resistance, trailoring treatment, 80–81
response to illness and disability, families
        under stress, 152–157
restructuring, 44–45

rituals, 33
roles, family therapy theories, 19
ropes, 27
rules, family therapy theories, 20

S

Satir, Virginia, 25–29
    goals, 25–26
    techniques, 27–28
    treatment, 26
scaling, 38
shamanism, family therapy and, 9
similarities, family therapy theories, 20
single working parents, work and family
        concerns, 191–192
situation/severity, tailoring treatment, 88–90
skeleton keys, 38
skill training, relapse prevention, 211–212
skills, tailoring treatment, 91–92
smart marriages, family therapy, 10
Snyder, D. K., 72–75
social formulation, 106
solution-focused theories, 36–39
    goals, 37
    techniques, 37–38
    treatment process, 37
special needs of families, treatment
        tailored to, 11–12
spirituality, family therapy and, 9
split-team intervention, 33
strategic family therapy theory, 39–42
    goals, 39
    techniques, 40–41
    treatment, 39–40
strategies for changing environment, family
        therapy, 1–2
stress management, relapse prevention
        and, 211
structural family therapy theory, 42–45
    goals, 43
    techniques, 43–45
    treatment, 43
style/status, tailoring treatment, 92–93
system, tailoring treatment, 90–91
systemic changes, families under stress,
        147–148

T

tailoring strategies
    family therapy, 134–139
    tailoring treatment, 95–96
tailoring treatment, 79–98, 143–165
    assessment, 87–95
    case conceptualization, 100–107
    case study, 99–119
    clinical protocol, 87–96
    culture impact, 121–122
    differential therapeutics, 86–87
    distress level, 86
    families and addiction, 144–149
    families under stress, 143–144
    family functioning level, 81–83
    family life values, 122–124
    implementation, 96
    individual functioning level, 84–85
    models, 79
    protocol, 79
    readiness level, 85–86
    relapse prevention, 210–211
    relational conflict level, 83–84
    resistance, 80–81
    situation/severity, 88–90
    skills, 91–92
    style/status, 92–93
    system, 90–91
    tailoring strategy, 95–96
    terminology, 80–81
    therapeutic strategy, 95
    treatment adherence, 199–200
    treatment suitability, 93–95
    work and family concerns, 167–194
techniques
    Adler, 21–22
    behavioral theories, 47–48
    Bowen, 24
    constructivist/narrative theories, 35–36
    integrative behavioral couples therapy, 66
    Milan theories, 32–34
    object relations theories, 49–50
    Satir, 27–28
    solution-focused theories, 37–38
    strategic family therapy theory, 40–41
    structural family therapy theory, 43–45
    Whitaker, 30–31
telephone chart, 32
terminology, tailoring treatment, 80–81
theories, family therapy, 17–51
    Adler, 19–22
    behavioral and cognitive-behavioral,
        46–48
    boundaries and intimacy, 19
    Bowen/intergenerational, 22–25
    coalitions, 19

theories, family therapy *(continued)*
  complementarity and differences, 20
  constructivist/narrative, 34–36
  experiential, 29–31
  family dynamics, 19–20
  goals, treatment process, and
         techniques, 17–50
  Milan, 31–34
  myths, 20
  object relations, 48–50
  patterns of communication, 20
  power, 19
  roles, 19
  rules, 20
  Satir/communication, 25–29
  similarities, 20
  solution-focused, 36–39
  strategic, 39–42
  structural, 42–45
therapeutic strategies
  dual-career couples, 185–187
  tailoring treatment, 95
therapist bias, work and family concerns,
         173–174
therapist's role, integrative behavioral
         couples therapy, 65
therapists *vs.* clients, case
         conceptualization, 102–104
transtheoretical therapy
  change levels, 59–60
  change processes, 58–59
  change stages, 59
  interventions, 60–61
treatment
  Adler, 21
  behavioral theories, 46
  Bowen, 23–24
  constructivist/narrative theories, 35
  object relations theories, 49
  Satir, 26
  strategic family therapy theory, 39–40
  structural family therapy theory, 43
  suitability, 93–95
treatment adherence, 195–200
  family-orientation, 199

family support, 200
family's perspective, 198–199
guidelines, 197–200
negotiation, 199
nonadherence, 197–198
tailor treatment, 199–200
treatment alliance, relapse prevention, 210
treatment efficacy, integrative
         treatment, 53–54
treatment focus, relapse prevention, 206–208
treatment formulation, 108–110
treatment process
  family therapy theories, 17–50
  Milan theories, 32
  solution-focused theories, 37
  Whitaker, 30

V

violence and abuse
  case study, 162–163
  families under stress, 158–162

W

Whitaker, Carl, 29–31
  goals, 29–30
  techniques, 30–31
  treatment process, 30
work and family concerns, 167–194
  consulting, 183–184
  dual-career couples, 184–191
  group strategies, 181–183
  integrative strategies, 179–181
  interpersonal-systems strategies, 177–178
  psychodynamic strategies, 178–179
  psychoeducational strategies, 175–176
  single working parent, 191–192
  therapist bias, 173–174
  work-family conflicts, 170–173
  work life and family life
         relationship, 168–170